LAST THINGS

Last Things

Emily Brontë's Poems

JANET GEZARI

OXFORD
UNIVERSITY PRESS

OXFORD

UNIVERSITY PRESS

Great Clarendon Street, Oxford OX2 6DP

Oxford University Press is a department of the University of Oxford.
It furthers the University's objective of excellence in research, scholarship,
and education by publishing worldwide in

Oxford New York

Auckland Cape Town Dar es Salaam Hong Kong Karachi
Kuala Lumpur Madrid Melbourne Mexico City Nairobi
New Delhi Shanghai Taipei Toronto

With offices in

Argentina Austria Brazil Chile Czech Republic France Greece
Guatemala Hungary Italy Japan Poland Portugal Singapore
South Korea Switzerland Thailand Turkey Ukraine Vietnam

Oxford is a registered trade mark of Oxford University Press
in the UK and in certain other countries

Published in the United States
by Oxford University Press Inc., New York

© Janet Gezari 2007

The moral rights of the author have been asserted
Database right Oxford University Press (maker)

First published 2007

British Library Cataloguing in Publication Data

Data available

Library of Congress Cataloging in Publication Data

Data available

Typeset by Laserwords Private Limited, Chennai, India
Printed in Great Britain
on acid-free paper by
Biddles Ltd., King's Lynn, Norfolk

ISBN 978–0–19–929818–1

1 3 5 7 9 10 8 6 4 2

For Sam and Vanessa

She lives on a moor in the north.
She lives alone.
Spring opens like a blade there.

Anne Carson, 'The Glass Essay'

Acknowledgements

This book has been a long time in the making, and I have many obligations that will go unmentioned. Like all those who write about the Brontës, I have an immediate debt to the scholars who have come before me. They include Margaret Smith, whose magesterial edition of Charlotte Brontë's letters has become indispensable, and Juliet Barker, whose biography has made so much new information about the lives of the Brontës available. I am grateful to Connecticut College for research grants supporting this project and to the American Brontë Society and Theresa Connors, who invited me to address an enthusiastic and informed audience at the New York meeting in the spring of 2003, where I presented a shortened version of Chapter 7. Friends and colleagues who have read the typescript during its course of development and provided necessary advice and criticism include John Fyler, Charles Hartman, Willard Spiegelman, Christopher Ricks, and Vanessa Gezari. I am grateful to Oxford University Press for its dedication to the Brontës, to Andrew McNeillie for his support for this project, and to the press's two readers, Christine Alexander and Alison Chapman, who confirmed my sense of what I was doing and provided genuinely helpful criticism. A version of Chapter 3 appeared in *ELH* in 1999.

The publishers wish to thank the Brontë Parsonage Museum Library and the British Library for permission to reproduce holograph manuscripts in their collections, and Faber and Faber Ltd. (UK and World) and Farrar, Straus, and Giroux, LLC (US) for permission to reprint 'Emily Brontë' from *Collected Poems* by Ted Hughes. Copyright 2003 by The Estate of Ted Hughes. Although every effort has been made to establish copyright and contact copyright holders prior to printing, the publishers would be pleased to rectify any omissions or errors brought to their notice at the earliest opportunity.

Contents

List of Figures

A Note on Texts

All references to Emily Brontë's poems are to *Emily Jane Brontë: The Complete Poems*, ed. Janet Gezari (London: Penguin Books, 1992). Poems are identified by their first lines, unless Emily Brontë has provided titles for them.

All references to *Wuthering Heights* are to the Clarendon Press edition of the novel: *Wuthering Heights*, ed. Hilda Marsden and Ian Jack (Oxford: Clarendon Press, 1976). To facilitate locating references in this or other editions of *Wuthering Heights*, citations in parentheses in my text include book, chapter, and page number.

1
And First

And first an hour of mournful musing
And then a gush of bitter tears
And then a dreary calm diffusing
Its deadly mist o'er joys and cares
And then a throb and then a lightening
And then a breathing from above
And then a star in heaven brightening
The star the glorious star of love

When I edited Emily Brontë's poems for the Penguin English Poets
series, I was surprised to discover so many poems and poetical fragments
that had the pure cry of genuine poetry, and then to see how little had
been written about them. Although Brontë's poems have always had
their admirers—Virginia Woolf thought they might outlast *Wuthering
Heights*—they have frequently been criticized as self-indulgent and
self-dramatizing, crude and extravagant, or lacking in judgement and
finish.[1] Like Emily Dickinson's poems, many have been thought to
begin better than they end, but unlike them, they have not been
redeemed from neglect as forerunners of high modernism and are
unlikely to be. Nor have they been restored to view by feminist critics,
who have rehabilitated so much nineteenth-century poetry written by
women. In my second chapter, I argue that it is the very uniqueness of
Emily Brontë's poems—the justice of Charlotte Brontë's observation
that no woman ever wrote poems like those her sister was writing—that
makes them less interesting to recent feminist critics than the poems of
either Elizabeth Barrett Browning or Mathilde Blind. My book seeks to
redress this neglect by offering new ways to read Brontë's poems and
new reasons for wanting to read them.

As a writer, Emily Brontë didn't suffer from either an anxiety of
influence or an anxiety of authorship. In her poems, she succeeded

in authorizing herself as the subject of her own experience, apparently without wondering whether that experience was eccentric and trivial or, contrarily, profoundly relevant to others. In life, she spoke infrequently but firmly, as in her curt response to Mary Taylor's having said that her own religion was nobody's business but hers and God's: 'That's right'. She had no patience with what Keats called 'poetry that has a palpable design on us—and if we do not agree, seems to put its hand in its breeches pocket'.[2] Her own poetry is always open-handed, although it continues to prove an elusive guide to what has interested most people: the daily life of the woman who produced it. The poems are at once personal and impersonal, in keeping with Yeats's twin insights: 'a poet writes always of his personal life, in his finest work, out of its tragedy, whatever it be, remorse, lost love, or mere loneliness,' and 'all that is personal soon rots.'[3] Their deep personality has to do with their faithfulness to Emily Brontë's own experience of anguish and intoxication, but their deep impersonality is connected to her motive for writing them. 'The impulse which urged her to create was not her own suffering or her own injuries,' Woolf writes, contrasting her with Charlotte Brontë, but the 'gigantic ambition' to say something about relations between 'the whole human race' and 'the eternal powers'.[4]

We can say of Emily Brontë what John Middleton Murry said of Thomas Hardy: her poems and novel are 'not the record, but the culmination of an experience' that contains 'within it a reaction to the universe'.[5] Brontë's daily life, the life of the poems and her novel, was not a life of doing with others but a life of watching alone. What she did, apparently with great pleasure, was the repetitive, inconclusive work required in a household: brushing the carpets, kneading the bread, feeding the dogs.[6] Anne Carson gives the most concise account I know of what she watched in 'The Glass Essay', Carson's extraordinary poem about Brontë and the denuding lacerations of love. In the poem, Carson adopts Brontë's usual spelling of 'watch' as 'whach,' which suggests that Brontë pronounced the word, often in contexts where inspiration is being sought, by breathing into it:

> She whached God and humans and moor wind and open night.
> She whached eyes, stars, inside, outside, actual weather.
> She whached the bars of time, which broke.
> She whached the poor core of the world, wide open.[7]

Kierkegaard located the core of romanticism in 'absolute loneliness, where not a breath of wind stirs, where no distant baying of hounds can be heard—and yet the trees incline to one another and repeat their childhood memories about when the nymphs lived in them, and imagination gorges itself in supreme enjoyment'.[8] Supreme enjoyment—an unqualified affirmation of the joy of being alive—is the core of Brontë's poems and is entirely compatible with her intimate knowledge of despair and her unflinching recognition of our human capacity for cruelty and ingratitude. The poems share this ground with *Wuthering Heights*. The early Romantic period was the period to which Brontë was affined not just by provincial isolation but by choice. Her dress, which E. C. Gaskell describes in her *Life of Charlotte Brontë*, belonged to that earlier time. Her fellow pupils in Brussels, where she studied for nine months in 1842, found it 'strange' that she wore leg-of-mutton sleeves 'long after they were "gone out"' and petticoats without 'a curve or a wave in them'.[9] Like Wordsworth's poems, Brontë's often emphasize the disjunction, or disproportion, between the emotions excited by an experience and the experience itself, but because the surplus of feeling in her poems is often more histrionic than it is in Wordsworth's, it may be less readily available to us as a warrant of sublimity. Although Brontë's poems have their own intimations of immortality, these have always to contend with her extraordinary love for the natural world in all its homely manifestations, what Swinburne calls her 'love of earth for earth's sake'.[10] She represents the ecstatic release associated with mystic experience more enduringly than the Romantics, but she is also more at home than they are in a natural world unimbued with moral significance. In her poetical fragments especially, she consecrates a moment, a feeling, or a sensory impression instead of making these the occasion for a poetic meditation or a more pointed and finished poem.

'Finally it matters little whether Emily Brontë really had what we call a mystical experience,' Georges Bataille writes, 'for she appears to have reached the very essence of such an experience.'[11] The vaunted mysticism of the poems, already present in the early poem or poetical fragment 'And first an hour of mournful musing', is not readily assimilable to Christian mysticism. What Brontë seeks isn't union with a transcendent deity but release into a state of undifferentiation where the subject is identified with its object and the imagination has sovereign authority. She doesn't rebel against Christianity so much as press beyond it. She did not lack faith, or lack it consistently, but she gives us no reason to doubt her assertion (in 'No coward soul is mine') that the 'thousand creeds | That move men's hearts' are 'unutterably vain'. In this poem, and in others, she registers her impatience with received doctrine and conventional belief.[12] Her poems stand as the record of a powerfully independent mind responding to her own inner experience in the world and seeking always an abrogation of human limits compatible with a stern morality. Her closest forebears on matters of principle are the Stoics. Their indifference to an afterlife, belief in a divine principle within human beings rather than external to them, and 'self-controlling self-reliance' are the primary articles of her faith.[13] The modern thinker who is most congenial to her is Bataille, who has written about *Wuthering Heights* in *Literature and Evil*, where he puts Brontë into the company of Baudelaire, Blake, and Sade. Like Bataille, Brontë is a self-taught philosopher whose audacity is related to her refusal to create or subscribe to a system.[14] Bataille's meditations on loss and anguish, unconditional expenditure, and sovereignty are always pertinent to the thinking Brontë was doing in her poems and have influenced my reading of them.

Information about Brontë's thinking, apart from what her novel and poems provide, is notoriously scant. In her edition of the French essays Charlotte and Emily wrote in Brussells, Sue Lonoff suggests that 'Emily's views emerge with startling clarity' in the nine essays of hers that survive.[15] Some of them do, and they are complicated and nuanced by the evidence of the poems. The essays open themselves to readings that emphasize Brontë's impatience with social conventions, her pessimism or misanthropy, her moral severity, and a dangerous inclination to speak plainly. In one of them, a music teacher declines an invitation to a pupil's musical party and does not hesitate to tell her how much she appreciates not having to witness her pupil's poor performance. In another, on filial love, Brontë offers her own version of the fifth commandment: not 'Honor thy father and thy mother: that thy days may be long upon the land which the Lord thy God giveth thee' but 'Honor thy father and mother if thou wouldst live.'[16] In Brontë's essay, humans must be threatened into honouring their parents. 'So powerful a prohibition', says Freud, writing about the commandment against murder, 'can only be directed against an equally powerful impulse.' In her version of the fifth commandment, Brontë seems to have anticipated Freud's insight: 'What no human soul desires stands in no need of prohibition.'[17] The poems are as open-eyed and severe as these essays, and they supply more than the charm the essays lack: they provide the emotional and spiritual context for them and for *Wuthering Heights* as well.

Emily Brontë's art is almost as elusive as her life, and any study of it confronts some insurmountable obstacles. The manuscript of *Wuthering Heights* has not survived to provide evidence of the novel's composition or revision, and we lack any record of authorial corrections to the first, carelessly printed edition. Although Brontë's creative experience is often the subject of her poems, we know very little about how and where she wrote them. She had no intimates, not even sisters, who observed her composing poems or with whom she shared her poems. Although the diary papers she exchanged with Anne refer to characters and events in Gondal, the imaginary imperial nation the two sisters collaboratively created, as well as to daily life, Anne merely mentions in one of them that Emily is writing 'some poetry' and wonders 'what it is about'.[18] Emily certainly wrote letters during the two brief periods she spent away from home and during the much longer periods her sisters, Anne and Charlotte, spent away from her, and it would be wonderful to have the sense they might give of her. Unfortunately, only three of Emily's letters survive, and they are 'tersely civil duty-letters' that were not written to her sisters; they include no information about her own activities, let alone those involving the composition of poems.[19] There have been efforts to reveal Emily at work, most recently Edward Chitham's in *The Birth of Wuthering Heights*, but his comments about the composition of the poems are conjectural, like these on 'Enough of thought, philosopher': 'A complex poem of 56 lines, it is likely to have taken several days to complete. It is likely to have provided a diversion from the novel, still in its early stages.'[20]

Gaskell's well-known image of the three sisters pacing up and down in the sitting room of the Parsonage while talking over their stories, reminds us that poems were not among the creative achievements shared during those evening sessions. When Charlotte, who knew that her sister wrote poems, came upon her *Gondal Poems* notebook in the autumn of 1845 and read some, Emily felt violated. Once persuaded to participate in Charlotte's publication project, she readied only twenty-one of her poems for printing. In the 1846 volume, her poems usually alternate with those of her sisters, so that relations between her poems are subordinated to relations between them and the contiguous poems of Charlotte and Anne. All of the poems Brontë selected for publication in 1846 came from the two books into which she had begun transcribing some of her poems about a year earlier, the *Gondal Poems* notebook and the so-called Honresfeld manuscript. After transcribing her poems, she almost always discarded earlier drafts. Her single-leaf manuscripts preserve many apparently unfinished or incomplete poems, usually described as fragments, and we cannot know what she intended to do with them. The posthumous publication of seventeen more poems in the 1850 edition of *Wuthering Heights* and *Agnes Grey* nearly doubled the number of Emily Brontë's poems available to nineteenth-century readers.[21] What knowledge we have about Charlotte Brontë's aggressive editing of these poems relies on a comparison of the manuscript versions in Emily Brontë's hand to the published versions and not on Charlotte Brontë's correspondence with her publisher about the edition, which says nothing about her editorial judgements. 1850 added one poem to the canon for which no holograph manuscript survives, 'Often rebuked, yet always back returning.' For generations of Brontë readers, as for T. J. Wise and J. A. Symington, this poem has sounded 'the keynote to her character',[22] yet its authorship continues to be disputed. In my last chapter, I argue that Charlotte, not Emily, is the author of 'Often rebuked, yet always back returning,' and that the poem promotes Charlotte's view of Emily, not Emily's view of herself or her own poetic project.

My title registers my starting place. A concern with endings, and with how we defy, resist, blur, or transcend them, characterizes Brontë's life, her art, and this book. In Carson's words, 'She whached the bars of time, which broke.' Brontë's approach to an end is most evident when death or memory is the subject of a poem, as it so frequently is. But there is no poet for whom immortality resolves less, or for whom ordinary temporal elements—night, day, evening, fall and spring—are more miscible. She gives us a vision of life *sub specie iterationis*. Her poems' formal resistance to endings can be seen in the recurrence of the word *again* both at the end of lines and at the end of poems, where it appears more often than any other word, disrupting our feeling that the experience the poem has recorded is over and done. Or in her fondness for circular structures and for outcomes that resemble openings rather than endings. If time is a prison that confines us, then Brontë's poems return again and again both to the prison site and to the prison break.

Although I do not discuss all her poems, the view of Emily Brontë's poems presented here seeks to be comprehensive. It relates to individual poems, to the progress she made from the beginning of her career as a poet to its end, to her poetical fragments and her writing practice, to her motives for writing poetry, and to the connections between her poems and her famous novel. When Brontë's ordinary life enters into my account of her poems, it does so to illuminate them, and not vice versa. I do not ignore the presence of Gondal in the poems, but I resist dividing poems that belong to a Gondal narrative from poems that probably do not, either because Brontë transcribed them into her

Honresfeld manuscript instead of her *Gondal Poems* notebook or because they include no references to Gondal characters or places. A specious distinction between 'Gondal' and 'personal' narrative contexts continues to thrive, especially when biographical interpretations are at stake.[23] Believing that a Gondal poem is less personal than a non-Gondal poem is like believing that *The Bell Jar* is less personal than 'Daddy'. Although she separated Gondal poems from non-Gondal poems by transcribing them into separate notebooks, Brontë composed both kinds of poems intermittently for as long as she wrote poems. For me, a Gondal poem is one in which a lyrical impulse converges with an occasion provided by a narrative about invented characters with aristocratic names. One way to look at Gondal is as intentional dreaming, a release like the one we experience in a dream when the self is freed to act various roles, but always under the aegis of an informing self-idiom that organizes and unifies whatever experience is being represented.[24] The chapters that follow endeavour to describe both the range and the distinctiveness of the experience Emily Brontë's poems offer.

2

Last Things

Did you ever read one of her Poems backward, because the plunge
from the front overturned you? I sometimes (often have, many
times) have—A something overtakes the Mind—

We don't know which poet Emily Dickinson read backward—
sometimes, often, many times swimming against the current of her
words. Susan Howe thinks that Emily Brontë and Elizabeth Barrett
Browning, both poets Dickinson admired, are the likely choices. She
suggests that Dickinson 'found sense in the chance meeting of words',[1]
but Dickinson's account of her backward reading points to a defensive
tactic for keeping her balance rather than an aleatory one for discovering
new meanings. She imagines herself as a person on horseback trying to
curb her horse's strength. Hurtling through space, the horse pitches its
rider forward (she is overturned by the 'plunge from the front') or leaves
her behind ('A something overtakes the Mind'). Given these terms of
engagement, Emily Brontë is more likely than Barrett Browning to be
the poet Dickinson reads backward. Charlotte Brontë's description of
her sister's progress toward death applies as well to the progress of her
poems: they do not linger. They often convey something of the speed
of her sensations and the urgency of her writing. An early poem, 'High
waving heather 'neath stormy blasts bending', communicates an excess
of vital stimulation and a readiness for sudden and fleeting visionary
flights and plunges with a gallop of present participles that imitates the
rapidly shifting motions of the natural world. In the poem she titled
'Wuthering Heights', Sylvia Plath evokes Brontë's nature worship and
its dangers for her:

> There is no life higher than the grasstops
> Or the hearts of sheep, and the wind
> Pours by like destiny, bending
> Everything in one direction.

I can feel it trying
To funnel my heat away.
If I pay close attention, they will invite me
To whiten my bones among them.

Brontë's 'High waving heather 'neath stormy blasts bending' offers its
reader an experience instead of describing one, and that experience is
ongoing and incomplete rather than recurrent or enduring. Nothing
lasts. Everything is 'Changing forever':

High waving heather 'neath stormy blasts bending
Midnight and moonlight and bright shining stars
Darkness and glory rejoicingly blending
Earth rising to heaven and heaven descending
Man's spirit away from its drear dungeon sending
Bursting the fetters and breaking the bars

All down the mountain sides wild forests lending
One mighty voice to the life giving wind
Rivers their banks in the jubilee rending
Fast through the valleys a reckless course wending
Wider and deeper their waters extending
Leaving a desolate desert behind

Shining and lowering and swelling and dying
Changing forever from midnight to noon
Roaring like thunder like soft music sighing
Shadows on shadows advancing and flying
Lightning bright flashes the deep gloom defying
Coming as swiftly and fading as soon

What Dickinson means by reading backward isn't obvious. What
happens to the punctuation she would have seen in all of Brontë's
published poems? Does the reader retain the order of the words in each
line while reversing the order of the lines, or does she retain the order of
the lines while reading each of them back to front? Perhaps she begins
at the end of a poem and reads it backwards, word by word. All of these
backward readings have something in common. As the eye moves from
left to right in a line, or from top to bottom in a poem, it moves from 'less
differentiation and more possibility toward more differentiation and less
possibility, and from global participation toward closure and cognitive
increment'.[2] At the least, a backward reading forecloses some of the
possibilities opened by a line or a poem, thereby reducing the burden of
speculation for a reader as imaginative as Dickinson. Dickinson would

have read only the thirty-eight poems attributed to Emily Brontë in the volumes published in 1846 and 1850. She asked to have one of them, 'No coward soul is mine', which she knew only in Charlotte's revised version of it, read at her funeral. The poem as Emily wrote it might have unsettled Dickinson as it did Charlotte, and one of the achievements of Charlotte's revisions is to slow the poem down. Here is the published poem's last stanza, read backwards, word by word, with line indentations neglected and punctuation omitted, except for the dash, which looks in two directions at once:

> destroyed be never may art THOU what And
> Breath and Being art THOU—Thou
> void render could might his that atom Nor
> Death for room not is There

The sense of these lines—their speaker's triumph over death and her impassioned exaltation of Breath and Being as divine principles—remains intact. Their rhythm has been joltingly altered, and their momentum has been slowed. The backward reading confirms the faith the poem could only posit at its beginning by transforming what was an outcome ('what THOU art may never be destroyed') into a premiss ('destroyed be never may art THOU what And').

Wuthering Heights takes reading backward about as far as it can go. The date affixed to the first chapter—1801—is not quite the narrative's endpoint, but it is close to it. An absence, that of Catherine, whose life ended many years earlier, haunts the Heights, presiding over the meanness of its domestic life, which the rest of the novel will oppose to the grandeur of the erotic life that Catherine's spectral persistence prolongs for Heathcliff. There are many pertinent accounts of the action of Chapter 3, in which Lockwood's sleep is broken by two nightmares. According to one of them, Catherine's presence in Lockwood's second dream is conjured out of her absence by the power of her written words. The dream reveals that reading can produce a Catherine ghost, a between-states figure, neither wholly present nor wholly absent, and therefore as difficult for Lockwood to dispel as she is for Heathcliff to recall or possess. Lockwood stands in for the reader as well as Heathcliff as he confronts the lacerations of love and loss this novel circles around. Reading the novel's events backwards has an effect related to that of filtering the novel's action through Lockwood and Nelly Dean. Both narrative devices keep us from being overturned or overtaken by the momentum the novel's story gathers as it plunges forward. If we miss the logic of these narrative choices, we miss something of Brontë's solicitude for our safety and our human weakness.

Appreciating the danger of Emily Brontë's poems is a necessary condition for admiring them, as it is for seeing their connection to *Wuthering Heights*. The list of poets who have admired Brontë's poems includes not just Dickinson and Carson but Swinburne, Hardy, Bridges, and Plath. Reviewing an anthology of poetry by English, Scotch, and Irish women in 1909, Oscar Wilde describes Brontë's poems as 'instinct with tragic power and quite terrible in their bitter intensity of passion, the fierce fire of feeling seeming almost to consume the raiment of form ... '.[3] Brontë haunts Ted Hughes's late references to his visit to Top Withins with Sylvia Plath, soon after their marriage. In his poem titled 'Wuthering Heights', published in *Birthday Letters*, the book of poems Hughes addressed to Plath, he describes her as 'jealous' and 'emulous' and 'Twice as ambitious as Emily'. This 'terrible' Emily Brontë has largely disappeared from view, except as the author of *Wuthering Heights*.

Some of the neglect visited upon Brontë's poems is long-standing and results from an idea of Victorian poetry as 'largely a male preserve',[4] with only small spaces carved out for Emily Brontë, Elizabeth Barrett Browning, and Christina Rossetti. Feminist critics have challenged this understanding of Victorian poetry, largely by displacing the critical programmes that have required a particular subject matter, thematic content, or point of view and undervalued women poets when their work didn't conform. But feminist critics have brought expectations of their own to the poetry of Victorian women, and these threaten to make Emily Brontë inconsiderable once again. As Barbara Herrnstein Smith points out, repeated citation and discussion of a writer's work in critical essays or repeated inclusion of it in literary anthologies 'not only promotes the value of that work but goes some distance toward creating its value'.[5] Virginia Blain's anthology of poetry by Victorian women poets, *Victorian Women Poets: A New Annotated Anthology*, published in 2001, is representative, not eccentric, in excluding Brontë. We can appreciate Blain's effort to 'provide a varied and wide-ranging coverage of the kinds of subjects and poetic treatments most often employed by Victorian women poets,'[6] and also share Charlotte's conviction that her sister's poems were valuable precisely because they were 'not common effusions' and not 'at all like the poetry women generally write'.[7] They don't abide by the restrictions that define the expressive range of nineteenth-century female poets like Augusta Webster, whose work Angela Leighton brings

Last Things

to light in *Victorian Women Poets: Writing against the Heart* (1992). They contribute little to the representation of nineteenth-century female figures that is Kathleen Hickok's subject in *Representations of Women: Nineteenth-Century British Women's Poetry* (1984). They don't readily support Isobel Armstrong's conclusion, in *Victorian Poetry: Poetry, Poetics and Politics* (1993) that 'it is undoubtedly the case that [Victorian] women wrote with a sense of belonging to a particular group defined by their sexuality.'[8] Although *Women's Poetry, Late Romantic to Victorian* (1999), deliberately turns away from Brontë, Barrett Browning, and Rossetti, whom the editors (Armstrong and Blain) describe as 'an established triad of middle-class poets', it nevertheless includes one essay on Barrett Browning and two essays on Rossetti but no essay on Brontë. Unlike Barrett Browning, Brontë wrote no poems that campaign for changes in the lives of women and the opportunities available to them; unlike Rossetti, she doesn't explore feminine subjectivity and female sexuality in her poems, or doesn't do so in a vocabulary yet familiar to us. Even more tellingly, the essays about other women poets mention Barrett Browning and Rossetti dozens of times, but Brontë only twice, and these two instances are revealingly old-fashioned: she is listed among the women poets who remained unmarried and among those whose poems have been mined for biographical facts.[9]

Plus ça change. If the value of Emily Brontë's poetry was not apparent in relation to the interests of critics of canonical Victorian poetry before the birth of modern feminist scholarship and theory, its value is no more apparent in relation to the interests that feminist critics are currently supplying to guide our reading. The advantage of any critical paradigm is that it brings some writers into focus; its disadvantage is that it blurs others. With respect to Emily Brontë, history comes full circle. Recent feminist criticism endorses Charlotte Brontë's judgement that no woman ever wrote poems like those her sister was writing, and this judgement may provide what she—Charlotte Brontë—couldn't have anticipated: an additional reason for not paying them any mind.

The assignment of Emily Brontë to the category woman writer has produced not just neglect but distortions, in our time as well as hers, and these distortions may be as great as those associated with her removal from all categories, the treatment of her as a *lusus naturae*. One distortion associated with the wave of feminist criticism and scholarship that preceded Armstrong (and supports her description of Brontë as an 'established' poet) has been to interpret Brontë's recurrently expressed difficulty contending with an inspirational force whose powers are awful and insidious as a specifically feminine difficulty. The idea is that a woman writer's relation to her muse is like the relation of women to dominant male figures in their culture, so that the muse's authority mimics the social authority men have historically exercised over women.

Both Margaret Homans and Irene Tayler have produced compelling accounts of Brontë's failure to claim a voice of her own or identify her muse as 'a power to serve her' rather than as a ' "self" cut off from her in disastrous alienation'.[10] But the feeling of being mastered by an external force is widespread among male as well as female artists. Picasso is only one of many who have expressed it, although his domination over living women makes him a useful example. 'La peinture est plus forte que moi, elle me fait faire ce'qu'elle veut,' he wrote at the end of one of his notebooks. Freud reminds us that the practice of locating agency outside the self is not limited to artists describing an experience of inspiration. In *The Question of Lay Analysis*, he uses the same language as Picasso to describe the ego's subjection to instinct: 'C'était plus fort que moi.'[11] The idea that ordinary socio-sexual relations between men and women reproduce themselves in the relations between an artist and his or her gendered medium or muse inevitably simplifies any artist's psychological transactions with his or her sources of inspiration and risks condescending to Brontë.

In my last chapter, I will argue that all of Brontë's poems about the operations of the imagination have been read through the lens of 'The Visionary', a poem created by Charlotte Brontë, attributed by her to Emily Brontë, and published posthumously in 1850. 'The Visionary' begins with the first twelve lines of 'Julian M. and A. G. Rochelle', lines which Emily Brontë had written but not published in 1846 as part of 'The Prisoner (A Fragment)', but Charlotte finishes the poem with eight lines of her own. As Lucasta Miller points out, Charlotte's lines were still being quoted in the *New Pelican Guide to English Literature* (1982) 'as typical of the younger sister' and 'showing her "true spiritual vision" '.[12] One way to describe the lens of 'The Visionary' would be to say that it feminizes the speaker of the poem's first twelve lines, those written by Emily Brontë, by transforming him into the heroine familiar to us from Charlotte's novels and her early writings, a faithful acolyte awaiting the visitation of a 'Strange Power'. Both 'The Visionary' and 'Often rebuked, though always back returning,' a poem that I will argue was entirely written by Charlotte, have profoundly influenced our understanding of Emily, just as Charlotte meant them to.

I agree with Nancy Chodorow that gender is 'part of what is often on people's minds' and 'part of what constructs (and constricts) their life consciously and unconsciously'.[13] More specifically, gender is a part of what constricted the life of Emily Brontë, although it is also a part of what freed her, most obviously from the economic responsibilities and professional expectations that contributed to her brother Branwell's collapse. The earliest evidence we have of Brontë's consciousness of the differences and disabilities she shared with other women appears in one of the school essays she wrote in Brussels, 'The Siege of Oudenarde', which describes women as 'that class condemned by the laws of society to be a heavy burden in any situation of action and danger' because they have been accorded 'degrading privileges'.[14] This is an old view of gender discrimination, one that Brontë would have found in Wollstonecraft and one that Charlotte Brontë, in *Shirley*, associates with Emily, on whose character she based Shirley's, when she shows her heroine's frustration at being sequestered at a safe distance from the anticipated battle between Robert Moore and his angry millworkers. Nor is this particular formulation of the condition of women Emily Brontë's only insight into the constraints of gender, which figure importantly in *Wuthering Heights*, though more there than in the poems. But at a time when gender is being so widely promoted as a political issue, it is easy to exaggerate the degree to which or miscomprehend the way in which Emily Brontë felt (or was) degraded or constricted by being a woman. My point is not that she avoided the constraints of the various double standards associated with the construction of gender in the mid-nineteenth century and certainly not that she was unaware of them, but that her chosen subject in the poems and in *Wuthering Heights* is the constraints that are general to humanity, not those that are specific to women. Many readers and writers have acknowledged—sometimes with dismay or resentment—that lyric poetry requires this subsumption of the personal into the impersonal, or the individual into the collective, or the social into the human. But a novel like *Wuthering Heights*, which has long been seen to supply a powerful social matrix, can provide an example of the degree to which the social markers of identity can be represented as an aspect, and an aspect only, of some larger, more universal human condition. So, when Catherine Earnshaw returns from her stay at Thrushcross Grange, she is dressed in the grown-up feminine costume that indicates her acceptance of standards of conduct appropriate to a young woman of her social class, but she soon finds herself bound not just by her clothes and the conventions associated with them but by the walls that shelter her, her closest familial relationships, and, last but never least, her own flesh.

Another distortion associated with Brontë's assignment to the category of 'woman writer' results from reading her representation of visionary experience as displaced heterosexual longing, as in these justly celebrated lines from 'The Prisoner (A Fragment)':

> He comes with western winds, with evening's wandering airs,
> With that clear dusk of heaven that brings the thickest stars.
> Winds take a pensive tone, and stars a tender fire,
> And visions rise, and change, which kill me with desire.

Stevie Davies comments: ' "He comes": we are made aware of the visionary experience as being linked with a sexual approach, as if this were the closest "normal" experience which the poet could think of to the meeting of self with other.'[15] Since writing this, Davies has changed her view of Emily Brontë's sexuality. In *Emily Brontë: Heretic*, she also disputes the 'cynical reductiveness' that explains the spiritual claims of women mystics as a form of sexual sublimation.[16] There isn't far to go from Davies's earlier presumptive reading to Ted Hughes's melodramatic characterization of Emily Brontë as another doomed female sufferer in his poem 'Emily Brontë':[17]

> The wind on Crow Hill was her darling.
> His fierce, high tale in her ear was her secret.
> But his kiss was fatal.
>
> Through her dark Paradise ran
> The stream she loved too well
> That bit her breast.
>
> The shaggy sodden king of that kingdom
> Followed through the wall
> And lay on her love-sick bed.
>
> The curlew trod in her womb.
>
> The stone swelled under her heart.
>
> Her death is a baby-cry on the moor.

Hughes likens Brontë not just to her own Catherine but to that other dark heroine, Cleopatra. Both suffer a specifically female death associated with disappointment in love and unnatural acts around breast and womb. No longer willing to sustain life (like Cleopatra), and unable to survive giving birth to it (like Catherine), Hughes's Brontë experiences her own death as gynaecological damage, petrification, or regression to a condition of infancy. Openness to the elements—the wind enters her ear, the stream her breast—reverses the natural course of events equally for a poet with her own tales to tell and a woman with her own fluids to discharge. Such openness transforms this poet's female, human body (womb and heart) into elements of nature, a marsh for curlews to tread or a place where stones grow. These violations are implicit in Hughes's language, and the effect is to reduce Emily Brontë's language to plaintive noise, a 'baby-cry on the moor'. Anne Carson suggests that a woman's language is primitive, monstrous, or unnatural so long as it is perceived as a 'piece of inside projected to the outside'.[18] Hughes imagines Emily Brontë alive as a silent victim. Her voice—or, more precisely, some non-verbal but audible emanation from her—demands attention only when she is dead. Sylvia Plath presides over this poem, as Brontë haunts Hughes's later poem, 'Wuthering Heights'.[19] Is death what matters most about Plath and Brontë and what ultimately serves to regulate or dismiss their too powerful, uncensored words?

Although sexual experience is more familiar to most people than visionary experience, this wasn't the case for Brontë, however fervently contemporary readers may wish to grant a sexual body to women writers or rend the veil of privacy that obscures their sexuality from us. Moreover, the assumption that sexual experience is heterosexual experience—an assumption in which our gendered pronouns are complicitous—is risky business, inviting merely tired interpretations of the poet's interactions with herself and her world. I am not suggesting that Brontë's sexual experience will be better understood as homosexual or onanistic experience. In her most recent effort to get closer to Brontë, Stevie Davies says as much: 'I would go so far as to say that only by self-love (itself forbidden and transgressive) could most nineteenth-century middle-class women have come to an understanding of sexual passion'; 'a self-enjoying "spinster" must be thought to know more of the erotic than her married contemporary.'[20] I am suggesting that the sexual metaphors in Brontë's poems will continue to resist our efforts to reduce them to familiar categories, especially the most familiar ones, which are those of heterosexual romance. This is one of the many lessons of *Wuthering Heights*, which has invited, resisted, and outlived so many misreadings of it as a romantic (rather than Romantic) novel. Although *Wuthering Heights* is a great love story, enjoyment of self or other—pleasure of any kind, even the quiet or passionate exchange of a kiss—is not its point. As Bataille puts it, 'the love of Catherine and Heathcliff leaves sensuality in suspension.'²¹ We are told that they share a bed before the death of Mr Earnshaw, but they come closest to a sexual embrace as adults with the intimate violence that marks their reunion after Heathcliff returns from his three-year absence. The drama of their assault on and resistance to each other when they meet after that absence and after Catherine's marriage to Edgar, narrative contracted to a scene and brought, at last, into supreme focus, is heightened by the physical damage they do. Catherine grasps Heathcliff's hair in her fist; her flesh purples with its involuntary resistance to his penetration.

What can we say about Emily Brontë's poems that will make it more likely that they will be experienced as valuable, or experienced at all? Suppose we try to take the lyric pulse of those lines from 'The Prisoner (A Fragment)' that I have already quoted:

> He comes with western winds, with evening's wandering airs,
> With that clear dusk of heaven that brings the thickest stars.
> Winds take a pensive tone, and stars a tender fire,
> And visions rise, and change, that kill me with desire.

The leisurely hexameter couplets, the balanced phrases and clauses, the steady, even placement of the caesura in the middle of the line, and the repetition of vowels and consonants, separately and in combination, create a feeling of openness and gradually intensifying anticipation. In the fourth line, alliteration is less prominent than in the preceding three, but the deft repetition of beginning and ending sounds in '*change which*' (as in 'thickest stars' in line 2) and of the consonants framing the long vowel sound in 'rise... desire' produce an effect like that of internal rhyme and bear witness to Brontë's fine musical ear. The physical qualities of the verse are intimate with her feeling for what it means to open oneself to one's own absence. What is it that gives such phrases as 'small rain' (from the anonymous Middle English lyric 'Western Wind') and 'thickest stars' (in Brontë's poem) their power to move us? Partly it is the instability of the modifiers, and their capacity to evoke the sensation of a parched throat or suffocated breath and the longing for release that is sexual, but not only sexual. The evening's wandering airs ignite the stars, but their flame is tender, and tenderly compatible with the pensive tone of the winds, as if deep thought and strong feeling had the same origin or joined in the same apprehension, as Coleridge maintained they should. Brontë's lines express the innocence and intoxication of existence when, as Bataille puts it, the 'isolated being loses himself in something other than himself'.[22] This is what dying with desire is like, or so Emily Brontë would have us believe.

Northrop Frye's idea that the 'private poem often takes off from something that blocks normal activity' or keeps the poet from 'carrying on with ordinary experience' is as pertinent to Brontë's poems as to the Petrarchan lyrics Frye cites, for which the block is conventionally frustrated love. Writing a lyric poem, Frye says, is a 'displaced activity, as when a chimpanzee crossed in love starts digging holes in the ground instead.'[23] What blocks normal activity for Brontë, the abiding motive for her poetry and for *Wuthering Heights*, a novel that gives enlarged narrative dimensionality to the shifting moods and performative utterances that figure so largely in the poems, is the consciousness Bataille names 'naked anguish'. Such anguish 'doesn't have an object except that we exist in time—which destroys us'.[24] Her poems are 'instinct with tragic power and quite terrible in their bitter intensity of passion' because anguish is one of her familiars. The word appears in poems written at all stages of her writing life, but turns up with increasing frequency in her late poems. From the beginning, anguish is intimate with death: there is the 'anguish | Of leaving things that once were dear' and the 'anguish of that last adieu'.[25] Towards the end of her poetic career, anguish is more fully adumbrated as a response to the irreducibly painful knowledge that so long as we exist as ourselves, we exist in time. Unlike the rest of the natural creation, we carry the knowledge of our mortality with us. Brontë's eponymous philosopher, reprimanded for thinking too much, laments the burden of human consciousness, and turns the apprehension of death into the wish for it, as Tennyson does in so many of his poems:

> 'Oh, for the time when I shall sleep
> Without identity,
> And never care how rain may steep,
> Or snow may cover me!'

Oh, for the time when time—the memory of the past, the hope or dread of the future—will be cancelled because we will cease to exist as ourselves in it. Although dying is one way of ceasing to exist as ourselves in time, Brontë's poems explore other ways too. They include night and day dreaming, existing as someone else (a Gondal character, for example), and mystical experience.

Brontë's philosopher doesn't sound like a philosopher, and the philosophy he expresses is not original or complex. He speaks a feeling rather than a thought, and the feeling is as simple as his language and syntax and as familiar as the hymn metre Brontë has chosen for him. The single abstraction—identity—is more transitory than the concrete rain and the snow. These natural elements, produced by changes in the seasons and the weather, literally remind us of a gravesite that is open to the elements, but they also stand in for all the other interminable changes that summon up care. Like many dramatic utterances in Brontë's poems, this one is difficult to read in our ordinary speaking voices. 'As pure unmediated speech,' Sharon Cameron writes, lyric speech 'lies furthest of all the mimetic arts from the way we really talk.' Cameron's lyric speech—'the way we would talk in dreams if we could convert the phantasmagoria there into words'—corresponds to what the poet hears in the dream recorded in *The Prelude*, when he holds the Arab's shell to his ear: 'articulate sounds' in 'an unknown tongue, | Which yet I understood'.[26] Lyric speakers like Brontë's philosopher are loosed from their social and historical contexts so that they can speak in this unknown tongue which yet we understand. This doesn't mean that the speakers of lyric poems aren't persons given to human utterances, or that these utterances lack specific historical coordinates, although recently the lyric poem has come under fire as 'a deplorably anti-social genre' and an exercise in the programmatic exclusion of otherness, difference, and history.[27] Lyric speakers typically pitch their voices above, or below, the voices we use for ordinary social intercourse. This is the point Edith Wharton makes about Henry James's reading of 'Remembrance', when she says that he was not afraid to 'chant' the poem, refusing to 'chatter high verse as if it were colloquial prose'.[28] Stanley Cavell's idea that it is difficult to teach someone to read a lyric poem makes a related point. 'You will have to demonstrate how it rests in the voice, or hauls at it, and perhaps will not be able to do that without undergoing the spiritual instant or passage for which it discovers release (that is, unable to say what it means without meaning it there and then) .... '[29] If we take these lines from 'The Philosopher' or the lines I have quoted from 'The Prisoner (A Fragment)' as examples, you may not be able to demonstrate how to read them without undergoing the spiritual instant for which these poems discover release, that is, without opening yourself to your own absence or dying with desire. From this perspective, reading a lyric poem is like dreaming the kind of dream that Catherine says has gone through her like wine through water and altered the colour of her mind.

Although this book is about Emily Brontë as a lyric poet, the distinction between her lyric and her narrative poetry, especially the

Gondal narrative poetry, is not at all clear-cut. Readers have long recognized that Brontë's narrative poems contain passages of pure lyric; some have lamented the degradation of these lyric passages by the inferior narrative context that surrounds them.[30] But apart from her fragmentary poems or poetical fragments, Brontë wrote hardly any lyric poems that do not have a powerful narrative dimension, whether they are poems belonging to the world of Gondal, like 'Remembrance', or poems she situated outside that world, like 'Death'. The strong narrative element of a poem like 'Hope', also among the poems Brontë selected for publication in 1846, is especially evident if we read it together with any of the three poems by Emily Dickinson on this topic, ' "Hope" is the thing with feathers' (P 254), 'Hope is a strange invention' (P 1392), and 'Hope is a subtle Glutton' (P 1547). Each of Dickinson's poems begins with a metaphor that defines Hope in terms of a specific kind of agency, but all three poems substitute duration, more or less timeless, for accomplished action. That is, there is no progress in the action being described and no development of the speaker's feeling about Hope as the poem threads its way from beginning to end. Dickinson's 'Hope is a subtle Glutton' determinedly evokes and insists upon the stasis of paradox: 'whatsoever is consumed | The same amount remain'. This is a zero-sum game without advances or withdrawals, gains or losses:

> Hope is a subtle Glutton—
> He feeds upon the Fair—
> And yet—inspected closely
> What Abstinence is there—
>
> His is the Halcyon Table—
> That never seats but One—
> And whatsoever is consumed
> The same amount remain—[31]

Brontë's poem on Hope works differently by striving to give duration to what appears simultaneous in Dickinson's poem. This difference is registered in the wider range of tenses and moods Brontë requires. Like Dickinson's, her poem begins by personifying Hope, but the personification serves the purposes of an allegorical narrative, not those of definition:

> Hope was but a timid friend;
> She sat without the grated den,
> Watching how my fate would tend,
> Even as selfish-hearted men.

She was cruel in her fear;
   Through the bars, one dreary day,
I looked out to see her there,
   And she turned her face away!

Like a false guard, false watch keeping,
   Still in strife, she whispered peace;
She would sing while I was weeping;
   If I listened, she would cease.

False she was, and unrelenting;
   When my last joys strewed the ground,
Even Sorrow saw, repenting,
   Those sad relics scattered round;

Hope, whose whisper would have given
   Balm to all my frenzied pain,
Stretched her wings, and soared to heaven,
   Went, and ne'er returned again!

Hope takes on various identities according to changes in the speaker's mood and feeling. She is first a 'timid friend', then a 'false guard', and finally a free spirit. Hope is a friend because she is near, a visible presence and perhaps a concerned one. But Hope's refusal to do anything but watch, and the speaker's belief that merely watching is selfish and cruel, produce feelings of alienation and abandonment, which are expressed when Hope turns her face away. This explicit separation of the speaker from Hope produces an enmity like that between a prisoner, who is trapped, and his guard, who is free to come and go. Finally, Hope does what the speaker can't do: she stretches her wings and soars to heaven.

The self is divided or dispersed in this poem. It experiences itself as both here—locked inside a prison or 'grated den'—and there—beyond the bars. This idea of a split or dispersed self is fundamental to *Wuthering Heights*, where it is most fully expressed in the relationship between Catherine and Heathcliff, and to many of the poems. 'Hope' manages to protract its speaker's struggle with herself over a (relatively) long stretch of time. It does this with its present progressive verbs, which gravitate from the beginning of the line in the first stanza ('Watching') to the ends of lines in the third and fourth stanzas. The fourth stanza, which describes Hope as 'unrelenting' while Sorrow is 'repenting' and refers to the scattering of the speaker's 'last joys', lengthens time further by teasing us with the hope that Hope will, at last, relent.

The precise way in which Brontë forestalls an ending in 'Hope' is a characteristic feature of her narrative practice. Hope departs in the last stanza, and the speaker informs us that she 'n'er returned again'. This formulation holds open the possibility of a return but not of an ending. *Again* is a word that appears with unusual frequency in Brontë's poems: eighty-two times, many of them in phrases including 'ne'er' or 'never', often at the end of a line and more often than any other word at the end of a poem. Bruno Snell observes that *again* is a typical feature of the opening lines of early Greek lyric poetry. He relates its use there to the poet's effort to extend his or her poem's temporal reach 'beyond the scope of the present'.[32] The use of *again* at the end of a poem extends that poem's temporal reach beyond the scope of the present not just by remembering the past but by anticipating a repetitive future. Again disrupts our sense that an experience is over and done with, even if a poem is over and done with. The frequency with which *again* rhymes with *pain* in Brontë's poems reminds us of Dickinson, whose pain 'cannot recollect | When it begun—or if there were | A time when it was not,'[33] but Brontë puts the stress on a future as relentless as the past and as endless as forever. Take, for example, 'I see around me tombstones grey, where the shadow of the tombstones stretches as far as the eye can see, and the 'silent dead' are said to be 'Forever dark, forever cold':

> For Time and Death and Mortal pain
> Give wounds that will not heal again—

When do you know that someone or something never returned again? Only when there is no more knowing. So long as there is consciousness, there is the possibility, and either the hope or the dread, of a repetition of what has been before. *Not for the first time* has easy relations with *not for the last time*, and 'never' or 'ne'er' has trouble undoing them. One of Brontë's undated fragmentary poems turns around this insight:

> All hushed and still within the house
> Without—all wind and driving rain
> But something whispers to my mind
> Through rain and air and wailing wind
>   —Never again
> Never again? Why not again?
> Memory has power as real as thine[34]

Hope whispers because she is intimate with the self, because a whisper requires a particularly attentive listener, and because whispers linger the way pain does. But what's on offer is a palliative, not a cure—'Balm to all my frenzied pain'. Hope's disappearance is prolonged, as the speaker watches her leisurely departure for heaven. What does it mean to say that Hope 'ne'er returned again'? This is what Hope does, Brontë tells us: she comes and goes. Though the line may not mean that Hope will not return, it knows that even if Hope returns, she won't stay.

Dickinson's and Brontë's poems about Hope embody two kinds of resistance to ending. Dickinson seeks to undo time by freezing it. Zeno's paradox of the tortoise represents spatially the paradox her poem represents temporally. Brontë protracts time almost beyond bearing. In 'Hope' and other poems, Brontë regularly does this by representing an event that has happened, is happening, and will happen again. 'For him who struck thy foreign string', a Gondal poem that Charlotte Brontë published in 1850 under her title 'The Lady to Her Guitar', shows Brontë again creating a world without end where effects outlast their causes so that whatever was persists in a timeless present. Perhaps because both are visionary poems, 'For him who struck thy foreign string' shares Kubla Khan's imagery of sunny spots enclosed by antique forests, shapes hovering on a watery surface, and timeless music. Like Shelley's guitar (in 'With a Guitar. To Jane'), Brontë's is inhabited by a spirit that can be tempted to betray the 'secrets of an elder day':

> For him who struck thy foreign string
> I ween this heart hath ceased to care
> Then why dost thou such feelings bring
> To my sad spirit, old guitar?
>
> It is as if the warm sunlight
> In some deep glen should lingering stay
> When clouds of tempest and of night
> Had wrapped the parent orb away—
>
> It is as if the glassy brook
> Should image still its willows fair
> Though years ago the woodman's stroke
> Laid low in dust their gleaming hair:
>
> Even so, guitar, thy magic tone
> Hath moved the tear and waked the sigh
> Hath bid the ancient torrent flow
> Although its very source is dry!

In 'In drear-nighted December', Keats contemplates the seasonal changes in tree and brook and envies an insensate inhuman world for which the present is all there is. The measure of human sorrow is what can always be recovered, but only as a recollection of what was, and is no longer:

But were there ever any
    Writhèd not of passèd joy?
The feel of not to feel it,
When there is none to heal it,
Nor numbèd sense to steel it,
    Was never said in rhyme.[35]

Brontë's insight is different but equally haunting. Does feeling that once flowed dry up, or does it remain available not just to memory in an act of recovery but to consciousness as itself, the water that bursts from the rock? 'Nay, I have done: you get no more of me,' Drayton says. Are we ever done? Those plaintive questions—'Never again? Why not again?'—hang in this poem's air, for there are some things, some feelings, we would like to be over and done with but cannot get out of our systems, however hard we try. This is different from 'The feel of not to feel it.' It is the feel of having to feel it again and again. As in Keats's poem, the pool doesn't long for the absent willows and the deep glen doesn't lament the disappearance of warm sunlight, but Brontë's speaker lacks even the small comfort of not feeling past joy as if it were present while at the same time knowing it is not. Her poem's speaker has been thrown into a tumult of feeling, a 'torrent' of tears and sighs. That the past is cumulatively present in us, yet not always wholly accessible, is time's mercy. But the opposite is also true. The capacity of the past to elicit not just a memory but 'an inner psychic constellation laden with images, feelings, and bodily acuities' is time's miracle.[36]

    The magical images of the two middle stanzas—the persistence of the sunlight after the disappearance of the sun and the retained reflection of willows in the brook after the trees have been cut down—provide analogies for the persistence of human feeling. Shelley uses the same image of pools of water that reflect the surrounding forest in 'To Jane. The Recollection', but the pools cannot maintain their loving view for long and so confirm the mutability of his own moods:

Like one beloved, the scene had lent
    To the dark water's breast,
Its every leaf and lineament
    With more than truth exprest;
Until an envious wind crept by,
    Like an unwelcome thought
Which from the mind's too faithful eye
    Blots one dear image out.—

The images in Brontë's glassy brook are like ghosts in being sufficiently unreal for her poem not to go farther than to claim a hypothetical ('as if') presence for them. Still, the music the speaker is making with her guitar is real, and it works its magic with feeling in a 'real' present. It matters that the music is present, although the object of feeling, whoever 'struck thy foreign string', is absent. Is the speaker deluding herself about having ceased 'to care' for him, or has she ceased to care for him without losing access to her feeling as if she still did care? We cannot resolve this ambiguity and should not try to. Brontë's poem is much less interested in the psychology of its speaker than it is in the archaic mechanism of remembrance. Remembrance, in this poem as in Brontë's better-known poem 'Remembrance', is involuntary and gives present life to what once lived and has only seemed dead. Both poems are about unresolved loss and mourning. In 'For him who struck they foreign string', one of the most familiar nineteenth-century emblems of mourning, the image of the 'gleaming hair' of the willows 'laid low in dust', confirms this. In all of Brontë's poems, the boundary between the past and the present is permeable and always in danger of collapsing entirely. Feeling is often cut loose from its source so that it persists without an objective correlative in present-time reality. Keats takes the measure of his loss in 'In drear-nighted December' and rationally balances his emotional accounts. Brontë perpetually relives the past in the present so that no emotional balance can be struck.

'Stars', another poem Brontë selected for publication in 1846 (Figure 1), may be her most successful poem about the rhythm of loss and recovery that characterizes a life in time. The poem has been read as both a celebration of imaginative escape from the ordinary world and an acceptance of the need to live in that world. For Robin Grove, 'Stars' registers the degree to which Brontë is 'alive to the raptures of the night-time world' and at the same time enables her to criticize her wish 'to return to that sheltering trance of nature rhapsodies and "mysticism" and the Gondal world which would not bear exposure to daylight.'[37] But the achievement of 'Stars' is larger and more impersonal. To view the poem's psychological landscape, we need the resources of a vocabulary that is not in thrall to biographical insights or too easily prepared to describe Brontë's desire for imaginative escape from the ordinary, daylight world as escapism, a turn away from 'reality' that is temperamental instead of philosophical, and cowardly instead of risky. We can find it in the essays of Brontë's contemporary, Ralph Waldo Emerson, one or more of which we know Charlotte was reading to her

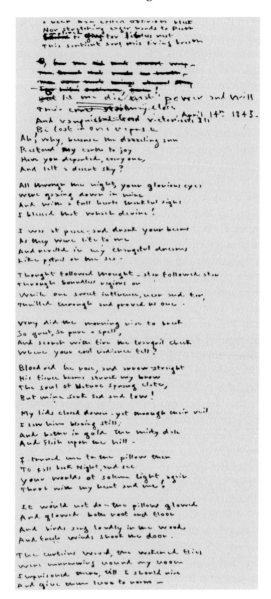

Figure 1. 'Stars', from a reproduction in facsimile of the Honresfeld manuscript, now missing. The first page of this manuscript is headed 'E. J. B.' and 'Transcribed February 1844'.

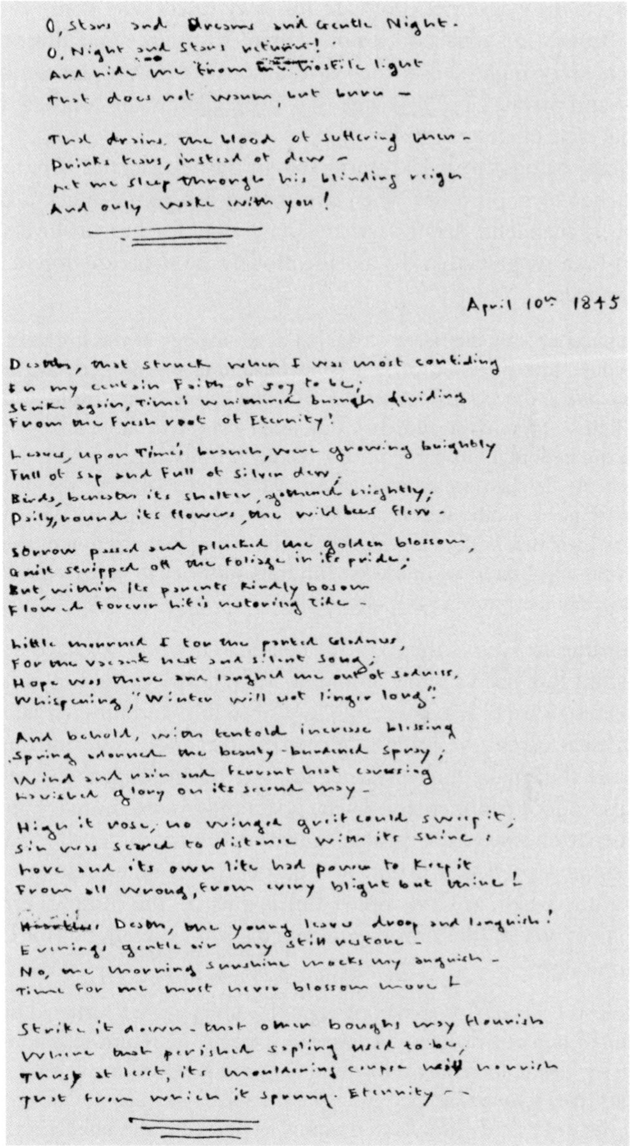

Figure 2. 'Stars' (continued) and 'Death,' from a reproduction in facsimile of the Honresfeld manuscript, now missing.

sister on the eve of her death. In his essay titled 'The Poet', Emerson, like Brontë in 'Stars', does not hesitate to praise 'that dream-power which every night shows thee is thine own; a power transcending all limit and privacy, and by virtue of which a man is the conductor of the whole river of electricity'.[38]

'Stars' belongs to an old genre, that of the aubade, but Brontë adapts it to her own purposes when she makes her gentle night a time to revel in changeful dreams rather than a time for human lovers. Allen Grossman suggests that the aubade models the structure of lyric poems in general:

For an example of the poem of waking as an analogy of the structure of lyric procedure (the direction of flow from beginning to end), see Shakespeare's *Romeo and Juliet*, act III, scene v, 1–36. The passage ends, 'Rom. More light and light—more dark and dark our woes!' The lyric begins by awakening from the dark night of participation, the night of having, in which there is no speech. As light grows, differentiation increases, the lark and the nightingale are distinguished, persons become identified and more separate. As light grows sorrow increases, as does knowledge. In this sense, the direction of the lyric is from participation to acknowledgment, from intimacy to strangeness, from the hour before dawn to the hour after dark.[39]

According to 'Stars', the night of having is a world we have access to daily but lose just as often simply by waking up. As light increases, the awakening sleeper becomes conscious of sounds and differentiates them from each other: the birds sing outside, the door rattles in the wind, and the flies make their presence known, murmuring their complaint against indoor confinement. As the poem progresses, intimacy gives way to alienation, heaven to history, and tranquillity to violence. 'Stars' is not about a particular dream or a particular dreaming self. It is about dreaming, when, as Christopher Bollas puts it, 'the complex reflecting self' gives way to 'the simple experiencing self', though not for long, or long enough:

Winnicott believed that each of us begins life unintegrated, scattered islands of organized potentials coming in to being. Perhaps we return to unintegration when we dream, loosening this self into an archipelago of many beings, acting various roles scripted by the ego in the theater of the night. Waking, we rise from these regressed states, both from the fetal place to the ambulatory posture and from the plenitude of selves to the discerning 'I' who reflects on his odd subjects.[40]

Stars

Ah! why, because the dazzling sun
  Restored our Earth to joy,
Have you departed, every one,
  And left a desert sky?

All through the night, your glorious eyes
  Were gazing down in mine,
And with a full heart's thankful sighs,
  I blessed that watch divine.

I was at peace, and drank your beams
  As they were life to me;
And revelled in my changeful dreams,
  Like petrel on the sea.

Thought followed thought, star followed star,
  Through boundless regions, on;
While one sweet influence, near and far,
  Thrilled through, and proved us one!

Why did the morning dawn to break
  So great, so pure, a spell;
And scorch with fire, the tranquil cheek,
  Where your cool radiance fell?

Blood-red, he rose, and, arrow-straight,
  His fierce beams struck my brow;
The soul of nature, sprang, elate,
  But *mine* sank sad and low!

My lids closed down, yet through their veil,
  I saw him, blazing, still,
And steep in gold the misty dale,
  And flash upon the hill.

I turned me to the pillow, then,
  To call back night, and see
Your worlds of solemn light, again,
  Throb with my heart, and me!

It would not do—the pillow glowed,
  And glowed both roof and floor;
And birds sang loudly in the wood,
  And fresh winds shook the door;

The curtains waved, the wakened flies
  Were murmuring round my room,

Imprisoned there, till I should rise,
And give them leave to roam.

Oh, stars, and dreams, and gentle night;
Oh, night and stars return!
And hide me from the hostile light,
That does not warm, but burn;

That drains the blood of suffering men;
Drinks tears, instead of dew;
Let me sleep through his blinding reign,
And only wake with you!

'Stars' expresses the wish not just that the night would last but that the stars would remain visible in the daylight sky. The fiction that they depart is, in this poem, no fiction at all, for the speaker cannot see them. They appear to have abandoned the sky but have indeed abandoned her. Like Wordsworth's 'Intimations Ode', 'Stars' weighs two kinds of vision against each other. The daylight vision, the world as it usually looks in Wordsworth's 'light of common day', is at first appealing to the dreamer. Although she awakens reluctantly, the sunlight is 'dazzling'. It restores the earth to 'joy', birds sing, and the winds that shake the door are 'fresh'. But the daylight vision is inimical to a different vision (associated by Wordsworth with the noon, by Brontë with the night), and Brontë's daylight is not just dazzling but coercive. The contrasts in 'Stars' are sharp: while the starlight shines with a 'cool radiance' that quiets and nourishes the speaker, the light of the sun scorches her cheek and its 'fierce beams' strike her brow.

Brontë's sun is monstrously masculine, and her stars are not just feminine but maternal and nurturing. The sun rises 'Blood-red' and 'arrow-straight', and instead of satisfying the speaker's thirst, it slakes its own. The daylight hides the night world and simultaneously reveals a world in which the self is forced to acknowledge its weakness and accept its dependency as an occasion for dominance. During the night, however, the stars were as intimate with her as a mother with her child. Her engagement with them involved a sensory exchange that evokes nursing: their 'glorious eyes' gaze down on her, while her eyes drink their beams. According to Bollas, being in the dream space is 'a continuous reminiscence of being inside the maternal world when one was partly a receptive figure within a comprehending environment'. The dreamer—'the productive intentionality that determines the dream we are in and that never reveals itself'—recreates or resembles the 'mother's unconscious, which although it does not "show itself," nonetheless produces the process of maternal care'.[41]

Although 'Stars' announces the loss of the night world in its first stanza, the separation between man and Nature that is the ordinary condition of being in time is fully acknowledged only in the sixth stanza, when the sun re-establishes the distance between them, driving the dreamer's soul and Nature's in opposite directions: 'The soul of nature, sprang, elate, | But mine sank sad and low!' The poem might have ended here, at what turns out to be its midpoint, but stanza seven goes on to describe the speaker's renewed efforts to block out the sun's brightness. How can a sun that steeps the dale in gold and flashes upon the hill not satisfy this viewer, or any viewer with eyes to see the poetry of nature and familiarity with Brontë's Wordsworthian diction? Despite the brightness of the dreamer's waking vision, it is a vision to which her heart doesn't throb. The last stanza surprises us by turning away from the dreaming self and toward 'suffering men' in general. The progress from intimacy to alienation, from heaven to history, and from self-experience to self-reflection requires this turn in 'Stars'. During the night, the speaker rides the waves of her 'changeful dreams'; during the day, she is unable to escape her fraught consciousness of human suffering. This consciousness, held at bay through an effort of the will despite the sun's rising, surfaces in the poem's last stanza.

In order to deal with the questions raised by the poem's last stanza, I want to review the course the poem has plotted somewhat differently. The speaker begins with a question that covers or stands in for an accusation. The stars have abandoned her, and she demands to know why. The body of the poem expresses more fully and perhaps more clearly than any other poem Brontë wrote just what she has known and lost. She makes an effort of will to bring back the stars, but has to acknowledge her defeat by the sun. The poem ends with a plea that modulates into a bitter characterization of the cruel world she is now forced to occupy, and then into a prayer. Although the poem has so far proceeded in closed quatrains, each one containing a single sentence, the end of the stanza before the last one appears to coincide with the end of a sentence but doesn't. Brontë indicts the ordinary world in the last stanza, where the light of the sun is not just 'hostile' but cruel. This is the patriarchal deity of Shelley's *Prometheus Unbound*, who drains the life and savours the tears of suffering men. The speaker has only to leave the safety of her dreaming in order to fall into a larger community of human sufferers cut off from a nurturing world. She prays for release, at least for herself:

> Let me sleep through his blinding reign,
> And only wake with you!

These lines invert the relation between the night-time and daytime worlds the poem describes. Like Keats, Brontë would have known Johnson's contrast between dreams, which come to us in a sleeping state, and visions, which appear when we are awake. Throughout the poem, she has called herself a dreamer, but in the last two lines, she emerges as a visionary. She proclaims that the world the stars light is as real as the world lit by the sun. In order to wake to it, we have to close our eyes to the life around us.

'Stars' is intimate in its setting and its details—pillow, flies, a rattling door. No other Brontë poem places us in the poet's bedroom. Yet 'Stars' tells us very little about the particular woman who occupies that bedroom, buries her head in her pillow, and sympathizes with the eagerness of the flies to escape confinement. The poem doesn't tell us, for instance, anything about the content of her dreams, although we know from *Wuthering Heights* that Brontë was fully aware of the psychological interpretations to which dreams lend themselves. Thus Catherine regards her dream of finding herself in heaven and longing to return to Wuthering Heights as evidence that she would be miserable in heaven, and also, when she translates the dream's manifest into its latent content, as a warning not to marry Edgar Linton. 'Stars' doesn't offer the content of its speaker's dream because the poet isn't interested in the psychology of its speaker but in the impersonal psychological activity of dreaming. Although the dream has ended, she writes about what it feels like to be caught up in it, not about what it feels like to contemplate it or to use it to better understand the waking self.

The dream state revealed in 'Stars' can be said to recreate or resemble the process of maternal care insofar as the poem represents the self as flowing with the world or feeling itself a part of the world so long as it is buoyed up by its 'changeful dreams'. The sea birds suggest that this self lives in two elements—air and ocean—but finds nourishment in only one of them. Brontë may be recalling Wordsworth's primal sympathy here, but she anticipates Winnicott's benign circle of maternal care and Freud's oceanic feeling. The content of these feelings is the same: boundlessness ('Thought followed thought, star followed star, | Through boundless regions, on') together with at-oneness with the environment ('While one sweet influence, near and far, | Thrilled through, and proved us one!'). Brontë's use of thought in 'Stars' is related to her assimilation of thoughts to feelings in 'The Philosopher', and has a precedent in Wordsworth's definition of thoughts as the 'representatives of all our past feelings'.[42] The dreamer's thoughts are said to follow each other only because this is our ordinary way of speaking, and only in the way that one star can be said to follow another when they are actually shining at the same time. Like the stars, the dreamer's thoughts are simultaneously present to her. Released from the constraints of time that decree succession, they participate in an original unity repeatedly lost to us in our waking, self-reflective state.

Dreaming almost always occurs at night in Brontë's poems, whether she is describing a 'dream of sleep' or silently musing on the threshhold of a dream while earth sleeps, as in 'The Night-Wind'. The exception is 'A Day Dream', also selected for publication in 1846, which has as its setting an afternoon in late May. Like 'Stars', 'A Day Dream' opposes daylight life to the imaginative or spiritual life in the poet and around her, but this daylight life is joyous, not hostile:

A Day Dream

On a sunny brae, alone I lay
　　One summer afternoon;
It was the marriage-time of May
　　With her young lover, June.

From her mother's heart, seemed loath to part
　　That queen of bridal charms,
But her father smiled on the fairest child
　　He ever held in his arms.

The trees did wave their plumy crests,
　　The glad birds carolled clear;
And I, of all the wedding guests,
　　Was only sullen there!

There was not one, but wished to shun
　　My aspect void of cheer;
The very grey rocks, looking on,
　　Asked, 'What do you here?'

And I could utter no reply;
　　In sooth, I did not know
Why I had brought a clouded eye
　　To greet the general glow.

So resting on a heathy bank,
  I took my heart to me;
And we together sadly sank
  Into a reverie.

We thought, 'When winter comes again,
  Where will these bright things be?
All vanished, like a vision vain,
  An unreal mockery!

'The birds that now so blithely sing,
  Through deserts, frozen dry,
Poor spectres of the perished spring,
  In famished troops, will fly.

'And why should we be glad at all?
  The leaf is hardly green,
Before a token of its fall
  Is on the surface seen.

Now, whether it were really so,
  I never could be sure;
But as in fit of peevish woe,
  I stretched me on the moor,

A thousand thousand gleaming fires
  Seemed kindling in the air;
A thousand thousand silvery lyres
  Resounded far and near:

Methought, the very breath I breathed
  Was full of sparks divine,
And all my heather-couch was wreathed
  By that celestial shine!

'O mortal! mortal! let them die;
  Let time and tears destroy,
That we may overflow the sky
  With universal joy!

'Let grief distract the sufferer's breast,
  And night obscure his way;
They hasten him to endless rest,
  And everlasting day.

'To thee the world is like a tomb,
  A desert's naked shore;
To us, in unimaginable bloom,
  It brightens more and more!

'And could we lift the veil, and give
    One brief glimpse to thine eye,
Thou wouldst rejoice for those that live,
    Because they live to die.'
The music ceased; the noonday dream,
    Like dream of night, withdrew;
But Fancy, still, will sometimes deem
    Her fond creation true.

More than any other Brontë poem, this one comes into repeated relation with the poems of Brontë's predecessors, not just because it is a familiar kind of poem, a dream vision in which authoritative figures communicate some doctrine or revelation to the dreamer, but because it generously echoes or alludes to earlier poems. Acknowledging that Brontë's poems call into play the words of previous poets goes against one of the most fundamental precepts about her: she prized the freedom to think her own thoughts in her own way so highly that she refused the influence of others or was immune to it.[43] As a student in Brussels, she opposed her teacher Constantin Heger's assignment of 'some of the master-pieces of the most celebrated French authors' as models for analysis and imitation. According to Gaskell, he thought that the Brontës were capable of 'catching the echo of a style, and so reproducing their own thoughts in a somewhat similar manner'. Charlotte accepted this plan and thrived on it, since it gave her opportunities for displaying her gifts as a pupil. Emily 'said she saw no good to be derived from it; and that, by adopting it, they should lose all originality of thought and expression'.[44]

A reader does not need to recognize the echoes in 'A Day Dream' in order to take Brontë's meaning. She may not have consciously sought them, but she would not have been likely to miss hearing them in her poem. They alert us to what John Hollander has called 'a private melody or undersong hummed during composition by the poet as a spell or charm'.[45] For the reader of 'A Day Dream', this undersong helps to mark the ground that Brontë's poem shares with some important predecessor poems. Thus, the memory of Macbeth, unnerved by the ghost of Banquo—'Hence, horrible shadow! | Unreal mockery, hence!'—surfaces in Brontë's image of the 'bright things' of spring, which will vanish 'like a vision vain, | An unreal mockery!' The mockery in Brontë's poem is not some 'horrible shadow' we long to dispell, the ghost of the good man whose assassination Macbeth has just had accomplished. It is the sunny springtime world we cannot keep time from dispelling. Why should Macbeth's guilty moment attach itself to Brontë's 'sullen' one? Certainly mourning, or the anticipation of it, shadows her reverie. In 'On Transience', a brief essay written in 1915 at the invitation of the Berlin Goethe Society, Freud describes an occasion similar to the one in 'A Day Dream':

Not long ago I went on a summer walk through a smiling countryside in the company of a taciturn friend and of a young but already famous poet. The poet admired the beauty of the scene around us but felt no joy in it. He was disturbed by the thought that all this beauty was fated to extinction, that it would vanish when winter came, like all human beauty and all the beauty and splendour that men have created or may create. All that he would otherwise have loved or admired seemed to him to be shorn of its worth by the transience which was its doom.[46]

Freud cannot dispute the transience of beauty—'what is painful may none the less be true'—but he does dispute the view that transience diminishes worth. 'On the contrary, an increase! Transience value is scarcity value in time.' This interpretation makes little impression on the poet. Freud then infers that the poet's judgement is impaired by a 'foretaste of mourning', which he describes in much the same way he describes it in 'Mourning and Melancholia', published after 'On Transience' but written a few months earlier. Freud tells us that his conversation with the poet took place in the summer before the war. Although he is writing 'On Transience' after the war has destroyed so much beauty, he does not acknowledge that his own powerful emotions may be involved in producing the faith that mourning, like beauty, is transient.

Although she has killed no one, Brontë's dreamer is guilty in the face of death because like Macbeth, she is a self-condemned outcast from the human community. In 'A Day Dream', the community that shuns the dreamer is the community that refuses to acknowledge and anticipate the death that nature owes. All except the dreamer are happy. Brontë emphasizes her dreamer's solitariness both in the poem's first line, where she lies 'alone' on a 'sunny brae', and later, when 'I took my heart to me' reminds us that she has no lover. She may or may not consciously echo Wordsworth's 'Intimations Ode' when she chooses the word 'sullen' to describe her dreamer. The coincidence of the word alone would not pull Wordsworth's poem into the orbit of 'A Day Dream,' but the poet's guilt when he imagines that his mood may not harmonize with nature's might:

> Oh evil day! if I were sullen
> While Earth herself is adorning,
> This sweet May-morning…

As an alien and disruptive presence at a wedding, Brontë's day dreamer also resembles Coleridge's Ancient Mariner, and Coleridge's is the language that resonates most fully in Brontë's ballad. Just after the wedding guest says that he fears the Mariner because he suspects that he is a ghost, the Mariner reassures him that he still lives:

> The many men, so beautiful!
> And they all dead did lie:
> And a thousand thousand slimy things
> Lived on; and so did I.

Brontë's 'thousand thousand gleaming fires' echo Coleridge's 'thousand thousand slimy things', which reappear—after seven days during which the mariner longs to die—as gorgeous water snakes belonging to the company of 'happy living things'. The Mariner loves and blesses them; the Albatross drops from his neck; he sleeps, dreams, and wakes to a vision:

> The upper air burst into life!
> And a hundred fire-flags sheen,
> To and fro they were hurried about!
> And to and fro, and in and out,
> The wan stars danced between.

One other poem is alive in 'A Day Dream', Wordsworth's 'Resolution and Independence', which may also be alive in the 'Intimations Ode''s reference to the 'timely utterance' that relieved the poet's grief. Like the poet in 'Resolution and Independence', Brontë's dreamer falls into 'a fit of peevish woe' out of which she is startled by a miraculous appearance. 'Now whether it were by peculiar grace | A leading from above, a something given,' Wordsworth's poet says upon seeing the leech gatherer. Seeing a 'thousand thousand gleaming fires' and hearing a 'thousand thousand silvery lyres', Brontë's dreamer echoes him: 'Now, whether it were really so, | I never could be sure …'. Although Wordsworth's leech-gatherer is a human presence in the scene, unlike Brontë's 'little glittering spirits', he is also internalized, so that he seems 'Like one whom I had met with in a dream'. The dream, which may have come to Wordsworth rather than having come from him, is like

Brontë's dream in having the power to restore the poet's faith in himself and the universe.

Whether or not Brontë intends her echoes of Shakespeare, Wordsworth, and Coleridge, she intends to write a dream vision poem and is familiar with its features: a framing narrative introducing a dreamer, sometimes a poet, who may or may not be depicted as depressed or anxious; a dream that includes a conversation with real or allegorical characters; and a setting, often a garden in May.[47] Dream visions, both secular and religious, were popular in medieval England and continued to figure in the work of writers Brontë knew, like Bunyan and Burns. In 'A Day Dream', Brontë's 'glittering spirits' offer the dreamer an apocalyptic vision. And, like all apocalyptic visions, this one does not enable her to witness and celebrate the end of time but promises that she would celebrate it if she could see it:

> 'And could we lift the veil, and give
> One brief glimpse to thine eye,
> Thou wouldst rejoice for those that live,
> *Because* they live to die.'

But the dreamer's apocalyptic vision has a specific psychological context. At the poem's start, she is already sullen and heart-sick. Her 'reverie', like Wordsworth's in 'Resolution and Independence', only sinks her deeper into despondency. The 'glad birds' so joyously carolling in the beginning of the poem now sing 'blithely', unaware, as the dreamer can't help being, that they are destined to become 'Poor spectres of the perished spring'. In 'The Darkling Thrush', Hardy will perversely derive hope from his aged bird's 'happy good-night air'. Since the desolation of the scene provides 'So little cause for carolings', the thrush must know something that the poet doesn't. But in Freud's words, 'what is painful may none the less be true.' What sense does it make to take the death of every living thing as evidence of eternal life, as Brontë does in 'A Day Dream'? The italics in her triumphant formula—'rejoice for those that live, | *Because* they live to die'—have an effect like that of the exclamation point when Freud rejects his poet's view that the transience of beauty involves a loss of value: 'On the contrary, an increase!' Both suspect that the claim being made has little to support it, though Freud presents himself as more rational than his poet, while Brontë presents her dreamer as one who glimpses the truth behind the veil. The final stanza of 'A Day Dream', which marks the end of the dream and completes the narrative that frames it, makes the smallest possible claim for the dream's truth. It is said to be 'Fancy''s creation, and even Fancy believes in her creation only intermittently.

Visionary experience in 'A Day Dream' not only alludes to the visionary experience of Coleridge's Ancient Mariner but anticipates that of Yeats's dreamer in 'The Man Who Dreamed of Faeryland'. In Yeats's poem, the meanest creatures keep the dreamer from being satisfied with his material and sensual life. Even after his death, the man continues to dream, as the worms circling his buried body

> Proclaim with that unwearied, reedy cry
> That God has laid His fingers on the sky,
> That from those fingers glittering summer runs
> Upon the dancer by the dreamless wave.

The word 'glittering', used here in relation to summer, echoes earlier uses, not just Brontë's 'glittering spirits' but the Mariner's 'glittering eye' and the mist that is 'glittering in the sun' in 'Resolution and Independence'. What we hear is partly a shared sense of the word itself, which describes a light that is brilliant but not steady and may lack lasting substance, however powerfully we are drawn to it. In her last poem, 'Why ask to know the date—the clime', Brontë uses the word 'glittering' to describe the 'toys his lightness loved— | The jewelled rings, and locket fair', things of beauty and emblems of transience. That Brontë's 'spirits' are 'glittering' does not diminish their attraction but may diminish their authority in anticipation of the poem's final stanza. But we also respond to the topos according to which glitter signals prophetic power and privileged experience, as it does in Coleridge's description of the Mariner's eyes. What Brontë's dream vision adds to the Mariner's dream vision, when the 'upper air burst into life', is a sense of her own participation in universal joy that connects her yet more closely to Wordsworth than to Coleridge. The 'thousand thousand gleaming fires' and 'silvery lyres' produce a new feeling in her that is linked to poetic inspiration: 'the very breath I breathed | Was full of sparks divine.' This new feeling is the soul of the poem and its warrant for the ongoing life from which, like Wordsworth in the 'Intimations Ode' or Yeats's man who dreamed of faeryland, she is most of the time cut off.

All of the poems I have considered so far involve imprisonment and the possibility of escape from it, whether the imprisonment is imagined as confinement in a grated den, in the ordinary daylight world, or in the physical body. They illustrate Brontë's habit of structuring a lyric meditation as a narrative of events taking place in endless time ('Hope'); her representation of images and feelings as timeless because they are perpetually subject to reiteration ('For him who struck thy foreign string'); her formulation of a fundamental dualism of existence in terms of two worlds or ways of being in the world and a self caught up in a perpetual rhythm of exchange or transport ('Stars'); and her revelation, or promised revelation, of last things in a dream that turns death into the aim of life and the trigger for life everlasting but isn't itself lasting ('A Day Dream'). When Brontë turned from writing poems to writing *Wuthering Heights* (though she never turned from writing poems in the sense of ceasing to write them during or after the composition of her novel), she had already expressed all of her novel's major themes in verse.

3

Fathoming 'Remembrance'

Remembrance has a Rear and Front—
'Tis something like a House—
It has a Garret also
For Refuse and the Mouse.

Besides the deepest Cellar
That ever Mason laid—
Look to it by its Fathoms
Ourselves be not pursued—

                                    Emily Dickinson

A poem titled 'Remembrance' would have raised certain expectations in 1846. Other titles Emily Brontë assigned her poems in the volume the three sisters published at their own expense—'Sympathy', 'Hope', 'The Prisoner (A Fragment)', and the inevitable 'Stanzas' and 'Song'—would also have been familiar to nineteenth-century readers, but 'Remembrance' is remarkable for its ubiquity in the period and for the particular associations it would have evoked. In 1846, 'Remembrance' was already the title of published poems by many poets, including Shelley, Byron, L. E. L., and Southey, whose 'Remembrance' Brontë probably read. It includes a phrase—'harass'd heart'—she used in two poems, including one on sleep beginning 'Sleep brings no joy to me | Remembrance never dies.'[1] Brontë's conviction that remembrance never dies, even in sleep, anticipates Freud. Recognizing that there is no cure for memory, psychoanalysis presents itself as a cure for forgetting or pretending to forget by turning symptoms, which are like monuments in the patient's psyche, into conscious memories, available for processing.[2] Brontë's protest against death requires the survival of remembrance, and like Freud, she is alert to how memory threatens that survival. Her poem 'Remembrance' turns on the axis of this dense psychological contradiction.

Freud explains the threat memory poses in his 'Notes upon a Case of Obsessional Neurosis':

I then made some short observations upon the *psychological difference between the conscious and the unconscious*, and upon the fact that everything conscious was subject to a process of wearing-away, while what was unconscious was relatively unchangeable; and I illustrated my remarks by pointing to the antiques standing about in my room. They were, in fact, I said, only objects found in a tomb, and their burial had been their preservation: the destruction of Pompeii was only beginning now that it had been dug up.[3]

Freud's distinction between conscious and unconscious memory has a mid-nineteenth-century analogue in the distinction between *recollection* and *remembrance*. In Brontë's time, *remembrance* differed from *recollection* by being involuntary. According to the *OED*, '*recollect*, when distinguished from *remember*, implies a conscious or express effort of memory to recall something which does not spontaneously rise to mind.' In *Sleep and Dreams* (1851), John Addington Symonds identifies 'two kinds of memory,—the one *passive*, the other *active*':

The simplest form of memory is the mere reproduction of a sensation or the return of a thought, or of a former emotion to the mind. When the recurrence of certain feelings and ideas is brought about by an effort of the will, such an act of the mind is denominated *recollection*. But when the past images come unbidden, we say that they are the products of mere *remembrance*.[4]

While the word *recollection* figures repeatedly in affirmations of memory's consoling powers in the Victorian period, the word *remembrance* is prominent in accounts of chronic and protracted grief. 'Precious recollections' are 'so pleasant yet so mournful', but the 'love that survives the tomb' lives '*on long remembrance*'.[5] One of the most potent divisions between the two families of *Wuthering Heights*, the Earnshaw family (including Heathcliff) and the Linton family, is their different relation to memory. Lintons recollect; Earnshaws remember. Thus Isabella Linton, when she reports having told Hindley that Catherine would still be alive if Heathcliff had not returned to the Heights, says that she told him she could 'recollect how happy we were—how happy Catherine was before he came' (II. iii. 223). The same sense of recollection as a voluntary effort of memory that tends to be comforting is active in Nelly's description of Edgar's 'resignation' to Catherine's death: 'He recalled her memory with ardent, tender love, and hopeful aspiring to the better world, where, he doubted not, she was gone' (II. iii. 226). Earlier, Nelly has warned Heathcliff against 'thrusting yourself into her remembrance, now, when she has nearly forgotten you, and involving her in a new tumult of discord and distress'. He counters that Catherine's remembrance of him is vibrantly alive: ' "You suppose she has nearly forgotten me?" he said. "Oh Nelly! you know she has not!" ' (I. xiv. 181). Heathcliff subscribes to an idea about memory that Nietzsche formulates: 'If something is to stay in the memory it must be burned in: only that which never ceases to *hurt* stays in the memory.'[6] In *Wuthering Heights* and in Brontë's poems, what never ceases to hurt survives as remembrance, not recollection.

Nelly's fear of the consequences of Heathcliff's encounter with Catherine after his three-year absence suggests her hope that remembrance, however perdurable, can slumber or remain buried. This idea about remembrance accounts for the currency of a contradictory nineteenth-century use of the word to refer not to a passive or involuntary return of former feeling but to something expressly designed to summon such feeling up. A keepsake or token of friendship and affection was, in this sense, a remembrance. The material sense of 'remembrance' shadows its immaterial sense, and is alive in Gaskell's formulation, when she writes that Charlotte Brontë, two years older than Emily, 'tried hard, in after years to recall the remembrance of her mother, and could bring back two or three pictures of her.'[7] Recalling the remembrance as two or three pictures of her mother, Brontë's memory acquires the concreteness, the stability, and the calmative ordinariness of a keepsake. Or does it? The only picture Gaskell provides is one of Charlotte's mother playing with the little boy whose birth, only fourteen months after her own, and whose greater value as the only son she probably experienced as traumatic. By the end of the nineteenth century, Freud would be addressing both reminiscences and gaps in the memories of hysterical young women. The 'reminiscences were cut-off bits of story somewhere between a day-dream and a memory. The huge gaps were due to an internalized prohibition on thinking those thoughts or feeling those feelings.'[8]

The considerable traffic in keepsakes or tokens of remembrance in the nineteenth century points to the period's efforts to manage the distresses associated with remembering and forgetting past feelings, especially those associated with the dead. The poems titled 'Remembrance' invoke the passing of years and seasons, the loss of childhood and youth, and the absence of the beloved dead. Several were published in the annuals in vogue from 1822, when Rudolph Ackermann brought out the first of them, his *Forget Me Not, a Christmas and New Year's Present for 1823*, until mid-century.[9] One of the annuals that began publication in the 1830s was called *The Remembrance*, another *The New Forget Me Not, or*

Ladies Fashionable Remembrancer. As the last title suggests, the audience for the annuals was largely female; they replaced manuals of conduct as presents for young ladies. One implication of this feminization of remembrance in the nineteenth century is that poems titled 'Remembrance', like others appearing in the annuals, were not supposed to challenge faith or question its consolations. Such poems were meant to be read easily. Southey characterized the annuals as 'picture-books for grown children', and Frederic Shoberl, the editor of the *Forget Me Not* series, advertised the 'cheering hopes and deepest convictions' to which they ministered.[10] Victorian society expected men to return to their public lives and to fill the places in their private lives left unoccupied by the dead fairly quickly. Women were supposed to remain faithful to the dead and, at the same time, to work through their grief, learning to supplant melancholy remembrance with calm recollection.[11]

When Emily Brontë prepared her poems for publication in 1846, she removed any references to Gondal characters, disguising the place of some of these poems in a larger Gondal narrative and maintaining the privacy of the world she and Anne had invented and explored. But her substitution of 'Remembrance' for 'R. Alcona to J. Brenzaida', the title of the poem in manuscript, goes further. It puts 'Remembrance'—the word appears only in the title—in dialogue with these other accounts of remembrance that transmute remembrance into recollection. Brontë's poem ministers to no cheering hopes and also bears on her deepest convictions about death in time and its human survivors. 'Remembrance' takes up the mortal grief that is a recurrent subject in her poems, and does so by exploring the injunction—familiar and directed particularly at women in the mid-nineteenth century—to remember. If remembering is, as Freud suggests, the beginning of a process of wearing away, while one of the uses of forgetting is to preserve the past intact, then the risks of remembering are related to those of mourning, conceived of as Freud conceived it in 'Mourning and Melancholia' as a process with detachment and consolation as its outcome. In response to a bereavement, pretending or seeming to forget may be the best way to resist resignation to a death and the inducement to consoling recollections.

In 'Remembrance' Emily Brontë sets out to express the idea that finality and composure in the face of deep and irrevocable loss are unattainable and to discover what happens when memory is dug up and brought in contact with the air. The essential information we lack about the poem's dramatic situation isn't information about R. (or Rosina) Alcona's relationship to J. (or Julius) Brenzaida in the missing Gondal narrative. It is information about what has thrust the dead beloved into the speaker's remembrance, which has for fifteen years preserved itself by a kind of burial that we could describe as the pretence of forgetting. The poem's extravagant references in its final stanza to 'memory's rapturous pain' and 'divinest anguish' together with the poet's highly disciplined warding off of closure respond to the many poems Emily Brontë would have read that insist on remembrance, like the ghost of Hamlet's father: 'Adieu, adieu, adieu! Remember me.' As if remembrance could die, or as if the act of remembering were less fraught and freighted than it is. As if it were more like Isabella's recollection of former happiness, or Edgar's recalling Catherine's memory in order to compensate for present loss with future gain. Tennyson responds to this charge in the *In Memoriam* lyric that marks the second Christmas eve after Hallam's death:

> O last regret, regret can die!
>   No—mixt with all this mystic frame,
>   Her deep relations are the same
> But with long use her tears are dry.

Although the speaker of Brontë's 'Remembrance' admits, in the poem's first half, that she has been 'beset' by 'Other desires and other hopes' during the fifteen years since her lover's death and asks forgiveness for forgetting, she denies the justice of this charge against herself in the poem's second half by reinterpreting forgetting as a false appearance—a 'Front', as Emily Dickinson punningly puts it. Instead, she describes a progress toward detachment that is always incomplete. Brontë's 'Where wilt thou go my harassed heart?' chimes feelingly with Dickinson's 'Ourselves be not pursued—.'

For convenience, I refer to the speaker of 'Remembrance' as female, even though this assumption, which is consistent for the poem's critics, relies for its substantiation either on the manuscript (which identifies the voice as Rosina Alcona's) or on the tendency to read Brontë's lyrics as if they were autobiographical utterances. The question of whether the experience the poem represents enables a reader to identify its speaker as female has not been discussed. I think it does, largely because some of the language—the insistence that the speaker has remained faithful to an 'only Love' or the description of that love's heart as 'noble'—is conventionally gendered as feminine in its period. The question of whether this poem represents Brontë's own experience is, however, much at issue in F. R. Leavis's once influential essay, 'Reality and Sincerity', first published in 1954. In it, Leavis repudiated his high estimate of 'Remembrance', which he had formerly praised as 'the finest poem in the nineteenth-century part of *The Oxford Book of English Verse*'. He objected both to the poem's flamboyant (or 'insincere') feeling, and to the absence of the concrete specificities that would substantiate the 'reality' of the experience it represents.[12] Leavis goes on in the later essay to contrast Brontë's satisfaction in 'dramatizing herself in a tragic role' with Hardy's 'conversational' or 'self-communing' intimacy in 'After a Journey', a poem in which Leavis sees the sceptical intelligence of the comfortably middle-aged male mourner triumphing over disorderly, disarming, and immature feelings.

C. Day Lewis makes the point that 'Sincerity is an active virtue only in personal poems,'[13] and 'Remembrance', as Henry James recognized in his reading of it, is not a personal poem. It is the kind of poem that is more than likely to cause a reader like Leavis to recoil, or any reader less ready to meet the human demands of embarrassment than James, whose reading of the poem Edith Wharton movingly records.[14] It is embarrassing to be transported by emotion in an address to a corpse, whose cold stillness proclaims his unresponsiveness, not to be able to present a coherent or wholly resolved self (even after fifteen years), and to be torn between justifying apparent facts and gesturing defensively at what they obscure. According to Wharton, when James chanted the poem, his 'stammer ceased as by magic ... and his ear, so sensitive to the convolutions of an intricate prose style, never allowed him to falter over the most complex prosody, but swept him forward on great rollers of sound till the full weight of his voice fell on the last cadence.'

Remembrance

Cold in the earth—and the deep snow piled above thee,
Far, far, removed, cold in the dreary grave!
Have I forgot, my only Love, to love thee,
Severed at last by Time's all-severing wave?

Now, when alone, do my thoughts no longer hover
Over the mountains, on that northern shore,
Resting their wings where heath and fern-leaves cover
Thy noble heart for ever, ever more?

Cold in the earth—and fifteen wild Decembers,
From those brown hills, have melted into spring:
Faithful, indeed, is the spirit that remembers
After such years of change and suffering!

Sweet Love of youth, forgive, if I forget thee,
While the world's tide is bearing me along;
Other desires and other hopes beset me,
Hopes which obscure, but cannot do thee wrong!

No later light has lightened up my heaven,
No second morn has ever shone for me;
All my life's bliss from thy dear life was given,
All my life's bliss is in the grave with thee.

But, when the days of golden dreams had perished,
And even Despair was powerless to destroy;
Then did I learn how existence could be cherished,
Strengthened, and fed without the aid of joy.

Then did I check the tears of useless passion—
Weaned my young soul from yearning after thine;
Sternly denied its burning wish to hasten
Down to that tomb already more than mine.

And, even yet, I dare not let it languish,
Dare not indulge in memory's rapturous pain;
Once drinking deep of that divinest anguish,
How could I seek the empty world again?

'Remembrance' opens with two lines that are punctuated to look like a complete sentence; they hover between being indicative and imperative in feeling, a lament about the long-ago death or a command hurled at someone who is dead but refuses to stay safely buried. The first complete sentence in the poem is the question that occupies the second half of the first stanza. Like the poem's other questions—the one which composes the second stanza, and the one with which the poem ends—this one is rhetorical. Its predictable answer is 'no, I haven't forgot to love thee.' Although Time claims to sever all 'at last', this lover has so far held out. The image of time as an ocean or stream, of life as a sea, and of death as a crossing figures often in the poetry of the period. The sea figures in 'Death and Despondency', the first poem by Emily Brontë in the 1846 volume, literally as that which separated father and daughter and figuratively as both an image of 'this world's life' and an analogue for the chasm between the living and the dead. In 'Faith and Despondency', the afterlife is imaged as a 'steadfast, changeless, shore' where the spirits of the dead survive, separated from the living by 'Time's wide waters', an image that owes a debt to two lines from Isaac Watts's 'A Prospect of Heaven Makes Death Easy': 'Death like a narrow sea divides | This heavenly land from ours.' To mark the shared imagery of 'Faith and Despondency' and 'Remembrance' is to mark as well the very different purposes it serves in two very different dramatic contexts. Unlike the speaker of 'Remembrance', who directs her speech to someone who is 'Cold in the earth', the child who addresses her father and speaks the part of faith in 'Faith and Despondency', is certain that the dead do not inhabit their graves: 'Their dust is mingled with the sod, | Their happy souls are gone to God!' If the rhyme of 'sod' with 'God' can be said to assert the incommensurability of human body and divine spirit, the rhyme of 'wave' with 'grave' in 'Remembrance' can be said to express the incompatibility of life, which is always in motion, and death, which stills the quick.

The question of where the dead are, and of the fate of the body, concerned the nineteenth century and Brontë as much as the question of when exactly death occurs. 'Where is she?' Heathcliff cries, in response to Nelly's account of Catherine's death. 'Not *there*—not in heaven—not perished—where?' (II. ii. 204). Although the burial service that would have been so familiar to Brontë proclaims the body's dissolution and the spirit's flight, Heathcliff will not believe that the dead Catherine is either under ground, or in heaven above it, or 'perished'. He digs up her corpse twice, once on the day of her burial and again on the day of Edgar Linton's burial. On the first occasion, he stops before opening her coffin because he feels her presence 'not under me, but on the earth' and is 'unspeakably consoled'. On the second, he opens the coffin and exposes her face—'it is hers yet'—though the sexton warns him that the air will change it (II. xv. 349—50). Heathcliff's 'distinct impression of her passionless features' provides another antidote to Nelly's description of Catherine's corpse as lying 'with a sweet smile on her face'.

The body's purity, signified by incorruptibility after death (as also by miraculous bodily closures—not eating, menstruating, or excreting in life), requires more dramatic substantiation in women's lives than in men's in Western culture, as Caroline Walker Bynum points out in her study of the lives of female saints.[15] I take it for granted that the mystery of Catherine's immunity to physical decay, her removal from the realm of flawed physicality and change, is as necessary to the myth of *Wuthering Heights* as Heathcliff's capacity to sense her earthly presence after her death—at her gravesite or, more memorably later, in the coffin-like press bed where Lockwood has his dream of Catherine at the novel's start and where Heathcliff dies still seeking her at its close.

But Catherine's long, physically wasting illness before death and the violation of her physical integrity by a birth that coincides with her own death, after a pregnancy the novel barely mentions, suggest how problematic the relation of spirit to body is, not just for Brontë but for her contemporaries. Does Catherine's miraculous preservation in the flesh deny the validity or interest of a Christian resurrection at the end of time? Does it prove that Catherine exerts more control over her body in death than she could in life? Is she, despite Heathcliff's earlier fears, unchanged and unchanging?

Philippe Ariès offers a likely natural explanation for the preservation of Catherine's body: the soil has peculiar qualities that enable it to embalm corpses.[16] Catherine's grave is 'on a green slope, in a corner of the kirkyard, where the wall is so low that heath and bilberry plants have climbed over it from the moor; and peat mould almost buries it' (II. ii. 206). But this explanation cannot exhaust the power of Heathcliff's image of Catherine's incorruptibility, or explain the relief provided by the preservation of her face, the sign of her continuing identity sixteen years after her burial, as well as by Heathcliff's intuition of her earthly presence outside the grave on the day she is buried. Moreover, these images and others associated with Catherine's survival after death are contradictory. Heathcliff dreams that he is 'sleeping the last sleep, by that sleeper, with my heart stopped, and my cheek frozen against hers' (II. xv. 349), but most readers of *Wuthering Heights* will remember that he removes one side of Catherine's coffin and bribes the sexton to remove the facing side of his after his burial so that their dust can mingle. Apparently, the dissolution of Catherine's body will occur, but only after Heathcliff's arrives to share it. At the same time, the folk legend that Heathcliff and Catherine walk the moors, hand in hand, preserves the possibility of a different union after death.

In *Wuthering Heights* and in the poems, Brontë expresses contradictory ideas about material continuity and the relation of body to soul or spirit. She imagines the body sometimes as a weight or enclosure, most famously in her poem 'The Prisoner (A Fragment)', first published in 1846, although not in the longer poem from which it has been excerpted, and in *Wuthering Heights*, where Catherine refers to her body as 'this shattered prison'; sometimes as the site of radical metamorphosis or transmogrification, as in 'Death', another poem she selected for publication in 1846; and sometimes as inseparable from identity, as in Catherine's dream of her expulsion from heaven or Heathcliff's discovery of Catherine's survival in the flesh sixteen years after her burial.

Only characters situated at a considerable psychological distance from their creator, like the child in 'Faith and Despondency' or Nelly Dean in *Wuthering Heights*, imagine a happy afterlife for disembodied spirits in a place resembling a Christian paradise or heaven.

'Remembrance' invokes three of the four elements in its first two stanzas—earth, water (in two forms), and air—thereby recalling images of mouldering flesh merging with the elements that are conventional in nineteenth-century poems about the dead, like James Thomson's *The City of Dreadful Night* (1874), where corpses 'dissolve and merge afresh | In earth, air, water, plants, and other men'. But the corpse in 'Remembrance' is said to be 'cold in the dreary grave', a condition that may imply physical continuity—as opposed to dissolution—like Heathcliff's dream of 'sleeping the last sleep', his 'cheek frozen' against Catherine's. The fourth element, fire, figures explicitly only in the second half of the poem, in words like 'light', 'morn', and 'burning', but attributing coldness to the dead lover already implies the living speaker's warmth. Heat figures again in the third stanza, with its image of cyclical change, the 'fifteen wild Decembers' that 'have melted into spring', and its opposing image of nature's endurance, the 'brown hills' that do not melt. The 'deep snow' of the poem's first line also suggests the speaker's long, numb silence; her feelings have congealed like the snow that covers the beloved's grave. As she overcomes her chilled and chilling reluctance to express her buried feelings, the snow of the poem's first line figuratively melts into the wave of the fourth line, and then literally melts with the advent of spring in the third stanza. The water that is first snow, then ocean, and then melting snow running in rivulets down hills emerges towards the poem's end as tears. In this respect, Brontë's imagery of changing states has a function that Peter Sacks, in his study of the English elegy, attributes to two of the elegy's formal conventions that figure in 'Remembrance', repetition and questioning. According to Sacks, such devices free the energy locked in grief or rage and keep the expression of grief in motion.[17] Tears are the sign of this vital grief.

Does seasonal change correspond to and reinforce a human pattern? Cowper, whose poems the Brontës read and admired, suggests not in his translation of a Latin poem by Dr Jortin: 'Spring returns, but not our bloom; | Still 'tis Winter in the tomb.' Cowper's poem influenced Henry Neele's contribution to the *Forget Me Not* annual for 1826, and Brontë might easily have read Neele's poem there. Here is its first stanza, which, together with Cowper's poem, may bear on 'No coward soul is mine' as well as 'Remembrance':

> Suns will set, and moons will wane,
> Yet they rise, and wax again;
> Trees, that Winter's storms subdue,
> Their leafy livery renew;
> Ebb and flow is Ocean's lot;
> But man lies down and rises not:
> Heaven and Earth shall pass away,
> Ere shall wake his slumbering clay.[18]

'Remembrance' differs from both these poems in contrasting seasonal change with human constancy rather than with enduring death. Despite the transformations the earth undergoes, remembrance survives unchanged. The poem neither holds out nor cancels the hope of bodily resurrection. Its concern with change and continuity does not focus on the clay that is 'cold in the dreary grave' but on 'the spirit that remembers'.

The elemental opposition of heat and cold in the poem is related to another opposition that shapes the speaker's understanding of her difference from her buried lover and marks her acknowledgement of his death. For while he is confined 'in the earth', with 'the deep snow piled above' him, she is hauntingly, tauntingly free. In Hardy's 'After a Journey', the dead woman the poet mourns is a visible, 'voiceless ghost', but in 'Remembrance', it is the speaker who is ghostlike; her winged thoughts 'hover' over the grave in which her beloved lies frozen. In a large number of the poems that Brontë wrote about the relation of death to life, she reverses these associations, representing the living as struggling against their confinement in the world and the flesh, while the dead have won release. This poem begins in the place where Keats's 'Ode to a Nightingale' leaves off, with its speaker deprecating the sensory deprivation and frozen immobility of the noble dead.

Sacks, who grounds his study of the English elegy in the work of mourning described by Freud in 'Mourning and Melancholia', cites the penultimate stanza of 'Remembrance' in support of his 'claim that the woman's mourning', like the man's, '*does* equally recapitulate not only her loss of the mother but also her internalization and identification with the idealized parental figure'. This is Brontë's stanza:

> Then did I check the tears of useless passion—
> Weaned my young soul from yearning after thine,

Sternly denied its burning wish to hasten
Down to that tomb already more than mine.

According to Sacks, the speaker internalizes a repressive mother who acts like the father by forbidding 'the child's regressive desire to remain in an undifferentiated state of union with the mother'. This pattern connects the work of mourning to the Oedipal plot: in both, as Sacks explains, 'an acceptance of mediation or substitution was the price of survival'.[19]

Sacks's reading of 'Remembrance' uses a psychoanalytic vocabulary to stigmatize as 'regressive' the indulgence of feeling Leavis criticized as immature. The fear that the boy (or girl?) will remain in an undifferentiated state of union with the mother produces the oversimplification Jessica Benjamin so intelligently criticizes: 'as long as the boy gets away from the mother, he has successfully become an individual.'[20] But weaning provides an image or model for loss and individuation different from that provided by the oedipal conflict. In the poem, the parallelism of checking futile tears and weaning a 'young soul', connects weaning specifically to the suppression of feeling rather than to detachment. Instead of signalling the completion of the work of mourning, an achieved composure in the face of death may signal a pathological repression, as British psychoanalyst John Bowlby suggests in *Attachment and Loss*, his three-volume study of how children respond to the loss of their mothers. Moreover, the infant who submits to the inevitable separation from her mother by no means submits to the displacement of the mother by any subsequent attachment. In the language of this poem, she learns instead 'how existence could be cherished, | Strengthened, and fed without the aid of joy.'

The absence of biological mothers in *Wuthering Heights*, let alone idealized or nursing ones, has often been noted, but nursing is eroticized as well as idealized in 'Remembrance' by being made contiguous with 'joy', 'passion', a 'burning wish', and—in the last stanza—'drinking deep of that divinest anguish'. If we seek to locate the sexuality of 'Remembrance', which is after all a poem spoken by a lover to a lover, we will discover that the poem's metaphors of desire are never specular and do not contribute to the story of a sexuality that Freud constructs as a story about looking. The senses that are active in the poem are touch and taste, the senses that are also active in nursing. Nursing always figures in Brontë's poems as the occasion of an active, physical pleasure, as in 'Stars', when the speaker imagines a lost bliss by evoking the 'glorious eyes' of the stars gazing down on hers, while she, instead of remaining passive as the object of their gaze, actively drinks their 'beams | As they were life to me'.

In 'Remembrance', Brontë connects detachment with deep cold and confinement and attachment with the emotional vitality expressed in the capacity to weep and drink, to take from the world what it has to offer and to give the world its due. The speaker's refusal, in the poem's last stanza, to drink 'deep of that divinest anguish', 'memory's rapturous pain', is expressed so as to constitute something other than a refusal. We may remember that Sacks focused his attention on the poem's penultimate stanza in his effort to bring 'Remembrance' into conformity with other poems about mourning which conclude with detachment and reparation or consolation. But attention to the last stanza of 'Remembrance' shows a poet who is determined to avoid concluding.

'Remembrance' ends with a question that holds the speaker's options in equipoise and with a word that emphasizes continuation, not termination. The sense of 'again' and the rising inflection of the question are in tension with the metre and the reader's sense of having come to the end of the poem, both of which require the full weight of the voice to fall on the last cadence. Although three ordinary words, 'me', 'thee', and 'away', turn up more often than 'again' at the end of lines within Brontë's poems (and one resource all these words share is the large number of English words available for rhyming with them), 'again' is the most frequently appearing last word in her poems. Rhyme is the 'recurrence of termination'[21] and 'again' puts the stress on recurrence, not termination. Brontë most often rhymes 'again' with 'pain', as here, suggesting that 'memory's rapturous pain', like Wordsworth's 'natural sorrow, loss, or pain' (in 'The Solitary Reaper'), 'has been, and may be again!' All the verbs in the last stanza, the present progressive 'drinking' and the conditional 'dare not let' and 'could I seek', also refer to continuous events. For a reader approaching the end of this poem with an expectation of closure, the contrast between the stillness of the buried beloved, who is 'cold in the dreary grave' at the beginning of the poem, and the speaker, who warms to her agency as the poem proceeds, will also work against any sense of finality or composure. Unlike the speakers of the English elegies Sacks studies, the speaker of 'Remembrance' does not turn away from death and toward life after a circumscribed period set aside for grieving. She asks whether such a turning is possible.

The refusal of termination in 'Remembrance' also is expressed in the poem's two most remarkable formal features, the doubling or repetition of words, phrases, and grammatical constructions; and the use of feminine endings, the sound of a voice pressing beyond a line's anticipated closing stress, in regular alternation with masculine endings. Hardy uses feminine endings to fine effect in 'After a Journey', but Hardy's poem, unlike Brontë's, enforces a feeling of finality and composure in its last stanza, partly by juxtaposing a human farewell with the dawn—an ending as well as a beginning—and partly by the calm certainty with which the speaker acknowledges his abandonment:

> Ignorant of what there is flitting here to see,
>   The waked birds preen and the seals flop lazily,
> Soon you will have, Dear, to vanish from me,
>   For the stars close their shutters and the dawn
>   whitens hazily.
> Trust me, I mind not, though Life lours,
>   The bringing me here; nay, bring me here again!
>   I am just the same as when
> Our days were a joy, and our paths through flowers.

In his essay on Swinburne, Housman admires his mastery of feminine rhymes, and notes that few English poets before him 'had used them much, and few without doing themselves an injury'. He goes on to 'mention one significant detail':

The ordinary versifier, if he employs feminine rhymes, makes great use of words ending in *ing*: they are the largest class of these rhymes, and they form his mainstay. Swinburne, so plentiful and ready to hand were his stores, almost disdains this expedient: in all the four hundred and forty lines of *Dolores*, for example, he only twice resorts to it.[22]

Brontë resorts to the 'ing' ending only once in 'Remembrance'—in lines 10 and 12, where she rhymes 'spring' with 'suffering', wrenching the accent for 'suffering' so as to produce a masculine instead of the usual feminine ending and a rhyme of one syllable, not two, to contrast with the poem's only triple rhyme ('Decembers/remembers'), which also appears in this stanza. In other poems, Brontë also uses feminine rhymes and endings very skilfully. 'The Prisoner (A Fragment)' uses a feminine rhyme only once, in its last two lines, rhyming 'given' with 'Heaven' so as to illustrate Arthur Hallam's insight that rhyme contains 'in itself a constant appeal to memory and hope'.[23] A particularly graceful use of feminine endings occurs in Brontë's two earliest surviving compositions, 'Cold clear and blue the morning heaven' and 'Will the day be bright or cloudy', where the unrhymed feminine endings—'heaven/water', 'cloudy/thunder', 'shadow/blossom'—are played off against masculine rhymes—'high/sky', 'begun/sun', and 'rain/vain/pain'. Her most remarkable development of the resources of masculine and feminine endings used in alternation, apart from 'Remembrance', occurs in 'Death', where the poem's regular feminine rhymes set off its only recurring rhyme, the masculine one of 'be' and 'Eternity' that closes both the first and last stanzas. This particular rhyme also gains force from the contrast between the extreme brevity of 'be' and the stretch of 'Eternity', and from the extra emphasis imposed by both metre and rhyme on the word's final syllable:

> Death! that struck when I was most confiding
> In my certain faith of joy to be—
> Strike again, Time's withered branch dividing
> From the fresh root of Eternity!

The feminine endings of 'Remembrance' participate in a rhythmical effect to which other metrical features of the poem also contribute. C. Day Lewis very beautifully describes this effect, which he attributes to the repeated substitution of a trochee for an iamb in the first foot of each line and a strong caesura after the second foot:

The effect of this rhythm I find extremely powerful, extremely appropriate. It is a dragging effect, as of feet moving in a funeral march; an andante maestoso: it is the *slowest* rhythm I know in English poetry, and the most sombre.[24]

A dragging effect, 'as of feet moving in a funeral march', or funeral train (which Brontë also rhymes with 'again'). The feminine ending can also be heard as a holding forth, or holding out. Christopher Ricks describes its cadence as 'always related either to a dying fall or to some act of courage in the face of death, or of something that falls away'. The voice has to 'hold out that second syllable like a flag, which is either limp or, as it were, patriotically out. It will fall away, that cadence, *unless* the voice holds it out ... .'[25] That the same words, the pronouns 'thee' and 'me' and their variants 'thine' and 'mine', which define the axis of mourning in 'Remembrance', appear at the ends of both even and odd lines, as stressed and unstressed syllables, creates its own pattern of rising and falling accents.

In 'Remembrance', we hear the rhythms of impassioned speech in syncopation with the poem's metre, which is iambic pentameter. This is also an axis, one that Henry Newbolt, writing in 1912, described as 'an antagonism, a balance, a compromise'.[26] The first lines of each of the first two stanzas of the poem stretch to contain twelve, not ten or eleven, syllables and include the maximum number of variant feet (initial trochee, medial anapaest, terminal amphibrach) compatible with the poem's metre. Twelve syllables contract to ten, swell with the third line's feminine ending, then extend again to accommodate the trisyllabic 'severing'. However resolutely the poem's speaker insists on her determination to live actively in a world that lacks the dead lover, the rhythms of this poem combine with its powerful images of melting, dissolving, and flowing to prolong her remembrance and her mourning.

Suppose, then, a mourning that prefers interminable emotional turmoil—a forever 'new tumult of discord and distress'—to the salvational poise of consolation, the 'melancholy sweeter than common joy' that Nelly attributes to Edgar. Readers of 'Remembrance' and indeed of elegy as a genre have been on the *qui vive* for ambivalence, whether of the kind that Jahan Ramazani uncovers in the modern elegy, whose mourners 'attack the dead and themselves',[27] or of the kind Andrew Elfenbein discovers in 'Remembrance' when he describes the speaker's 'elaborate rhetoric of grief' as 'a mask for a woman filled with ambition's pride'.[28] But the contradictions and reversals of 'Remembrance' derive from the impersonal psychological activity the poem represents, not from the personal psychology of its speaker. This psychological activity revolves around what it means to remember—and forget—someone who has died.

One of the few differences between the manuscript and published versions of 'Remembrance' is the substitution of the adjective 'all-severing' for 'all wearing' in line 4. Authorial revisions aren't always improvements, and this one has the effect of hedging the poem's bets by asserting that Time, over a long period, does separate the living from the dead. The manuscript version of the line represents separation as gradual, like weaning, and also protracted. Not even 'those brown hills', which do not themselves melt, are immune to time. They change their appearance with the seasons, but they also undergo smaller changes in a geological time frame far vaster than a year or even fifteen of them. According to Adam Phillips's analysis of the passage I have quoted from Freud's 'Notes upon a Case of Obsessional Neurosis', Freud 'presents the Ratman with what is at best a paradox and at worst a double-bind'. Because remembering is 'a wearing away', it is 'a way of killing off the past', while forgetting, or repressing remembrance, keeps remembrance in ' "relatively unchangeable" storage'.[29] Burial is literally a kind of storage, and in 'Remembrance', winter burial, beneath snow as well as earth, is cold storage, a deeper freeze. Actively remembering the dead, like exhuming a corpse, carries the risk the sexton puts before Heathcliff when he uncovers Catherine's face: exposure to the air will change it. Apparent forgetting, however, cannot be construed as evidence that the speaker does not remember; it may signal instead a perfect remembrance, making 'forgive, if I forget thee' consistent with the lines that precede it: 'Faithful, indeed, is the spirit that remembers | After such years of change and suffering.'

In an undatable, untitled, fragmentary poem, Emily Brontë opposes memory to death:

> All hushed and still within the house
> Without—all wind and driving rain
> But something whispers to my mind
> Through rain and air and wailing wind
>   —Never again
> Never again? Why not again?
> Memory has power as real as thine

This poem, with its imagery of inside and outside, whether house or tomb, and the turbulence of its inner and outer weather, is as unmistakably Emily Brontë's as the lines from *The Prelude* that De Quincey famously said he would have recognized as Wordsworth's had he met them in the desert. Although the poem does not name 'Death', it is death's power that memory outlasts. The fulcrum of the poem is the short line—'Never again'—possibly a first thought awaiting excision in a later act of revision, certainly an occasion when we can glimpse the poet at her work. 'Never again?' The question generates an answer, the metre requires one, and the poet supplies it. 'Never again? Why not again?' Brontë's poems and *Wuthering Heights* repeatedly pose these questions.

Edgar Allan Poe's poem 'The Raven' was published in 1845 and widely read in England as well as the United States. Charlotte Brontë quotes its refrain in a letter to W. S. Williams about 'the void Death has left'.[30] Poe's essay on how he composed 'The Raven' and especially his account of the moral of the bird's repeated word, 'Nevermore', reminds us that Brontë's questions about memory in 'Remembrance' were arousing considerable interest in both England and America in the mid-nineteenth century:

The reader begins now to regard the Raven as emblematical—but it is not until the very last line of the very last stanza, that the intention of making him emblematical of *Mournful and Neverending Remembrance* is permitted distinctly to be seen.[31]

Melancholy disdains present time because it contains no fulfilment, and Romantic poets thrilled to present time because it held out the hope of something evermore about to be. Most readers will feel that Neverending Remembrance is less melancholy and more exhilarated in Emily Brontë's 'Remembrance' than in Poe's 'The Raven'. The difference is as final and as lasting as that between the sombre, dipping voice with which Poe's raven chimes his 'Nevermore' and the full weight of the voice falling on the rising cadence of Emily Brontë's last words. 'How could I seek the lonely world again?' or 'Never again? Why not again?'

4

Outcomes and Endings

That Emily Brontë's career as a poet is framed by poems looking ahead to outcomes that are dazzling and poems looking back on outcomes that are unmitigatedly bleak sketches a progress that we can understand in various ways, psychologically in relation to Brontë's life, dramatically in relation to an extended Gondal narrative, or mythically in relation to the topoi of romance and irony. The wild child and murderous foster parent of Brontë's last completed poem are the spiritual opposites of the characters who figure in her three earliest poems, a visionary, a happy child, and a loving mother. My aim in this chapter is not to establish some narrative progress for Brontë's poems that this account of poems written at the inception and close of her career as a poet may suggest. The picture that her poems taken all together provide is more complicated and more varied. What they show is that Gondal never stopped providing occasions for powerful poems and never was 'a self-contained alternative to the actual world'.[1] It was a way to write about that world. As a Gondal poet, Brontë began by thinking about individual lives and intimate relations and ended by thinking about social conflict and the nature of evil.

Brontë composed the earliest poems that have survived in 1836, the year before Victoria became Queen[2] (Figure 3). They announce beginnings and contemplate outcomes. 'Cold clear and blue the morning heaven,' probably composed a few weeks before her eighteenth birthday, describes a bright winter Gondal scene, with water mirroring sky:

> Cold clear and blue the morning heaven
> Expands its arch on high
> Cold clear and blue Lake Werna's water
> Reflects that winter's sky
> The moon has set but Venus shines
> A silent silvery star

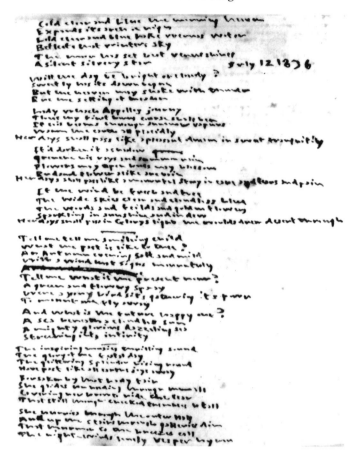

Figure 3. 'Cold clear and blue the morning heaven', 'Will the day be bright or cloudy', 'Tell me tell me smileing child', 'The inspiring musics thrilling sound'. 'Will the day be bright or cloudy' is dated 12 July 1836; poems written on the same leaf are conjecturally dated in relation to it. From the collection in the Brontë Parsonage Museum Library at Haworth, Yorkshire.

This poem alludes to one of Sappho's fragmentary lyrics (the phrase 'The silver moon is set' was attributed to her in the nineteenth century) but departs from the dominant tradition of nineteenth-century women poets singing Sappho's song. For most of the century and for most of the women poets writing in it, Sappho figures as an icon of suicidal passion; her fatal leap from the Leucadian Cliff is a recurrent theme in pictures and verse.[3] Brontë would have had ready access to this representation of Sappho, but as Lawrence Lipking points out, her poem 'reproduces the birth of an identity', not some leap into the abyss.[4] The identity may be that of A. G. A., the primary female figure in Brontë's Gondal saga, but we don't need to recall how difficult it is to kill her (her murder is the subject of a longer, later poem, 'The Death of A. G. A.') to see that Brontë's allusion to Sappho does not celebrate her suicidal end. The allusion to a great woman poet, the reference to the dawning of a female star, and the image of a sea that reflects not just the sky but a female moon and planet are appropriate to a poem announcing the birth of a female poet. 'Cold clear and blue the morning heaven' testifies to the cool self-assurance with which an adolescent Brontë launches herself as a woman poet in the tradition of Sappho, but not in the tradition of the Victorian Sappho.

In her next poem, 'Will the day be bright or cloudy', a woman watches the sky to learn the fate of her first-born child, a daughter. 'Will the day be bright or cloudy' bases three different predictions on three different changes in the day's weather: a life of 'sweet tranquillity', one full of 'care and tears and pain', or one passed 'in Glory's light'. The third and happiest destiny requires weather exactly like that pervading 'Cold clear and blue the morning heaven': a fresh, free wind and 'wide skies clear and cloudless blue'. Brontë's third poem, 'Tell me tell me smiling child', invokes a promising future even more confidently. Its image of an infinite sea echoes the ambitious image of heaven's expanding arch in 'Cold clear and blue the morning heaven':

> And what is the future happy one?
> A sea beneath a cloudless sun
> A mighty glorious dazzling sea
> Stretching into infinity

All three poems express a vital optimism that is appropriate to a boundless heaven and horizon and a self with ready access to the sources of her own joy. Although these are dramatic poems, words for Gondal characters, all of them involve self-figuration. The spirits who preside over these beginnings—a shining goddess, a loving mother, and a happy child—make up Brontë's pantheon.

Brontë gives a date of May 1848 for her last surviving poem, 'Why ask to know what date what clime', the only poem she is known to have written after the publication of *Wuthering Heights* (Figure 4). This twenty-five-line poem marks Gondal's enduring claim to imaginative

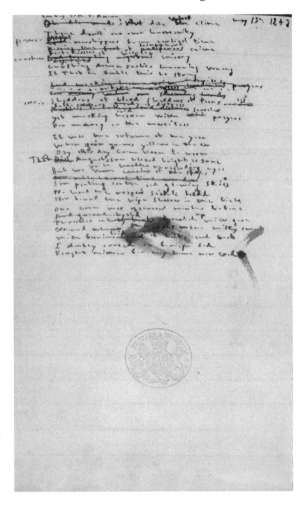

Figure 4. 'Why ask to know what date what clime', the last poem in the *Gondal Poems* notebook. The first page of this manuscript is headed 'Emily Jane Brontë' and 'Transcribed February, 1844'; the title 'Gondal Poems' appears in flourishing script. From the collection in the British Library.

space, last as well as first. The poem, which is incomplete, reworks the opening thirty or so lines of the much longer poem that precedes it in Brontë's *Gondal Poems* notebook, 'Why ask to know the date—the clime.' This poem, which has a composition date of 14 September 1846, is the last poem Emily Brontë completed, although it is unfinished in the sense of being still under revision. The poem is heavily revised after line 156, a double disruption of her usual practice. She has previously used the *Gondal Poems* notebook for fair-copy transcriptions, not for drafts, and this draft shows more evidence of revision than any other surviving draft.

We know something, but not enough, about the compositional time frame of 'Why ask to know what date what clime', Brontë's sure-handed revision of the opening lines of 'Why ask to know the date—the clime'. She wrote 'Why ask to know what date what clime' in the last months of her life when she was, according to one theory, blocked as a writer by Charlotte's discovery of her poems and their publication in 1846, and, according to another, occupied with a second novel, the manuscript of which (like that of *Wuthering Heights*) has not survived.[5] Neither of these theories explains the poem's unfinished state, but Brontë's attention to revising 'Why ask to know the date—the clime'—first sometime between 14 September 1846 and May of 1848, and then again in May of 1848, when she composed 'Why ask to know what date what clime'—tells us more about her commitment to this poem than does her leaving it unfinished in the end.

Anne also composed a Gondal poem on the same day that Emily wrote 'Why ask to know the date—the clime'. Her poem, 'Z___'s Dream', has enough in common with Emily's to suggest that the dramatic occasion for both poems is the same civil war and that the Gondal narrative provided each poet with a framework for a different poetic experience. Like Emily's poem, Anne's describes a situation in which 'dearest friends turn deadliest foes' (l. 94),[6] but while Emily's centre of consciousness is a professional soldier fighting for pay, Anne's is one of Gondal's Republican heroes. Anne's speaker dreams about a loving friendship during his boyhood, then remembers that he has killed and mocked the man who was once his friend:

> These eyes had watched, without a tear,
> His dying agony;
> These ears, unmoved, had heard his prayer;
> This tongue had cursed him suffering there,
> And mocked him bitterly!

> (ll. 99–103)

Emily's speaker recalls a similar death-watch:

> I watched his ghastly couch beside
> Regardless if he lived or died—
> Nay, muttering curses on the breast
> Whose ceaseless moans denied me rest:
>
> (ll. 124–7)

After a momentary '[u]nwonted weakness', Anne's speaker rationalizes killing the man who was once his friend: both he and his friend have changed over time; the deed is done and, whether right or wrong, it cannot be undone; his political cause is just, and he would sacrifice his own life as well as the lives of others to it. Anne's poem, unlike Emily's, finds a steady resolution in its final lines, which confirm its speaker's resolve:

> Advanced this far, I'll not recede;—
> Whether to vanquish or to bleed,
> Onward, unchecked, I must proceed.
> Be Death, or Victory mine!
>
> (ll. 147–50)

Anne's soldier is heroic, whether we read his heroism as determined or dogged, and the poem locates its moral interest in his loss of friendship and the innocence that made friendship possible. There is no evidence that she recoils from the swashbuckling ease with which her soldier overcomes his regrets and dedicates himself to his mission, although she may have done. Emily's poem is differently focused: its subject is the easy brutality and unremitting cruelty of humans at war. The decision to make a mercenary her centre of consciousness signals her refusal to take sides in the war the poem describes or allow her soldier an easy political justification.

Emily Brontë's two poems, both 'Why ask to know the date—the clime'—which may be complete even though it is unfinished in the specific sense of being a draft that is incompletely revised—and 'Why ask to know what date what clime'—which is incomplete because it stops short of its finish—begin by describing a war-torn landscape.[7] In both poems, she evokes the autumn setting of 'Tell me tell me smiling child', but there are no crops to harvest in fields laid waste by battle and no hands to be spared for holding sickles instead of weapons. Her surreal imagery of 'milky sweet' corn 'Threshed out and kneaded-up with gore' suggest that human beings are themselves the crops that have been harvested, not just that the grain that was planted was wasted when growing fields became killing fields. Roper cites the civil wars in Scotland in the late sixteenth century, as described by Scott in *Tales of a Grandfather*, as background for this poem, but the hunger and fear that haunt its opening lines may mark Brontë's engagement with the active public debate surrounding the Irish Famine in the months preceding September 1846, when she composed 'Why ask to know the date—the clime'.[8] Yet the questions with which both poems open do more than register their speaker's impatience with an unidentified audience. They announce her unwillingness to specify the time and place of the events about to be narrated and mark his story as a story for all times and places. These poems are apocalyptic, like Lockwood's dream of the battle in the Chapel of Gimmerden Sough, where every man's hand is against his neighbour:

> Why ask to know the date—the clime?
> More than mere words they cannot be:
> Men knelt to God and worshipped crime,
> And crushed the helpless even as we—

Jonathan Wordsworth notes the surprise of the rhyme word 'crime' at the end of line 3. 'The reader has been tricked, has identified too easily with the conversational tone, and now finds himself taking part in the everyday business of crushing the helpless and worshipping crime.'[9] The phrase 'even as we' is cooperatively ambiguous: do we belong to the ranks of the helpless ('even as we are crushed') or are we counted among those who crush them ('even as we crush the helpless')?

The ambiguity is deliberate: Brontë assimilates victims to victimizers. This principle emerges early on in one of her grimmest poems, 'I am the only being whose doom'. This poem was composed in 1839 but dated two years earlier by C. W. Hatfield because of its reference to being 'friendless after eighteen years' and then read by C. Day Lewis as evidence that Brontë believed herself to be damned.[10] Both Hatfield and Lewis imagine the historical Emily Brontë speaking autobiographically, but 'I am the only being whose doom' is probably also a Gondal poem. It may have been influenced by another poem attributed to Sappho in the nineteenth century. Here is Sappho's first stanza, as represented in *Collections from the Greek Anthology* (1833), where Brontë might have read it:

> Unknown, unheeded, shalt thou die,
>   And no memorial shall proclaim,
> That once beneath the upper sky
> Thou hadst a being and a name.[11]

And Brontë's:

> I am the only being whose doom
> No tongue would ask no eye would mourn
> I never caused a thought of gloom
> A smile of joy since I was born

As a mature poet and as a novelist, Brontë did not shrink from the view of human nature she expresses in the last stanza of this early poem:

> 'Twas grief enough to think mankind
> All hollow servile insincere—
> But worse to trust to my own mind
> And find the same corruption there

For the most part, Brontë's revisions to the 1846 poem improve it. For example, she cancels two groups of lines. The first (lines 149–56) relays the contemptuous words the poem's speaker hurls at his captive as he lies dying; the second (lines 172–89) contains the speaker's assertion that God exacts punishment for the deeds that 'turn his earth to hell' as well as his memory of his captive's look, which he takes to be a silent plea to God for mercy. The poem is strengthened by the omission of these lines, both because the speaker's words to his captive are so much weaker and less compelling than his crass act—he has just stolen his captive's remaining valuable property—and because his thoughts about divine retribution offer a cruder version of the poem's moral economies than does the narrative as a whole.

The twenty-five-line poem, 'Why ask to know what date what clime', transcribed on a fresh page in the *Gondal Poems* notebook, moves even further in the direction of allegory than the opening lines of 'Why ask to know the date—the clime'. These last lines Brontë wrote are unflinching in their account of the evil that men do:

> Why ask to know what date what clime
> There dwelt our own humanity
> Power-worshippers from earliest time
> Foot-kissers of triumphant crime
> Crushers of helpless misery
> Crushing down Justice honouring Wrong
> If that be feeble this be strong
> Shedders of blood shedders of tears
> Self-cursers avid of distress
> Yet Mocking heaven with senseless prayers
> For mercy on the merciless

It was the autumn of the year
When grain grows yellow in the ear
Day after day from noon to noon,
That August's sun blazed bright as June

But we with unregarding eyes
Saw panting earth and glowing skies
No hand the reaper's sickle held
Nor bound the ripe sheaves in the field

Our corn was garnered months before,
Threshed out and kneaded-up with gore
Ground when the ears were milky sweet
With furious toil of hoofs and feet
I doubly cursed on foreign sod
Fought neither for my home nor God

The men who 'knelt to God and worshipped crime' in 1846 become 'Power-worshippers from earliest time' in 1848. The phrase 'earliest time' tells us that the strong have oppressed the weak since the time-before-time, or before our longest memory of it. Insistent syntactical parallels and verbal repetitions emphasize the continuity of the events being narrated and make any change in their course unlikely. Are the 'shedders of blood' also the 'shedders of tears', or are there two parties to this transaction? The difficulty of deciding has something to do with the presence of *shed* in these two formulations: we shed other people's blood but shed our own tears. Brontë's assimilation of victims to victimizers is bolder in these lines than it was in 'Why ask to know the date—the clime': those who cause others to bleed and weep will themselves weep. They are self-destructive, or in the poem's language, 'Self-cursers' who are 'avid' of their own distress as well as that of others. They mock heaven by praying for mercy when they are themselves merciless, just as their victims mock heaven by offering the same prayers and being no more merciful than their enemies. What does it mean to call their prayers 'senseless'? *Senseless* is a word Brontë uses in only one other poem, 'The Philosopher', where the philosopher describes death as 'senseless rest' and contrasts it with his 'sentient soul' and 'living breath'. In 'Why ask to know what date what clime', as in 'The Philosopher', *senseless* has the primary meaning of lacking feeling, not judgement, and the secondary and corroborative meaning of ignoring the evidence of the senses: the eyes are 'unregarding'.

The speaker of these twenty-five lines—someone who fights 'neither for my home nor God'—is identified as a mercenary in the longer draft poem, where we also learn that this is a civil war fought 'For Loyalty, and Liberty'. The compression—not fought by those who stood for loyalty against those who sought their liberty, but simply fought 'For Loyalty, and Liberty'—emphasizes the moral equivalence of the combatants' opposing standards. There is no explanation for the shift from the timeless events of the opening stanzas to the story of events located in imagined if unspecified historical time, but the poem implies that the speaker is himself facing death, 'that last hour when most are true':

> Go with me where my thoughts would go;
> Now all today and all last night
> I've had one scene before my sight—

The scene that haunts him is another death-scene, and the poem unsparingly records the insults and taunts he and his captain directed at the dying man. It is as if the grim jailer in 'Julian M. and A. G. Rochelle', the Gondal poem that was revised to become 'The Prisoner (A Fragment)' in 1846, had been developed into the voice of this poem, or as if the character of Julian had been fundamentally altered so that he maintained the pitiless, scoffing manner he brought with him into his dungeon instead of being moved to mercy, pity, and desire by his prisoner. As the opening stanzas predicted, there is neither mercy nor pity in 'Why ask to know the date—the clime'. Even the motive of simple self-interest is awakened only in the last minutes of the dying man's life, and by then it is too late for the speaker to recall his insults or alter his actions. Both seem to spring directly from the core of his being. In 'Julian M. and A. G. Rochelle', the jailer contrasts his master's 'bland and kind' aspect with his own 'rough and rude' aspect. He likens his master's soul, 'hard as hardest flint', to his own 'rough ... hidden ghost', although his master's actions will prove him wrong about one of their souls. In 'Why ask to know the date—the clime', the speaker tells us that 'there were fates that made me feel | I was not to the centre, steel,' but the remembered death-scene makes a strong case against him. He curses the dying man for keeping him awake during the night, taunts him gratuitously, plunders his jewels and memories, and, as his death nears, refuses to let his daughter see him. When the speaker learns that his own son has been captured and destined for death, he begs his son's life from his captive, who grants it:

> And O my soul longed wildly then
> To give his saviour life again.

But heedless of my gratitude
The silent corpse before me lay

'Why ask to know the date—the clime' has an outcome rather than an ending, and it issues in two parts. The first part of the outcome is the speaker's lasting remembrance of his own inhumanity, or, as Brontë sees it, his own humanity. Damnation is not a part of this outcome anymore than it is in 'I am the only being whose doom'. Brontë took a Stoic position on future rewards and punishments. In her translation of Epictetus (1758), Elizabeth Carter points out that 'Epictetus never asserts either. He strongly insists, that a bad Man hath no other Punishment, than being such, and a good Man, no other Reward.'[12] The second part of the outcome concerns the surviving child who is orphaned by battle. She is full of 'savage woe' and 'anguish wild', and the poem closes with her release or abandonment by the poem's speaker, who had assumed guardianship over her after her father's death.

'Tragedy and tragic irony', Northrop Frye writes, 'take us into a hell of narrowing circles and culminate in some such vision of the source of all evil in a personal form.'[13] The personal form of evil in this poem is war without end and war as an end in itself. Its central consciousness belongs to a mercenary because a mercenary is someone for whom war is an occupation and a provision, someone with a professional interest in prolonging it. Its representative human victim and survivor is a damaged child. These features connect the poem to *Wuthering Heights*, which Brontë had sent off for possible publication just two months before composing it. The most plausible account of Heathcliff's activity during his three-year absence from the Heights is that he has been a mercenary in a foreign war, and Heathcliff is one of the novel's many damaged children, all of whom inflict damage on others, including other children. But the largest connection between the poem and the novel has to do with the ways in which the poem takes up the novel's themes of transgression and atonement.

If the outcome Brontë describes in 'Why ask to know the date—the clime' is not the promised end, it is another image of its horror. The comparison with *King Lear* is justified not just by the way in which this poem, like the play, invokes the end but also by the way in which an action taken has consequences that cannot be recalled and by the role assigned to a child. Brontë isn't content to restrict her cruel speaker's relation to this child to his refusal to let her see her father on his deathbed. She defies realistic probability by having the dying man accuse his captor of stabbing his child not once but four times. 'Twice in my arms twice on my knee' is the father's rhythmical, hyperbolic, unnerving indictment. He dies hoping that death has also ended his daughter's suffering, and her punishment torments him more than his own defeat, humiliation, or approaching death. When he orders that his captor's son, now in the hands of his own forces, not be killed ('Write that they harm no infant there | Write that it is my latest prayer'), he provides the poem's only instance of human sympathy: 'Yet not to thee not even to thee | Would I return such misery.'

In the poem, as often in *Wuthering Heights*, the mainspring of action is the desire to inflict pain on another and the wish to avoid pain oneself. In both the novel and the poem, the characters are differentiated according to their strength or weakness, not their capacity for good or evil, which is equivalent: 'If that be feeble this be strong.' Bataille fleshes out Brontë's insight about human behaviour in both this poem and her novel. 'In the practice of life,' Bataille writes, 'humanity acts in a way that allows for the satisfaction of disarmingly savage needs, and it seems able to subsist only at the limits of horror.'[14] In her discussion of Bataille's observation, Barbara Herrnstein Smith points out that classic utility theory offers

material aggrandizement and the survival of the individual-as-bodily-organism as the inevitable, fundamental, and/or ultimate 'goods' to which all human activity is subordinated. What he will offer in opposition to this—and implicitly in opposition to every rational/economic account of human action or to what he sees as the definitively bourgeois 'reasoning that balances accounts'—is the evidence of a fundamental human need for 'nonproductive *expenditure*' and interest in 'absolute *loss*': that is, a loss that is not otherwise compensated or reciprocated and thus does not operate as a means to some gainful end.[15]

In both *Wuthering Heights* and 'Why ask to know the date—the clime', Brontë rejects the idea of balancing accounts, by means of either good acts in return for benefits received, or bad acts in return for damages suffered. In the novel, Heathcliff's savage revenge, his effort to balance his accounts with Hindley Earnshaw and Edgar Linton, is doomed from the start. However great the damage he inflicts on his enemies, he never more than temporarily mitigates his own pain. He acknowledges this when he describes his acts of violence after Catherine's death as 'moral teething'. (Even this analogy breaks down, since teething has an end, not just in the sense of a purpose—the relief of pain—but in the sense of a termination—the production of teeth, whereas Heathcliff's pain can terminate only in his own death.) In 'Why ask to know the date—the clime', the mercenary also fails to balance his accounts, although he longs to repay his captive's generosity by saving the life of either his captive or his captive's child.

In Emily Brontë's cosmos, whenever human lives or loves are at issue, there are no equivalencies. Her resistance to a conventional Christian balancing of accounts by means of judgement and an afterlife runs very deep. 'Why ask to know the date—the clime' turns on a living man's inability to balance his accounts with a dead man, but it would be a mistake to believe—as the character does—that if only the dead man had survived, these accounts might somehow have been suitably adjusted. Brontë shows us that the principle of non-productive expenditure is fully operative with respect to war itself. The poem imagines a civil war without end, but if there were ever to be an end to this war, there could be no reparations that would balance the accounts of the opposing factions, whether winners or losers. The outcome envisioned by this poem, and at least one of the outcomes envisioned by *Wuthering Heights* as well, is absolute loss. In 'Funeral Music', Geoffrey Hill offers a related vision of war and its outcome:

> At noon
> As the armies met, each mirrored the other;
> Neither was outshone. So they flashed and vanished
> And all that survived them was the stark ground
> Of this pain ... .

The word *outcome*, referring to the visible or practical result or effect of something, is itself a nineteenth-century word, and one related to but different from *ending*, which carries the sense of a boundary or termination. The savage child's escape at the end of 'Why ask to know the date—the clime' is the outcome of the events that have been narrated, but by ending with the speaker's abandonment of her rather than with her father's death, the poem avoids a closural gesture and evokes another narrative, a sequel in which a child made savage by the horror of her experience will figure more largely. Providing new occasions for narrative was one of the operating principles of Anne and Emily's Gondal collaboration, as it was of Charlotte's and Branwell's Angria collaboration. Nevertheless, the subject of 'Why ask to know the date—the clime'—war and the human transactions associated with it—requires the refusal of an end. When Catherine tells Nelly that she has had 'dreams that have stayed with me ever after, and changed my ideas; they've gone through me, like wine through water, and altered the colour of my mind,' she marks a consequence of dreaming that is similarly the starting point for new experience. Emily Brontë didn't lack what Emily Dickinson called the grace to terminate,[16] but she preferred to write poems we can see as stretching into infinity rather than concluding. A sense of an enduring outcome usually replaces a sense of an ending in her poems.

What difference does publication make to Brontë's sense of an ending? Two poems composed at around the same time as 'Why ask to know the date—the clime' provide an occasion for thinking about publication as a motive for Brontë to seek a more determined kind of closure for a poem than that poem has in manuscript or than her poems usually do have in manuscript. Brontë created one of them, 'The Prisoner (A Fragment)', for publication in 1846. The 152-line poem that is the source of 'The Prisoner (A Fragment)', 'Julian M. and A. G. Rochelle', first became available to readers only in 1938, when the Shakespeare Head Press published a slim volume titled *Gondal Poems by Emily Jane Brontë*. In my reading of these two poems, I argue that the poem that is identified as incomplete in the 1846 volume, a part of something once larger or more nearly whole and complete, by the parenthetical words in its title—'A Fragment'—is more conclusive than the longer poem, the whole from which it was formed. In other words, the specific grace Dickinson saw in the capacity to terminate was largely a social grace in the case of 'The Prisoner (A Fragment)'. With 'The Prisoner (A Fragment)', we see Brontë acknowledging her engagement with an audience whose expectation of closure in poems she understands and is sometimes willing to satisfy. This sense of the value of an ending may explain one aspect of the punctuation of the poems in 1846: more than half of them close with the strongest mark available to Brontë, the exclamation point, although most of the poems are unpunctuated in the manuscripts. 'Remembrance' is the only poem published in 1846 that ends with a question (and a question mark), although Brontë wrote many poems that end with questions. In her role as Emily Brontë's first editor, Charlotte Brontë included no poems by her sister that appear incomplete in the 1850 selection of poems she offered readers along with *Wuthering Heights* and *Agnes Grey*. In the one instance in which she published a portion of a poem, the first twelve lines of 'Julian M. and A. G. Rochelle', lines which were omitted from 'The Prisoner (A Fragment)', she added eight lines of her own to complete it. In other instances, she added or revised lines to strengthen the resolution of her sister's poems.[17]

In the Gondal story 'Julian M. and A. G. Rochelle', Julian is casually visiting his own dungeons when he discovers a prisoner named Rochelle, a childhood playmate, and falls in love with her. The prisoner tells her visitor that she has been sustained by nocturnal visionary flights and longs only for death. Nevertheless, she accepts the release from imprisonment he offers her and, after months of illness through which he nurses her, comes to love him. When she revised the poem for publication in 1846, Brontë shortened it by omitting lines from the beginning, the middle, and the end. She removed twelve lines that open the poem and connect it to other poems about visionary experience that she had written during the previous spring ('Stars') and summer ('Anticipation'); twenty lines in the middle of the poem, when the prisoner recognizes her visitor and both remember their childhood friendship; and sixty-two lines at the end, which tell the story of the prisoner's release from the dungeon, Julian's care of her during her long illness and recovery, and how he wins her love. She added a four-line stanza at the new poem's end: in these lines, the visitor abandons the prisoner in her cell with the certainty that her approaching death has put her beyond human assistance or control.

How should we understand Brontë's own parenthetic description of the poem she published as a fragment? First, as a simple acknowledgement that she has excerpted this poem from a longer one. Next, as evidence of her familiarity with the Romantic practice of identifying and publishing as a fragment a poem either intentionally unfinished or—in Marjorie Levinson's language—'approved by the poet in and for its accidental unfinishedness'.[18] Brontë's decision to publish the poem in a truncated version—and her revisions to it—confirm her full participation in the 1846 volume and work against the theory that she was blocked as a writer by her sister's discovery of her poems.

Most readers will agree that 'The Prisoner (A Fragment)' is self-sufficient or, in Balachandra Rajan's language, unfinished but not inviting completion.[19] Although the published poem is derived from 'Julian M. and A. G. Rochelle', it culminates more conclusively than the longer poem. It does so both by not allowing the prisoner the opportunity to choose freedom from imprisonment in preference to death, a choice that values life more than death, and by providing a four-line coda that promises death. These are the only lines Brontë added to the published version of the poem:

> She ceased to speak, and we, unanswering, turned to go—
> We had no further power to work the captive woe:

> Her cheek, her gleaming eye, declared that man had given
> A sentence, unapproved, and overruled by Heaven.

The cessation of the prisoner's speech, the wordless departure of her jailer and visitor, the visitor's acknowledgement of his powerlessness to carry out the sentence of imprisonment, and his perception of a divinely devised end in store for his prisoner: all these elements of the new stanza establish an end-point or resting place from which the activity of the preceding narrative can be assessed. At the same time, the feminine endings in the last couplet, the only feminine endings in the poem, have a destabilizing effect, especially in the poem's last line. Contending against two decisive, legalistic words there—'sentence' and 'overruled'—the feminine ending strains towards release, reminding us that for the prisoner who awaits death nothing is yet finished.

Emily Brontë's most recent editors have chosen to regard the 1846 version of 'Julian M. and A. G. Rochelle' as a separate utterance that embodies a new intention. The same claim could be made for the other twenty poems Brontë published in 1846, although her revisions to them are much more modest. Nevertheless, special difficulties arise with respect to 'The Prisoner (A Fragment)' not just because the poem is so substantially different from the manuscript version but because most readers have preferred the published poem, thereby calling into question the textual primitivism that has been an important strain in the study and editing of Romantic poetry and, specifically, Emily Brontë's poetry. C. Day Lewis called lines 37–60 of 'The Prisoner (A Fragment)' 'the greatest passage Emily Brontë wrote,' and Caroline Spurgeon placed these lines among 'the most perfect mystic poems in English'. For Lewis, the famous lines show up the rest of the poem as 'superficial, insipid' and, 'unreal'.[20] Barbara Hardy contends that the verses of 'Julian M. and A. G. Rochelle' that Brontë omitted in constructing the fragment are 'undistinguished in language and uninteresting in character and action', so that the 'visionary feeling', although present in the longer poem, is 'greatly intensified and transformed when background, story, and character are eliminated'.[21] Hardy also deplores the readiness with which the prisoner apparently accepts her freedom in lieu of death in the longer poem. In Hardy's view, this turn is unmotivated and undermines the authority of the prisoner's commitment to her visions, and perhaps of the poet's commitment to hers.

I do not dispute the success of 'The Prisoner (A Fragment)', but the preference for it has obscured the longer poem's differently embodied intentionality, particularly its different account of imaginative or visionary experience, its wider representation of the conditions of confinement, and its substitution of what is properly an outcome for the published poem's effort to provide an ending. What we have lost sight of is Brontë's effort, not entirely successful but largely so, to put two different stories about visionary experience into relation with each other in 'Julian M. and A. G. Rochelle', one with Julian as the main character, the other with A. G. Rochelle in that position. We can locate both stories in other poems by Brontë, and in other better-known Romantic poems as well.

In 'The Prisoner (A Fragment)', Brontë chooses to tell the story of A. G. Rochelle, and so omits the verses from 'Julian M. and A. G. Rochelle' that develop Julian's story. In this story, the prisoner's confinement in her dungeon is a metaphor for her confinement in her flesh, and any possibility of her liberation from her prison is far less thrilling than her nightly flights, when her spirit is loosed from its clay. This is a story that recurs often in Brontë's poems, appearing for the first time in a poem written seven years before 'Julian M. and A. G. Rochelle' as well as in other poems selected for publication in 1846:

> I'm happiest when most away
> I can bear my soul from its home of clay
> On a windy night when the moon is bright
> And my eye can wander through worlds of light
>
> When I am not and none beside
> Nor earth nor sea nor cloudless sky
> But only spirit wandering wide
> Through infinite immensity

In 'The Prisoner (A Fragment)', this story of escape from bodily constraints—the flight that is either nightly or intermittent in other poems—is combined with an imagination of death as a final escape. This view of death is not the only one on offer in Brontë's poems. They also imagine death as 'senseless rest' or as an eternal exile from identity, which is grounded in the memory of lived experience.

The other story, the one that belongs to 'Julian M. and A. G. Rochelle' but not to 'The Prisoner (A Fragment)', has Julian as its main character. He falls in love with A. G. Rochelle at first sight; she then comes to prefer life to death and accepts the release from imprisonment he offers her; he then proves his love by devoting himself to her recovery; and she rewards him by loving him in return. The last twenty lines of 'Julian

M. and A. G. Rochelle', which describe Julian's care of A. G. Rochelle, reverse the roles played by Hope and Death during A. G. Rochelle's imprisonment. While for the prisoner, the messenger of Hope brings tidings of Death, which Hope represents as 'eternal liberty', for Julian, 'Death gazed greedily | And only Hope remained a faithful friend to me.' Julian resists the taunts of his kindred, who charge him with cowardice for remaining at home instead of seeking a soldier's and patriot's fame abroad, but the poem does not close with a marriage, not even a fatal marriage like the one in Keats's *Lamia*. The whole poem creates a mystery about its narrative—not a mystery about the identity of the speaker or the Wanderer who visits him nightly but about the peculiar way of life they have together devised. It is a life outside domestic comforts, private yet open and ongoing, and lacking an end or a consummation.

Julian's story, which has paled alongside A. G. Rochelle's, is significantly shaped by the twelve lines with which the poem in manuscript begins. These lines, the lines that Charlotte Brontë published as the beginning of 'The Visionary' in 1850, have puzzled readers in their original context. In a persuasive reading of 'Julian M. and A. G. Rochelle', Margaret Homans identifies the speaker of these lines as the poet, 'apparently the same as the "I" of the poems of imagination in the non-Gondal notebook':

> Silent is the House—all are laid asleep;
> One, alone, looks out o'er the snow-wreaths deep;
> Watching every cloud, dreading every breeze
> That whirls the wildering drifts and bends the groaning trees—
>
> Cheerful is the hearth, soft the matted floor
> Not one shivering gust creeps through pane or door
> The little lamp burns straight; its rays shoot strong and far
> I trim it well to be the Wanderer's guiding-star—
>
> Frown, my haughty sire, chide my angry Dame;
> Set your slaves to spy, threaten me with shame;
> But neither sire nor dame, nor prying serf shall know
> What angel nightly tracks that waste of winter snow—

According to Homans, the ' "I" idly straying in the dungeon crypts' in the next line of 'Julian M. and A. G. Rochelle' (this line is the opening line of 'The Prisoner [A Fragment]') is still the poet 'searching for an adventure to recount' and now 'taking on the persona of Julian'.[22] Homans's idea that the first-person speaker in the opening lines of the poem is the poet, is figuratively if not literally persuasive, but the corollary—that the 'I' then casts about for an adventure to recount and takes on the persona of Julian—is misleading. Instead, we should acknowledge that the elevated, archaic diction of the poem's opening lines ('Frown, my haughty sire, chide my angry Dame') makes it unlikely that the poet is speaking in her own voice. The voice we hear in 'Stars' or other poems about visionary experience copied into the Honresfeld manuscript is an ordinary and familiar voice. The elevated diction of 'Julian M. and A. G. Rochelle''s beginning alerts us to a dramatic occasion, and to the strange, romantic quality of the world Julian and A. G. Rochelle inhabit. Julian is, however, like the poet in that he watches and waits for A. G. Rochelle's nightly visits. She has become the free spirit she longed to be while in prison, and she may or may not leave tracks in the snow. 'Julian M. and A. G. Rochelle'—like Catherine's and Heathcliff's story in *Wuthering Heights* and unlike Jane's and Rochester's in *Jane Eyre*—avoids concluding with a marriage precisely so that it can leave us adrift in the kind of frozen world that traps Lockwood but provides no obstacle to the ghost-child who appears at his window. Comfortably protected from the elements outside by hearth, pane, and door, Julian is intently restless in his expectation of his beloved's visits. She enters the House more like a dream than an earthly lover. As in *Lamia*, worldly obligation and ambition—the distractions noted in the last twenty lines of 'Julian M. and A. G. Rochelle'—are incompatible with the wise passiveness that sustains Julian during these nightly vigils and makes possible the different order of achievement marked by the Wanderer's appearances. By identifying this achievement as other-worldly and imaginative, we restore Julian to his position as the second centre of consciousness in 'Julian M. and A. G. Rochelle' and avoid reducing the poem to a story about happy human lovers.

Where do we situate Emily Brontë, the poet, in relation to the two stories she brings together in 'Julian M. and A. G. Rochelle'? As the large number of Gondal poems she wrote will suggest, playing a part, or dramatizing herself in a role, is for her a habitual exercise in negative capability. In 'Julian M. and A. G. Rochelle', she gives poetic agency, what Jonathan Wordsworth, commenting on the central lines of 'The Prisoner (A Fragment)', calls the 'passionate loss of self in creative identification', to Julian as well as to the prisoner. Although readers have been willing to see only one of these characters—the prisoner—as like the poet, the poem's language connects Julian's Wanderer, the 'angel' who 'nightly tracks that waste of winter snow' with the prisoner's 'messenger of Hope', who visits her nightly. Both Julian and A. G. Rochelle are versions of the poet-figure in 'Stars' who is confined to her bedroom and exiled from the night of dreams she longs to recover. Both have access to a mode of self-experience in which the self flows with the world or feels itself an undifferentiated part of it. Brontë's decision to represent the social isolation and obsessive concentration necessary for the creation of art as a love story produces the impression that Julian profits from his prisoner's helplessness. His prisoner's turn to him will require that she be transformed from a powerful bird of prey stooping to dare the final bound into a 'wounded dove'.[23] But the opening twelve lines of 'The Prisoner (A Fragment)'—lines that are not 'undistinguished in language', as Charlotte Brontë must have felt when she made them part of a new poem, 'The Visionary'—restore initiative and authority to the captive, who is now free. They work against Charlotte Brontë's reformulation of imaginative experience as visitation by a powerful male figure, who is also a lover, in the eight lines she adds to her sister's twelve to produce 'The Visionary', and against a reading of 'Julian M. and A. G. Rochelle' as another story about how the female poet is silenced or consigned to an unproductive passivity in relation to a threateningly powerful, dangerously externalized male figure.

'Julian M. and A. G. Rochelle' has the same temporal structure as 'Why ask to know the date—the clime'. Both poems substitute an outcome located in a timeless, dateless, enduring present for an ending. Both begin with that outcome, which gives way to the narrative of a recollected event, Julian's visit to his dungeons where he discovers A. G. Rochelle or the mercenary soldier's haunting memory of his enemy's death. The relationship between Julian and the Wanderer that is sketched at the beginning of 'Julian M. and A. G. Rochelle' is less conclusive than the death promised at the end of 'The Prisoner (A Fragment)'. By providing an ending, 'The Prisoner (A Fragment)' more fully meets the expectations of readers in 1846, but by preferring an outcome to an ending, 'Julian M. and A. G. Rochelle' better evokes the repetitive rhythms of loss and recovery, confinement and escape, that tease us out of time.

5

Fragments

Start out ... forget it ... don't conclude. As far as I'm concerned
that's the right method and the only one able to deal with objects
that resemble *it* (resemble the world).

Georges Bataille

If we know something about what Emily Brontë meant by the word
'Fragment' in the title of her poem 'The Prisoner (A Fragment)', we
know much less about what she meant by the many fragments she
left behind on the sheets of paper she used for draft versions of her
poems. They consist of pairs of lines and four-line stanzas as well as
slightly longer units of verse that sometimes end abruptly in the middle
of a line or with a line or two at odds with an established metrical
pattern. Although in some instances the holograph manuscripts on
which the fragments survive are themselves fragments, these poems are
not fragments in the sense of having been broken off from larger wholes,
either deliberately like 'The Prisoner (A Fragment)' or accidentally like
the surviving tatters of Sappho. They may be the beginnings of longer
poems that remained unaccomplished, although *beginnings* isn't right
in both its senses, since some of the fragments look more like endings
than beginnings: they may be the poet's first written response to her
inspiration, although they are not the lines with which her poem (her
hypothetical poem) begins.[1] Some fragments may have enough integrity
and coherence to establish their claim to be completed poems. Others
may be successive parts of a poem in the process of composition.
What constitutes closure is only one of the questions Brontë's poetical
fragments and fragmentary poems raise for readers. What kind of
progress characterizes her briefest lyrics or one of her poems still in the
process of composition? What relationships between the parts of such a
poem might shore up the claim that they participate in or belong to the
same whole?

Most of the time, Brontë destroyed her draft versions of poems after transcribing them into one of her fair-copy manuscript notebooks. Where draft versions of poems survive for comparison with the transcriptions, there are few revisions. (The heavily revised draft of 'Why ask to know the date—the clime', which survives in the *Gondal Poems* transcript notebook, is the exception to this practice.) In this respect, Brontë's compositional habits resemble Byron's more than Wordsworth's: like Byron, she conceived of her poetry as process more than product and as expression more than communication.[2] Brontë's view of novel writing, as opposed to poetry writing, was different, at least partly because publication was the understood objective when she began writing *Wuthering Heights*. Where her poems were concerned, what mattered to her, as to Wallace Stevens, was not that they would survive but that she had written them.[3] It makes some sense to treat Brontë's transcript notebooks as a form of self-publication, but her fury when her sister found the *Gondal Poems* notebook and read one or more of the poems in it suggests that she was self-communing in the notebooks, not writing for an audience. She was the only monk in her imagination's monastery: 'What my soul bore, my soul alone | Within itself may tell!' ('My Comforter'). Even though she agreed to publish some of her poems after her sister discovered them, the usual distinctions between planned, authorized, or unfinished fragments and unplanned, accidental, and incomplete fragments operate weakly in relation to the writing of a poet for whom publication was never the horizon in view.[4]

If the fragments that survive are poetry that didn't invite revision or transcription, how do we know which fragments seemed to Brontë to be complete, even if they were unfinished in the sense of not having been revised? Philippe Lacoue-Labarthe and Jean-Luc Nancy's distinction between 'a piece that is struck by incompletion' and 'another that aims at fragmentation for its own sake' simplifies the range of available accounts of a poet's practice.[5] There is no evidence that Brontë aimed at fragmentation for its own sake, but it does not follow that her posthumous fragments were 'struck by incompletion' or that she would have brought them to some different conclusion but was prevented from doing so, either by death or by some other incapacitation or intervention. I hope to demonstrate the interest and value of Brontë's fragments both as poetical fragments that are incomplete, lyric seeds capable of taking root and producing future harvests,[6] and—in some cases—as fragmentary poems, lyric wholes lacking conventional narrative or discursive development or providing it without also providing the rhetorical transitions between the parts of a poem that help to sustain its continuity. The term *poetical fragment* as I use it here refers to poetry that can be identified as incomplete, potentially at least a part of something larger that remained unaccomplished, while the term *fragmentary poem* refers both to brief lyric poems that are often described as fragments but are complete in themselves, even when they are unfinished in the sense of not having been revised, and to longer poems that are made up of poetical fragments. I use 'fragmentary poem' in preference to Marjorie Levinson's term, 'fragment poem', to distinguish the objects of my attention from hers, which are unfinished poems in which 'irresolution invites assimilation as a formal directive and thus functions as a semantic determinant'.[7]

The poetical fragments and fragmentary poems I bring into view have received little critical attention. Some of them consist of only a few lines, and Brontë did not indicate her approval of any of them by transcribing them into one of her fair-copy notebooks.[8] One reason for attending to them is that a high proportion of Brontë's most vital, compelling, and characteristic poetry appears, from the very beginning of her career as a poet, in these fragments. They show what she could accomplish when she was in what Schiller called a 'poetic mood', a phrase Wittgenstein glosses as 'a mood of receptivity to nature in which one's thoughts seem as vivid as nature itself'.[9] They also reveal her debt to Romantic poetry more clearly than many of her better-known poems by showing her genius for what Wordsworth called remarking 'affinities | In objects where no brotherhood exists | To common minds'.[10] Establishing where poems that survive only as drafts begin and end is difficult because Brontë's graphic signals can be ambiguous.[11] In this chapter, I will argue that there are two poems composed of poetical fragments that we should identify as complete poems even though their narrative development is not linear and transitions between the parts of both poems are missing. These poems exaggerate tendencies in Brontë's poetry as a whole, and even in *Wuthering Heights*. In his *Defense of Poetry*, Shelley asserts that these are tendencies of Romantic poetry *per se*. The best a poet can do by means of 'labour and study', Shelley writes, is to provide artificial connections between passages of genuine poetry that are the products of inspiration.[12]

Even the briefest of Brontë's poetical fragments and fragmentary poems identify the occasions that stimulated her to compose poetry and some of her characteristic techniques for generating poetic language, including riddling, prophecy, incantation, and the cultivation of meditated emotion. Between May and July of 1838, for instance, a period in which she composed three poems that she revised and

copied into her *Gondal Poems* notebook, she also composed ten poetical
fragments and fragmentary poems of two to five lines each that survive
on a single leaf of paper (Figure 5).[13] Their rhythm is the most common

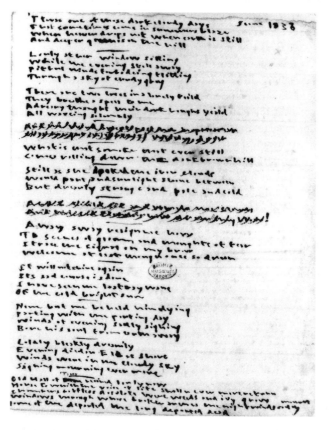

Figure 5. Poetical fragments: "'Twas one of those dark cloudy days', 'Lonly at
her window sitting', 'There are two trees in a lonely field', 'What is that smoke
that ever still', 'Still as she looked the iron clouds', 'Away away resign me now',
'It will not shine again', 'None but one beheld him dying', 'Coldly bleakly
drearily', 'Old Hall of [Elbë] ruined lonly now'. The first poetical fragment
on this manuscript leaf is dated June 1838; the poems written below it are
conjecturally dated in relation to it. Roper transcribes the first pair of cancelled
lines on the page as follows: 'And the wind swept past her hopeless ear/ Was
nought on earth so wildly drear'. From the collection in the Brontë Parsonage
Museum Library at Haworth, Yorkshire.

one in Brontë's poetry, the four-beat line that is closely related to song and chant rhythms. In them, she introduces a character, describes a setting, or asks the sort of question ('What is that smoke that ever still | Comes rolling down that dark brown hill'?) with which large numbers of her other poems begin. She also makes the kind of impassioned assertion ('Away away resign me now') with which other poems by her both begin and end.

The stanza below is evenly divided into two parts, one of which looks like a beginning, the other an end. Although lines 2 and 4 of this stanza have only three actual beats, we can hear the stanza, which is familiar to us as ballad metre and as common measure in hymns, with a strong virtual beat at the end of lines 2 and 4:[14]

> There are two trees in a lonely field
> They breathe a spell to me
> A dreary thought their dark boughs yield
> All waving solemnly

The power of this image—two trees in a lonely field—depends on Brontë's personification of the field and the trees, and this personification expresses her own deep connection to nature. The connection is antecedent to language, especially written language, as is the spell the trees 'breathe' to her. For the ancient Greeks living in an oral society, 'breath is consciousness, breath is perception, breath is emotion,' Anne Carson writes.

This attitude pervades archaic poetry and is strikingly present as well in the perceptual theories of the ancient *physiologoi*. Empedokles' celebrated doctrine of emanations, for example, maintains that everything in the universe is perpetually inhaling and exhaling small particles called *aporrhoai* in a constant stream.[15]

The breath of the trees is this kind of emanation in Brontë's lines, and she receives it with the whole of her being. Her image captures the magic of the wind and the priestly solemnity of the trees and expresses her hope that she will be the bearer of the primeval power that spells have to make things happen. The transition from the respired spell of line 2 to the 'dreary thought' of line 3 marks a step towards meaning, the power of spells having more to do with the sound of words than with their meaning and the power of thought having more to do with the meaning of words than with their sounds. The arrival at meaning is the consequence of inspiration that we may be anticipating. It is part of what we look for in a poem, this meaning that description discloses. In the end, however, the poet prefers not to examine the content of her 'dreary thought'. Or she remains content with the wordless exchange that has occurred. The slight dramatic action the stanza represents, a communication from the wind to the poet, and its transmission from her to her reader, is delicately expressed in the continuation of the sound of 'breathe' in 'dreary thought', and then, in the fading of the sound of 'dreary thought' into the sound of 'dark boughs'. What begins as sound, the quiet sound of breathing, ends in silence, or the barely perceptible vibration of a waving bough. Housman would have had no difficulty identifying these lines as poetry, 'though not in the highest, yet in the highest definable sense'. In the Leslie Stephen Lecture he delivered in 1933, he distinguishes between thought, which a poem may transmit to a reader, and emotion, which poetry *transfuses*. 'And I think that to transfuse emotion—not to transmit thought but to set up in the reader's sense a vibration corresponding to what was felt by the writer—is the peculiar function of poetry.'[16]

Brontë's four graceful lines can stand as an unusually pure manifestation of what C. Day Lewis calls 'the lyric impulse', which, 'when it possesses a poet, asks one thing of him above all, a pure commitment without reserve or circumspection to the creature of his love.'[17] The creature of Emily Brontë's love here is not just the natural world but the natural world as Wordsworth described it to Isabella Fenwick, 'as something not apart from, but inherent in, my own immaterial nature'.[18] In Brontë's effort to embody this world in her verse, she is especially attuned to motion (or change) and rest (or identity), which Emerson calls 'the first and second secrets of nature'.[19] Parting day and parting clouds, evening gradually dying, a quickly rising storm, breaking sunlight or starlight—all these compel her to attention and provide the inspiration for poetry that transfuses emotion or sets up a vibration in a reader corresponding to what was felt by the writer. In this series of ten poetical fragments or fragmentary poems, she focuses on changes of weather perceptible in the external world and in its human occupants, describing 'one of those dark cloudy days | That sometimes come in summer's blaze'; a woman 'Lonely at her window sitting | While the evening stole away'; sunlight flashing between parting clouds; a 'signal on thy brow'; the last waning ray of the sun; a man 'dying | Parting with the parting day'; and evening dying on Elbë's shore.

Two lovely poetical fragments turn on the balance of stillness and movement that is the characteristic modality of the Romantic epiphany,

Wordsworth's sublime Alpine waterfall in *The Prelude* or his steadying conviction of a 'motion and a spirit' that 'rolls through all things' in 'Tintern Abbey'. The first fragment takes the form of a riddle:[20]

> What is that smoke that ever still
> Comes rolling down that dark brown hill

Riddles often provide a description of one thing in terms of another, and we understand without difficulty that the smoke the poet sees is not smoke at all. The point of the poem, however, is not to name the thing (or answer the question, as it is when one faces a riddle) but to see what one is looking at in a new way and to know it differently or for the first time. The operation of eye and mind is similar in the second fragment:

> Still as she looked the iron clouds
> Would part and sunlight shone between
> But drearily strange and pale and cold

There is nothing to suggest that these two fragments belong to the same poem, but both fragments formulate a perception of relentless motion and stasis and take the expressive capacity of the word *still* to its limits. In the first fragment, Brontë contrasts the movement of the mist with the fixity of the 'hill' with which the word 'still' rhymes. Just outside the boundaries of this fragment but germane to it is the poet's knowledge, and the reader's, that this 'dark brown hill' actually not still but 'Rolled round in earth's diurnal course', as the 'brown hills' in 'Remembrance' are actually not immune to change, although they manifest it on a time scale vaster than that of the seasonal change that causes the snow to melt. The movement of the mist is continuous—it is 'ever still' rolling down the hill—but the mist is also itself 'ever still', like Wordsworth's water-fall. In the second fragment, the woman is still—like the hill, she is fixed in her place—and the 'iron clouds' are themselves at once 'still' (rigid like iron, as well as the colour of iron) and still parting. Though there are no rhymes in these three lines, there is the stilling semantic consonance of Brontë's first and last words, 'still' and 'cold', and the sonic consonance of the last words in the first and third lines, 'clouds' and 'cold'. A slight shift in the position of one consonant (the *l* in 'clouds' moves to the other side of the vowel in 'cold') is all that is required to produce so great a difference in meaning, and this is part of what Brontë's lines apprehend or summon into awareness. The three adjectives in the final line—'strange', 'pale', and 'cold'—are all unusual in their application to either sunbeams or eye-beams; they affirm the uncanny bond between the watcher and the watched, the woman who catches sight of the sunlight and the sunlight that shines on her through the parting of the iron clouds, which open like lids of flesh. These two fragments report related poetic occasions and use some of the same poetic resources to do so, but the first of them looks more like the beginning of a poem than the second, which has some of the sense and a lot of the sound of an unsettling end.

Three more stanzas sound even more like the ends of poems and may be exercises in producing them. The reference to 'Elbë's shore' in one of them identifies it as belonging to Brontë's Gondal narrative; it is likely that the stanza beginning 'None but one beheld him dying' also has a Gondal context. From one perspective, all the Gondal poems Brontë wrote may be considered fragments, surviving portions of a grand ruin, some of whose elements we see without perceiving their articulation in relation to each other or to the structure as a whole. By choosing only six poems from her *Gondal Poems* notebook for publication in 1846, less than half the number she culled from the Honresfeld manuscript, Brontë herself may be thought to have indicated a preference for her non-Gondal poems, but Gondal gave rise to two of the most deeply imagined poems she published in 1846, 'Remembrance' and 'The Prisoner (A Fragment)'. The fragments that are identifiable as Gondalian make the case that Gondal experiences and states of feeling are fused with autobiographical ones.[21] The Gondal narrative functioned for Brontë much as *A Vision* did for Yeats. If *A Vision* had not survived, we would be able to derive some of its schemes from the poems it inspired, but we would be unwise to do so, since *A Vision* exists for the sake of the poems, and not vice versa.[22] Yeats said that *A Vision* gave him metaphors for poetry. Brontë might have said the same about Gondal. Brontë's dungeons are as much metaphors for poetry as Yeats's phases of the moon.

Metaphors are also motives for poetry, and because Brontë's poetical fragments survive without the narrative context in which they may have been imaginatively embedded at the time of composition, they help to illuminate the places where a lyrical impulse and a narrative motive converge.

> It will not shine again
> Its sad course is done
> I have seen the last ray wane
> Of the cold bright sun
>
> .   .   .   .   .   .
>
> None but one beheld him dying
> Parting with the parting day

Winds of evening sadly sighing
Bore his soul from earth away
. . . .
Coldly, bleakly, drearily
Evening died on Elbë's shore
Winds were in the cloudy sky
Sighing mourning ever more

The second of these stanzas describes an event, probably a Gondal event, that Brontë also describes in many other poems, including 'A Death-Scene', one of the six Gondal poems she published in 1846. The poem begins with this stanza:

'O Day! he cannot die
When thou so fair art shining!
O Sun, in such a glorious sky,
So tranquilly declining;'

Before Edward can die in 'A Death-Scene', the light will have to pale, the sun set, the breeze sink, and the dews fall, in a catalogue of signals that create in the reader the sense of an ending. The feminine endings, located in the even lines of the poem's first two stanzas, will also have to shift to the odd lines in the poem's last two stanzas (as in the fragment), causing the masculine endings that have closed all the lines in the intervening stanzas to chime with the last words of these stanzas.

Brontë repeatedly dramatizes the contest between life and death, both the struggle that takes place within the dying person, and the struggle that pits the living observer, who survives the death and would forestall it, against the dying person, who presses towards an end. Alternating feminine and masculine endings in a stanza help to express this conflict and its resolution, where there is one. In 'None but one beheld him dying,' the feminine ending expresses both the living person's desire to prolong life and the burden a prolonged life imposes on the one who is dying ('Winds of evening sadly sighing'), while the masculine ending speaks forcibly for the appeal of death, which is in keeping with Nature ('Parting with the parting day') and liberating for the sufferer ('Bore his soul from earth away'). In her classic account of poetic closure, Barbara Herrnstein Smith describes the effect of 'lines which involve references to terminal *motion* (such as falling or sinking)'. She writes that 'there is a kinaesthetic aspect to our responses, as if we were subliminally, but nevertheless physically, participating in the motion so described', so that we get 'a sense of what it feels like to be engaged' in the event instead of a picture of it from the outside.[23] In the three poetical fragments above, the waning of the sun, the parting of day, and the death of evening invite this kinaesthetic response, but in two of them, the present progressive verbs and participles—'dying', 'parting', 'sighing', and 'mourning'—associated with the winds as well as with the human who witnesses a death invite the opposite kinaesthetic response: they reaffirm her investment in an ongoing life.

I have introduced these poetical fragments as experiments in lyric endings, but none of them is obviously incomplete. Incompletion is one typically Romantic theme associated with fragments; others are interruption and inexpressibility.[24] Interruption or occlusion is thematically more pertinent to Brontë's fragments than incompletion or inexpressibility, simply because incompletion and inexpressibility are usually associated with the inadequacy of language to vision. For Brontë, it is vision—not language—that fails: the poetic mood required for visionary flight cannot be induced or cannot be sustained. In several fragments, she laments her loss of poetic authority ('In dungeons dark I cannot sing'), or reacts against being mocked by the usual sources of her inspiration ('Woods you need not frown on me'), or asks forgiveness for unfaithfulness to her muse ('I know not how it falls on me'). These same themes turn up in some of the poems by her that have elicited the most critical attention, including 'Stars' and three of the poems Charlotte Brontë published in 1850, 'Shall Earth no more inspire thee', 'The Night-Wind', and 'Ay—there it is! it wakes to-night'.

The two fragments I juxtapose below present experiences of inspiration imagined in relation to confinement and release from it. Rosalind Miles identifies the first fragment, probably composed in 1837 and already quoted in full as the epigraph to my first chapter, as Brontë's 'first unmasked treatment of the onset of mystical experience'.[25] Edward Chitham suggests that the second one, probably composed about a year later, may have been inspired by Brontë's feelings of confinement in Law Hill,[26] the school in Halifax where she briefly taught:

> And first an hour of mournful musing
> And then a gush of bitter tears
> And then a dreary calm diffusing
> Its deadly mist o'er joys and cares
>
> And then a throb and then a lightening
> And then a breathing from above

And then a star in heaven brightening
The star the glorious star of love

.   .   .   .

I paused on the threshold I turned to the sky
I looked on the heaven and the dark mountains round
The full moon sailed bright through that Ocean on high
And the wind murmured past with a wild eerie sound

And I entered the walls of my dark prison-house
Mysterious it rose from the billowy moor

The first fragment is organized as the narrative of an experience that develops sensational stage by sensational stage until a climax is reached. The experience is mystical, and the imagery is sexual as well as mystical, as it is in the famous lines from 'The Prisoner (A Fragment)' that I discussed in my second chapter. In the first stanza, 'mournful musing' gives way to a burst of 'bitter tears', which gives way to 'a dreary calm': first sadness, then anguish, then numbness. In the second stanza, the poet mounts from insensibility to sudden feeling. A throb is tactile, a vibration from deep within, sometimes associated with the pulse, and a lightening is both tactile and visual. As a tactile word, *lightening* registers the lifting of the burden of the 'deadly mist', which blankets the speaker's feelings. As a visual word, it is the first sign of the speaker's attention to something going on outside her own body. The 'breathing from above', an emanation like the spell of the two trees in a lonely field, is felt as a vibration as well as heard. Together, the breathing from above and the brightening star draw her out of herself and, at the same time, affirm that self. She identifies the star as 'the glorious star of love'.

Although this fragment anticipates Brontë's classic representation of mystical experience in 'The Prisoner (A Fragment)', there are notable differences. Calm is 'soundless', not 'dreary' in 'The Prisoner (A Fragment)', where it is followed by 'Mute music' and 'unuttered harmony'. Brontë's 'unuttered harmony' is as superior to the kind of thing we do utter as Keats's 'unheard' melodies are to those pitched to the human ear. At the height of this experience, sensory reception is generalized to the whole being, not localized in eyes or ears. Instead of 'the glorious star of love', what dawns in 'The Prisoner (A Fragment)' is 'the Invisible' or 'the Unseen'.[27] In the later poem, access to what is outside ('the Invisible' or 'Unseen') is represented also as access to what is inside. An awakened 'inward essence' follows a loss of 'outward sense'. Writing about Novalis, whom he describes as 'in good part a Mystic', though not 'indeed what we English, in common speech, call a Mystic', Carlyle shows how close Brontë's formulation of this experience is to the formulations of German idealist writers like Novalis: 'The Invisible World is near us; or rather it is here, in us and about us; were the fleshly coil removed from our Soul, the glories of the Unseen were even now around us; as the Ancients fabled of the Spheral Music.'[28]

The second fragment has a structure different from that of the first, which proceeds linearly from event to event and culminates in a transfiguring release from confinement. When the second fragment begins, its speaker is about to undergo confinement, but pauses instead of entering her 'dark prison-house'. In the first four lines, she notes the sky, dark mountains that already intimate enclosure, a full moon that sails through the sky, and an eerie wind that drives the moon-ship. The two lines that follow, possibly the beginning of a second stanza that Brontë abandons, both recall the images of the preceding four lines and expand their significance. The 'dark prison-house' recalls the 'dark mountains round', and the unusual formulation—not 'I entered my dark prison-house' but 'I entered the walls of my dark prison-house'—reminds us of the contrast between the boundless sky and the circle of mountains with which the fragment begins. The description of the prison-house itself—'Mysterious it rose from the billowy moor'—(if this is a description of the house and not a return to the moon) recalls the full moon sailing through a sky she has imagined as an ocean, both because the house is endowed with a movement characteristic of the moon (it 'rose') and because the moor is made to swell or undulate like the sea. The moor is 'billowy' because of the wind, but the eeriness associated with the wind is projected onto the prison-house, which is 'Mysterious' or rises mysteriously, as if it did not belong to the scene at all or was the creation of inhuman forces. If this is an account of Brontë's resistance to her confinement as a teacher at Law Hill, as Chitham suggests it is, it expresses none of the distress Charlotte felt about her sister's situation: 'I fear she will never stand it—'.[29] In the first fragment, the personal pronoun 'I' was omitted; in the second fragment, it is prominent as the subject in three lines. Where the lyric 'I' is not asserting itself, those familiar lyric objects—the moon, the wind, and the mysterious prison-house—take its place. Although this is a poem about retreating from an inspiring scene, its language and structure suggest that the poet has been transfigured by what she has seen and felt. As in Coleridge's 'Kubla Khan', the dream vision may be lost to the poet or the poet may be kept from it, but it continues to exist, beckoning her back even as she closes herself off from it. If 'Nature is a Haunted House', as Dickinson says, Art is 'a House that tries to be haunted'. I have been reading this poetical fragment as if it described a literal scene, however instinct with visionary power, but the dark prison-house need not be a house at all. A house is a familiar image for the body, and this speaker's re-enclosure within the 'walls of her dark prison-house' may convey the wandering human spirit's inability to remain any longer at large. Such a reading brings this fragment into relation with Brontë's lines from 'The Prisoner (A Fragment)', lines in which she describes more fully the escape from the body and the return to it.

The poetical fragment 'The night is darkening round me', which appears in my edition of Brontë's poems as a poem in three distinct parts or as three poems that have been composed in relation to each other, raises different questions for readers. At the time of its first publication in 1902, and in all subsequent editions of Brontë's poems, 'The night is darkening round me' was printed as an independent poetical fragment, and the two poetical fragments that I associate with it were treated as separate from it. In the holograph, lines 1–12 ('The night is darkening round me') are centred on the page, with lines 13–28 ('I'll come when thou art saddest') and lines 29–35 ('I would have touched the heavenly key') located below it, side by side. Charlotte Brontë provided a precedent for pairing poems when she printed the poem titled 'A.E. and R.C.' in the *Gondal Poems* notebook under the title 'The Two Children' in 1850, although subsequent editors have printed this poem as two independent poems, one beginning 'Heavy hangs the raindrop', the other beginning 'Child of Delight! with sunbright hair'. The issue is not whether these are discrete poems or not—they are—but whether they are companion poems, composed and imagined in relation to each other, like Blake's paired poems in *Songs of Innocence and of Experience*, available for reading independently of each other but designed to be read in closer relation to each other than to other poems in the *Songs*. Although the first twelve lines of 'The night is darkening round me' have often been printed independently and may be familiar to readers under the title 'Spellbound', this fragment gains interest from being read as part of a triptych of poems that represent an exchange involving a spellbound speaker (lines 1–12), an answering voice (lines 13–28), and an altered speaker (lines 29–35). These last six lines, the weakest in the poem, both record and represent the poet's loss of inspiration and then access to her own feelings; line 35 is unfinished, breaking off in its middle: 'And then I felt … ':

The night is darkening round me
The wild winds coldly blow
But a tyrant spell has bound me
And I cannot cannot go

The giant trees are bending
Their bare boughs weighed with snow
And the storm is fast descending
And yet I cannot go

Clouds beyond clouds above me
Wastes beyond wastes below
But nothing drear can move me
I will not cannot go

.　　.　　.　　.　　.　　.　　.

I'll come when thou art saddest
Laid alone in the darkened room
When the mad day's mirth has vanished
And the smile of joy is banished
From evening's chilly gloom

I'll come when the heart's [real] feeling
Has entire unbiased sway
And my influence o'er thee stealing
Grief deepening joy congealing
Shall bear thy soul away

Listen 'tis just the hour
The awful time for thee
Dost thou not feel upon thy soul
A flood of strange sensations roll
Forerunners of a sterner power
Heralds of me

.　　.　　.　　.　　.　　.　　.

I would have touched the heavenly key
That spoke alike of bliss and thee
I would have woke the entrancing song
But its words died upon my tongue
And then I knew that hallowed strain
Could never speak of joy again
And then I felt

'The night is darkening round me' has been read as a Gondal fragment that has survived without our having the benefit of a fuller narrative context that would explain 'what was happening, to whom, and why'.[30] Juliet Barker provides a detailed account of one proposed Gondal narrative context in her note to the poem in *The Brontës: Selected Poems*:

> In a few words she manages to sketch a graphic picture of a snowscape and a fast descending snow storm. Despite the approaching storm and impending nightfall, the poet is held by a 'tyrant spell' which denies her all freedom of choice and prevents her seeking refuge: she 'will not, cannot go'. It is difficult to discover exactly what the 'tyrant spell' is: if Fannie Ratchford … is right in placing the poem in a Gondal context, then it seems likely that it relates to an incident when one of the heroines exposes her child to die on the mountains in the depths of winter. Although she cannot bear to watch the child die, as a mother she is unable to tear herself away from the place and the 'tyrant spell' is therefore her maternal emotions.[31]

Ratchford's story of infanticide lacks psychological plausibility, especially when it identifies the 'tyrant spell' with the feelings of a mother who is about to expose her child to the elements. Additionally, although the scene represented in the fragmentary poem is wild and a storm is predicted, there is no evidence in the poem that the lyric speaker feels threatened by it. In this case, the lost Gondal prose fiction has provided an excuse for inventing a narrative that is unsupported by the poem that the narrative has been invented to explain.

The psychological narrative being constructed in these twelve lines and in the twenty-three lines that follow them in the companion fragmentary poems is, I propose, closely related to the one in the fragmentary poem beginning 'And first an hour of mournful musing'. 'The night is darkening round me' expresses the sadness, anguish, and numbness of the first stanza of that poem but uses different means to do so. The darkening night; the cold, wild winds; the preternaturally enlarged trees bending under the weight of the snow; the vast sky above and the wide wastes below—these are the elements of a typically haunted Brontë landscape. Some of them turn up in the first stanza of 'Julian M and A. G. Rochelle' where they are part of a description of Julian's anticipation of a visitor, the Wanderer, who is related to the visitor who promises to come in the fragment:

> Silent is the House—all are laid asleep;
> One, alone, looks out o'er the snow-wreaths deep;
> Watching every cloud, dreading every breeze
> That whirls the wildering drifts and bends the groaning trees—

At the same time that they belong to an imagined landscape, these natural elements are also components of a haunted mindscape that is familiar to us from other poems: the speaker feels stupefied; she suspects that she is bewitched; she has the sensation of being burdened by a heavy weight; and she feels her own corporeal insignificance or diminishment in a vast space that stretches limitlessly above and below her. Her physical location is not clearly established, not even whether she is outside or inside. Nor is the refrain clear in its meaning. 'And I cannot cannot go'; 'And yet I cannot go'; 'I will not cannot go.' The small variations seem to mark subtle shifts of feeling: incapacity, frustration, defiance. Where is this speaker not going, or where is she unwilling to go? The answer comes in the second poetical fragment and comes in the form of a promise of release. Were the conditions right, the lyric speaker's spirit would be borne away:

> I'll come when the heart's [real] feeling
> Has entire unbiased sway
> And my influence o'er thee stealing
> Grief deepening joy congealing
> Shall bear thy soul away

This promised liberation occurs at the end of the second stanza of 'And first an hour of mournful musing' and occurs more explicitly in 'The Prisoner (A Fragment)':

> 'Then dawns the Invisible; the Unseen its truth reveals;
> My outward sense is gone, my inward essence feels:
> Its wings are almost free—its home, its harbour found,
> Measuring the gulf, it stoops, and dares the final bound.'

But in the last six lines of 'I'll come when thou art saddest', the soul fails to find its wings or dare the final bound. The lines themselves document an urging that feels and sounds increasingly forced and futile:

> Listen 'tis just the hour
> The awful time for thee
> Dost thou not feel upon thy soul
> A flood of strange sensations roll
> Forerunners of a sterner power
> Heralds of me

The metrical shift in these lines signals the poet's loss of momentum. The metre of lines 1–24 relies on three strong beats in each line, with a variable arrangement of iambs, anapaests, spondees, and amphibrachs. But the rhythm breaks down in line 25, when a steady iambic tetrameter takes over. No feminine endings here, or in any of the lines that follow. Neither the appeal to past experience ('Listen 'tis just the hour') nor the exhortation ('Dost thou not feel upon thy soul | A flood of strange sensations roll') can produce what the poet desires: the return of inspiration. In the final unfinished poem, lines 29–35, the speaker is reduced to documenting her desire for a release that has not occurred—'I would ... I would ... '. The conditional verbs recall the honest, troubled verbs of 'The night is darkening round me': 'cannot cannot ... cannot ... will not cannot'. Her effort to become a living soul is doomed, and she is driven to the most despairing conclusion, which, for a poet, is no conclusion at all but an enforced termination:

> And then I knew that hallowed strain
> Could never speak of joy again
> And then I felt

A particular kind of textual instability characterizes those fragments that may be parts of longer poems. Disagreements about whether poetical fragments are independent of each other or successive parts of longer poetic compositions can originate whenever such fragments appear on the same manuscript leaf and Brontë has not unambiguously signalled a poem's end. Such disagreements are registered in the publication history of these fragments, but they are unlikely to be resolved there. Brontë may have been composing poetical fragments, or she may have been composing a poem, or she may have been composing poetical fragments that she would later have given the appearance of a poem. Marjorie Levinson supplies a precedent for this last practice in the work of John Merivale, who published a poem with a note acknowledging that 'several unconnected fragments of verse' have been 'brought together as component parts of a larger poem' that were written 'without any such design'.[32]

I begin with three fragments that were first published as a single poem in 1910. The external evidence cuts two ways: the first fragment—now located on a torn scrap of paper—once belonged to the same manuscript leaf as the second and third fragments,[33] but the second and third fragments—still located on the same manuscript leaf—are separated from each other by the short, horizontal mark (indicated below by asterisks) that ordinarily signals the end of a poem in Brontë's draft manuscripts:

> Heaven's glory shone where he was laid
> In life's decline
> I turned me from that young saint's bed
> To gaze on thine—

> It was a summer day that saw
> His spirit's flight
> Thine parted in a time of awe
> A winter-night
>
> ***
>
> Upon her soothing breast
> She lulled her little child
> A winter sunset in the west
> A dreary glory smiled
>
> ***
>
> I gazed within thine earnest eyes
> And read the sorrow brooding there
> [I saw] thy young breast heave with sighs
> And envied such despair
>
> Go to the grave in youth's [first] woe
> That doom was written long ago

What about the internal evidence? The metre varies from fragment to fragment, the metre of the first fragment—alternating tetrameter and dimeter lines—being unusual for Brontë. There is only one poem in which she uses dimeter lines at all, 'Sleep brings no joy to me', and in it she uses them, as Keats does in 'La Belle Dame sans Merci', at the end of a four-line stanza, where their effect is similar.[34]

> Sleep brings no joy to me
> Remembrance never dies
> My soul is given to misery
> And lives in sighs

The collapse of four beats into two creates a feeling of foreboding appropriate to both 'La Belle Dame' and 'Sleep brings no joy to me'. But the alternation of two beats with four sounds dismissive or perfunctory: this is a metre giving news of its own diminishing momentum. Rhythm here also suggests that the first fragment is finished after eight lines, when the metre shifts from alternating tetrameter and dimeter lines into fairly regular trimeter and then into tetrameter.

The awkwardness of the stipulated dramatic occasion for the first fragment—the speaker turns from one deathbed to the other even though the deaths occur at different times—suggests that Brontë is working at some distance from her subject. This fragment, and the others below it, are probably Gondal fragments. Since one deathbed is occupied by a young saint, and since the fragment is structured by the oppositions or balances it invokes—two stanzas, each divided into two parts; a summer day and a winter night—we may be moved to identify the occupant of the other deathbed as a sinner, whether young or old. This provides a link to the third fragment, which may be complete. In it, a speaker observes a young man or woman who is dying in despair. He or she, however, has 'earnest eyes', and the speaker envies the despair that more years could only diminish. Apart from their having very different rhythms, then, these two fragments also represent two very different occasions and two very different responses on the part of the lyric speaker to them. The third fragment, which can only with difficulty be connected to the one that precedes it, shares a winter setting with the first fragment, but the times are differently specific ('A winter-night'; 'A winter sunset'). The mother and child who appear in the second fragment seem to belong to a different narrative or reverie, although there is a connection between soothing breasts and graves (though less of one between breasts and deathbeds), as well as between death and the sunset. Associations like these may be behind Brontë's rapid shift of scene and character, if indeed the presence of these poetical fragments on the same manuscript leaf signifies their having been composed more or less contemporaneously, as it may.

My argument for the integrity of two of Emily Brontë's poems, 'Deep deep down in the silent grave' and 'The battle had passed from the height', requires a defence of their formal and semantic coherence as well as a willingness to believe that they may be complete, at least in the way that a poem in draft is complete. Such poems may remain available for revision but do not lack any component essential to their integrity or present any insurmountable obstacle to their being read by a reader as coherent wholes. For a poet like Brontë, the avoidance of closure in a poem makes as persuasive a stopping place as its achievement. Her poems often move us towards a door and then spring rather than fasten its latch.

The publication history of 'Deep deep down in the silent grave' is inconsistent. In my edition of the poems, I treat this line together with the seventeen lines that follow it in Brontë's manuscript as a complete poem of eighteen lines. These eighteen lines were first published in 1902, together with twenty-four further lines that appear below them on the same manuscript leaf. Hatfield (1941) and Roper (1995) both represent the eighteen lines as four independent poetical fragments. In my edition of the poems, I represent the horizontal marks that appear after lines 2, 6, and 10 in Brontë's manuscript with a broken line. But as my note to the poem indicates, the marks after lines 2, 6, and 10 are shorter

than the mark that follows line 18; this longer line clearly separates the
eighteen-line poem from the poetical fragment that appears below it.

> Deep deep down in the silent grave
> With none to mourn above
> - - - - - - - -
> Here with my knee upon thy stone
> I bid adieu to feelings gone
> I leave with thee my tears and pain
> And rush into the world again
> - - - - - - - -
> O come again what chains withhold
> The steps that used so fleet to be—
> Come leave thy dwelling dark and cold
> Once more to visit me
> - - - - - - - -
> Was it with the fields of green
> Blowing flower and budding tree
> With the summer heaven serene
> That thou didst visit me?
>
> No 'twas not the flowery plain
> No 'twas not the fragrant air
> Summer skies will come again
> But *thou* wilt not be there—

The metre of all the stanzas of this poem is fairly consistent: three lines
of iambic or trochaic tetrameter are followed by a fourth line of iambic
trimeter. The opening two lines of the poem are also written in iambic
tetrameter and iambic trimeter, but the four lines that follow, lines
3–6, substitute a fourth line of iambic tetrameter for a fourth line of
iambic trimeter. This substitution maintains the forward momentum
of the stanza that is appropriate to the action being described and to the
questionable claim being made.

> I leave with thee my tears and pain
> And rush into the world again

The claim is questionable in two ways: as bravado that the rest of
the poem will undermine, and as containing a potent unresolvable
ambiguity. Does the speaker leave her tears and pain behind her at
the gravesite, or does she take them with her when she rushes back
to the world? If she carries her tears and pain with her, then she
doesn't really leave at all. Apart from the meter, the consistency of

the dramatic occasion of the poem—a speaker addresses someone who has recently died—and of the relationship between the speaker and her audience—always expressed as an 'I-thou' formulation—argues for the poem's unity. The first line, 'Deep deep down in the silent grave', anticipates 'Remembrance': 'Far, far, removed, cold in the dreary grave!' (l. 2) Repetitions in both poems—not just 'deep down in the silent grave', but 'Deep deep down' and not just 'far removed' but 'Far, far, removed'—tell us what we know: we cannot express our distance from the dead in any usual way. A significant difference between the two poems is that the mourner in 'Remembrance' has had fifteen years to attempt to come to terms with the death she confronts, while the death in this poem is fresh. We have some additional information about the death in 'Deep deep down in the silent grave': there are 'none to mourn above'. This is ambiguous, meaning perhaps that there is only one living person (the speaker) who mourns; or that her mourning is invisible, so that it appears that no one mourns; or, possibly, that mourning is interdicted, at least the kind of protracted mourning that characterizes the grief of someone who refuses to accommodate herself to a death and get on with her life.

The plot of the poem, its progress from beginning to end, is not obscure. The first two lines announce a situation to which the following stanzas react: the dead person has been buried, removed from the place still inhabited by the living. In lines 3–6, the speaker tries out the myth of burial as conclusive. What the living do is to return to life, leaving their feelings behind, buried with the corpse, in the grave. Positioning herself at the grave, she bids 'adieu' to feelings that are 'gone'. Her haste to leave the grave is unseemly, but her plaintive cry ('O come again') soon confirms the impossibility of burying her 'tears and pain' and her desperate longing for reunion in the place of the living, even if it takes the form of a single visit. This longing for a return of the dead will dominate Heathcliff's life after Catherine's death, and it is not resolved in this poem any more than it is in *Wuthering Heights*. In both the poem and the novel, the mourner is torn between a wish to tempt the dead person to struggle against the burial and a doubt that the dead sufficiently exert themselves to rejoin the living. In the last eight lines of the poem, the mourner asks a question about the relation between the renewal of the natural world and human renewal and then answers it: she faces the fact that human beings do not participate in the enduring life of nature. Spring and summer recur, but the dead remain absent to the living, or at least outside the field of our senses.

This poem does not lack closure. The repetitions that link lines 7–10 and lines 11–18 ('O come again ... Summer skies will come again'; 'Once more to visit me ... That thou didst visit me') may indicate that these twelve lines compose a more sustained effort at a poem than do

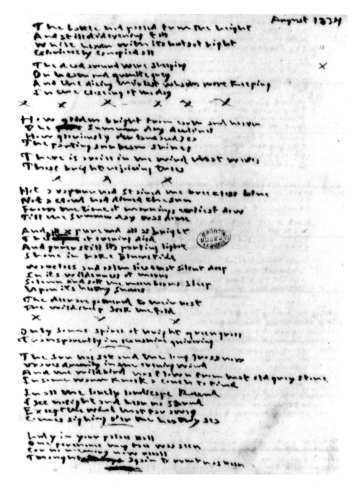

Figure 6. 'The battle had passed from the height', The sun has set and the long grass now', and 'Lady in your Palace Hall'. The date August 1837 appears at the top of the manuscript leaf. From the collection in the Brontë Parsonage Museum Library at Haworth, Yorkshire.

the preceding six lines, or all eighteen lines taken together. Still, the eighteen lines taken together have the sound of a poem in the making, and this poem is successful in expressing the mourner's feelings of anger, distress, resentment, resignation, and inconsolable grief.

The four fragments that compose 'The battle had passed from the height' are located on a single manuscript leaf and comprise thirty lines in all (Figure 6). These fragments also have an inconsistent publication history. They were first published in 1902 as parts of one poem that incorporated two further fragments (of eight lines and four lines, respectively) that also appear on the same manuscript leaf. They were then published as four independent poetical fragments in 1923 (Shorter), 1941 (Hatfield), and 1995 (Roper). In my edition of Brontë's poems (1992), I present them as parts of one poem. The fragments are separated from each other by rows of crosses rather than by the horizontal marks that ordinarily signify the end of a poem in Brontë's manuscripts; these horizontal marks appear at the bottom of the thirty lines and again below two other poetical fragments on the same manuscript leaf. The poem is primarily written in quatrains, but there is a precedent for its six-line second section (and its ten-line third section) in 'Cold clear and blue the morning heaven':

> The battle had passed from the height
> And still did evening fall
> While heaven with its hosts of night
> Gloriously canopied all
>
> The dead around were sleeping
> On heath and granite grey
> And the dying their last watch were keeping
> In the closing of the day
> - - - - - - - -
> How golden bright from earth and heaven
> The summer day declines
> How gloriously o'er land and sea
> The parting sunbeam shines
>
> There is a voice in the wind that waves
> Those bright rejoicing trees
> - - - - - - - -
> Not a vapour had stained the breezeless blue
> Not a cloud had dimmed the sun
> From the time of morning's earliest dew
> Till the summer day was done

And all as pure and all as bright
The [beam] of evening died
And purer still its parting light
Shone in Lake Elnor's tide

Waveless and calm lies that silent deep
In its wilderness of moors
Solemn and soft the moonbeams sleep
Upon its heathy shores

The deer are gathered to their rest
The wild sheep seek the fold
- - - - - - - -
Only some spires of bright green grass
Transparently in sunshine quivering

The setting is a battlefield at the close of day. In the first stanza, evening is falling, and its progressive changes are contrasted with the end to human activity brought about by the battle's end. Yet even the dead in the second stanza are accorded an ongoing life: they are 'sleeping' in the company of the 'dying', who are still 'keeping' their 'last watch'. The next six lines turn back to the scene, which is instinct with the motion of the declining summer day, the 'parting sunbeam' that shines, and the 'voice in the wind that waves' the trees. Like the lines that precede them, these lines present a scene that is 'gloriously' full of light. The trees are not 'dark' or 'waving solemnly' but 'bright' and 'rejoicing', oblivious to the human carnage.

The absence of protest or self-consciousness in the poet's representation of this contrast enables her to produce a pastoral vision of death in the next fourteen lines. Like the human dead of the first part of the poem, the moonbeams 'sleep' on the 'heathy shores' of Lake Elnor. The poet does not specify the kind of sleep the human dead endure in the poem's second stanza, but the sleep of the moonbeams is 'Solemn and soft'. The human occupants of this scene are present by association, first with these moonbeams, then with the deer and sheep:

The deer are gathered to their rest
The wild sheep seek the fold

Like the last stanza of Keats's 'To Autumn', these lines express a perfect and satisfying composure in the presence of death by conveying the poet's sense of nature's changes and its permanence. In both poems, animal activity at the close of day is also a confirmation of unceasing life, whether by Keats's 'gathering swallows' that 'twitter in the skies' or by

Brontë's silent deer being 'gathered to their rest' and wild sheep seeking the fold. While the absence of end-rhyme works toward openness in the two lines about the deer and the sheep, the long vowel sounds that connect these lines to the lines that have preceded them promise closure: 'wild' recalls the final words of a previous stanza ('bright', 'died', 'light', 'tide') and 'deer', 'sheep', and 'seek' echo 'deep' and 'sleep' in the stanza immediately preceding. The moving parallels between human and non-human worlds—the sleeping dead; the watching dying; the resting deer and the sheep seeking enclosure; the solemn, sleeping moonbeams; evening's parting light; the 'silent deep' that lies 'Waveless and calm'—are what Keats meant by 'touches of Beauty' that make the reader 'content', not 'breathless': 'the rise, the progress, the setting of imagery should like the Sun come natural natural too him [*sic*]—shine over him and set soberly although in magnificence leaving him in the Luxury of twilight—'.[35]

These two lines achieve the poetic closure that Barbara Herrnstein Smith defines as announcing and justifying

the absence of further development; it reinforces the feeling of finality, completion, and composure which we value in all works of art; and it gives ultimate unity and coherence to the reader's experience of the poem by providing a point from which all the preceding elements may be viewed comprehensively and their relations grasped as part of a significant design.[36]

But these two lines are not the final two lines of the poem, which continues with a second unrhymed pair:

> Only some spires of bright green grass
> Transparently in sunshine quivering

These lines have the effect of extending the poem, an extension that is palpable in the length and lightness of the last line, which swells to ten syllables while maintaining the three-stress rhythm of the line we would have anticipated, on the model of 'Upon its heathy shores' and 'The wild sheep seek the fold'. Brontë's two lines recall the closing couplet of Hardy's poem 'The Walk':

> Only that underlying sense
> Of the look of a room on returning thence.

Hardy might have read Brontë's lines in the 1902 edition of her poems in which they were first published, and almost certainly would have read them (after writing 'The Walk') in the 1923 edition of Brontë's poems he owned. Here is the last stanza of 'The Walk':

> I walked up there to-day
> Just in the former way:
> Surveyed around
> The familiar ground
> By myself again:
> What difference, then?
> Only that underlying sense
> Of the look of a room on returning thence.

In this poem too, something remains to be said, although it can hardly be communicated in terms more precise than those evoking a barely perceptible change in a room once occupied by someone who can no longer be left behind.

What difference, then, between Brontë's ending her poem at line 28 and her ending it at line 30? The word 'bright' appears in each section of the poem except the first, where its sense is supplied by 'Gloriously', but the colour green appears for the first time in line 29, in vital contrast to the 'granite grey' of the first section. 'Spires', not 'blades', of grass because of the assonance with 'bright' and the suggestion of a cathedral, in keeping with the poem's holy mood and the poet's attention to the interpenetration of human and non-human worlds. Brontë may be remembering the 'green spires' of the grass in Marvell's 'Upon Appleton House'. The word 'quivering', which describes the grass and may also describe the sunshine, is a human word and suggests the presence of an observer on whose senses the delicate motion of the light and grass can impress themselves as well as the excited, silent life of the inanimate world. These lines mark a shift in the poet's perspective. In the rest of the poem, she looks from a distance, her view taking in the battle that had 'passed from the height', the deep lake, and the vast stretches of sky and moor. A quiet calm rules the scene, and the tranquillity of the deer and wild sheep confirms the calm of the sleeping dead and even the calm of the dying seeking death. The tall spires of a cathedral, were there one in this landscape, might be seen from this distance, but the 'spires of bright green grass' can be seen or felt only at close range, and their quivering would be perceived by only the most attentive observer.

'The battle had passed from the height' shows what Brontë could accomplish, from an early date, when she was in a poetic mood. With the juxtaposition of the last two stanzas, the temporal mode of the poem's action trembles between three versions of present time: there is the simple present of 'are gathered' and 'seek', verbs that suggest an action being completed and an action moving towards completion, and there is the different time register of 'quivering', the only instance of a present progressive tense in a poem that has a remarkably wide temporal range. The poem is elegiac, celebrating the unnamed dead and dying by praising the fecundity of the natural world and the moving life to which the dying are gradually becoming oblivious and to which the dead already belong. Like so many of Brontë's other poetical fragments and fragmentary poems, 'The battle had passed from the height' doesn't seek to transmit a thought but to transfuse emotion by setting up in the reader's sense a quivering vibration corresponding to what the poet herself was feeling. It adds to the evidence that Gondal was enabling, not distracting, for her as a poet, even (and perhaps especially) when it provided opportunities for imagining experiences she couldn't have had. It tells us something about how she composed her poems—quickly, intermittently, often in fits and starts.

6

The First Last Thing

The four last things to be ever remembered are Death, Judgment,
Hell, and Heaven.

The Penny Catechism

Because that Death is final,
However first it be ...

Emily Dickinson

In January of 1996, when I was in London beginning to write about
Emily Brontë's poems, the Church of England determined that judge-
ment, hell, and heaven were all real. This was the unanimous conclusion
of a report by the Church's Doctrine Commission published as *The Mys-
tery of Salvation*. Earlier in the month, the first of the four last things had
been called into question when a woman named Daphne Banks died and
came back to life. More precisely, Mrs Banks went beyond her doctor's
ability to measure her vital signs and was pronounced dead and taken to
the mortuary at Hinchingbrooke hospital, where, about an hour later,
the undertaker noticed a varicose vein in her right leg twitching. Signs of
breathing and sounds of snoring followed. Mrs Banks, who would have
been placed in a sealed mortuary tray in another hour, came back to life.
Unlike her namesake, the nymph pursued by Apollo, Daphne Banks
wasn't granted everlasting life. Unlike Thomas à Kempis, the fifteenth-
century monk whose coffin was said to show evidence of scratch marks
on the inside, she wasn't buried alive either.

With our current interest in boundaries, we tend to think of the
one between life and death as there to be crossed, or breached, or
transcended. These metaphors have the luster of transgression; they
mask our helplessness, vulnerability, and lack of agency in the face of
death. Over time, we have improved our instruments for determining

death—mirrors have given way to stethoscopes, and stethoscopes to electroencephalograms—but we have no instruments for charting the experience of dying. Perhaps we would do better not to speak of a boundary line at all, a moment when spontaneous breathing stops, or there is no longer a heartbeat, or no brain function can be discerned—these being the criteria for death endorsed in the United States by the 1981 Uniform Determination of Death Act. Instead, we could think of a space of time that is occupied on one or the other side of a determination of death, which we would then imagine less as a discrete event than a process, like the sun's setting. This is how Emily Brontë imagines dying in the last four stanzas of a poem she titled 'A Death-Scene' and published in 1846:

> Paled, at length, the sweet sun setting;
> Sunk to peace the twilight breeze:
> Summer dews fell softly, wetting
> Glen, and glade, and silent trees.

> Then his eyes began to weary,
> Weighted beneath a mortal sleep;
> And their orbs grew strangely dreary,
> Clouded, even as they would weep.

> But they wept not, but they changed not,
> Never moved, and never closed;
> Troubled still, and still they ranged not—
> Wandered not, nor yet reposed!

> So I knew that he was dying—
> Stooped, and raised his languid head;
> Felt no breath, and heard no sighing,
> So I knew that he was dead.

Between the first and last lines of the final stanza—'So I knew that he was dying' and 'So I knew that he was dead'—something happens that the speaker registers with the primitive instruments at hand: skin ('Felt no breath') and ear ('heard no sighing'). The three stanzas that close this poem describe the process of dying. In the stanza that precedes them, the sun sets and night develops. While the landscape and skyscape are paling and quieting but still in motion, the dying man's eyes express only *troubling*, a human agency even more minimal than weeping, changing, ranging, or wandering. These natural events are implicitly different: the sun is setting once more, but the dying man's head is drooping once and for all.

The balances and repetitions of the poem's second to last stanza are precise, economical, and unnerving. The eyes that 'Never moved, and never closed' are those of a dead man, even though the dying is still in train, and the image of clouded orbs, heavy with moisture, reminds us that eyes are disconcertingly like both sea and sky. 'Troubled' had long been obsolete as an intransitive verb when Brontë wrote this poem, but she probably had in mind the passage from Job that supplied the title for Branwell's unpublished novel: 'There the wicked cease from troubling; and there the weary be at rest' (5: 17). In the death for which Job yearns, kings, counsellors, miscarried foetuses, stillborn infants, and prisoners all find an equal rest. In the third line of Brontë's stanza, 'still' (in both its senses) works like a fulcrum to support the chiasmus, which could be said to end with the dash or to flow through it to settle, finally, on 'reposed'. For me, the last line of 'A Death-Scene' has an effect like that of the last line of Blake's 'The Chimney Sweeper' in *Songs of Experience*: 'So if all do their duty they need not fear harm.' The childlike 'So' with which both lines begin confidently asserts a consequence that the poems put in deep doubt. What exactly does it mean to know that someone is dead?

The Church Doctrine Commission's report and the revival of Daphne Banks—events occurring within a few weeks of each other in 1996— touched the two primary anxieties about death current 150 years earlier when Emily Brontë was alive: how to determine it, and how to understand the judgement that was supposed to follow it. Live burial wasn't just a Gothic nightmare or a metaphor for repression in a period that saw the invention of a coffin equipped with a bell to ring and a flag to wave above the ground in case its occupant's chest moved beneath it. In his comprehensive text, *Human Physiology* (1835), John Elliotson refers both to a well-known error of Vesalius, who began to dissect a female in a paroxysm, and to a recent play by Leigh Hunt, *The Legend of Florence*, in which a young lady is entombed alive. Elliotson's directions for handling the dead are specific: wait for putrefaction, however late it may be in beginning, 'for many have died because deprived of their previous covering and put into a room without a fire in winter, from the belief that they were dead. The odour should be that of putrefaction, not that merely earthy smell which may be perceptible before death.'[1] Conviction about death was hard to achieve, but conviction about punishment in the afterlife was required of the faithful. In 1846, a clause affirming eternal punishment was added to the Evangelical Alliance's expanded confession of faith, and in 1853, F. D. Maurice was dismissed from his chair at King's College because of his lax views. He defended himself by maintaining that 'whilst he hoped for a universal salvation, he never affirmed that this would in fact be the case'.[2] The idea of universal salvation, so dangerous in the mid-nineteenth century, looks a lot like the Church Doctrine Commission's view in the late twentieth century. *The Mystery of Salvation* insists on hell but allows that it may be empty. Our modern hell is a place of annihilation, not torment, and ultimate salvation, including for unbelievers, is said to be in God's hands.

Brontë was familiar with the theological disputes current in the mid-nineteenth century (she calls them 'the thousand creeds | That move men's hearts' in 'No coward soul is mine'), but her novel and her poems advocate no particular creed, not even the belief in a universal salvation Anne promotes in *The Tenant of Wildfell Hall*.[3] Instead, both *Wuthering Heights* and the poems represent judgement, heaven, and hell as humanly irrelevant. As Marianne Thormählen points out, several characters in *Wuthering Heights* do invoke heaven and hell to describe their earthly experience. Cathy's and Linton's disagreement about the pleasantest way to spend a hot July day (a conversation she reports to Nelly, when she confesses to her clandestine meetings with her cousin) produces competing visions of heaven: Cathy finds Linton's 'only half alive' and soporific; he finds hers 'drunk' and suffocating (II. x. 301–2). We are probably meant to be reminded of Catherine's dream of being flung out of heaven and her own interpretation of it: 'I've no more business to marry Edgar Linton than I have to be in heaven' (I. ix. 99–100). But such references lack the theological weight and point of the accounts of heaven and hell as states of mind produced by living with or being separated from God that Thormählen associates with them.[4] In the poems, hell appears infrequently, and when it does, it figures either as a metaphor ('This hell shall wring thy spirit too') or a curse ('Hell snatch thy worthless soul away!'). Although heaven appears more frequently in the poems, this can be explained by the word's standing in for sky (as in 'summer's heaven' or 'nature's heaven'). Together, heaven and hell turn up in the poems as halves of an outcome imagined indifferently, as in these lines from 'The Prisoner (A Fragment)':

> 'Yet I would lose no sting, would wish no torture less,
> The more the anguish racks, the earlier it will bless;
> And robed in fires of hell, or bright with heavenly shine,
> If it but herald death, the vision is divine!'

Or these lines from 'The Philosopher', which pit human desire and will against whatever heaven and hell have on offer:

'No promised heaven, these wild desires,
Could all, or half fulfill;
No threatened hell, with quenchless fires,
Subdue this quenchless will!'

As one half of an eternal outcome, heaven is also represented as an inadequate compensation for human suffering or as a bad bargain in which identity, constituted by consciousness or memory, is exchanged for everlasting rest. From this non-theological perspective, heaven looks as much like annihilation as hell.

Unlike judgement, heaven, and hell, death is humanly relevant for Brontë. Ordinary and inevitable, death is also profound and intolerable. She was more familiar with death than most people, even in the nineteenth century, living as she did in one of the unhealthiest places in England, a rural town with a mortality rate equalling that of the most crowded cities. The Parsonage overlooked the crowded churchyard cemetery, and as the Vicar's daughter, she attended frequent funerals and worshipped in a church beneath which her mother and two oldest sisters were buried. Juliet Barker notes that during the seven and a half months of Emily's mother Maria Branwell Brontë's final illness, there were sixty-three burials in Haworth.[5] That's two or three dyings a week. In the British Library, there is a letter Charlotte Brontë hopefully wrote to a London specialist about ten days before Emily's death. It describes her sister's condition, requests advice about treatment, and closes with a warning that the patient opposes medical treatment:

Her resolution to contend against illness being very fixed she has never consented to lie in bed for a single day—she sits up from 7 in the morning till 10 at night. All medical aid she has rejected—insisting that Nature shall be left to take her own course ... [6]

How should we understand Brontë's determination to let nature take 'her own course'? Like Macbeth, she was determined to die in harness. Charlotte emphasizes her sister's resolve (and her stubbornness), which she sees in relation to her battle against illness and, not wrongly, her desire to live. What Charlotte doesn't see, or at least doesn't acknowledge, is the way God has disappeared from this scene. In Emily Brontë's death story, there are only two players: the individual and nature. If there is resignation, it is not resignation to divine intention or plan (like Anne's or Charlotte's) but acceptance of the unpredictable and unwilled course of natural events.

Nature so often takes her own course in *Wuthering Heights* that we may fail to attend much to the outcome, thereby accommodating ourselves better than we might have imagined to the novel's social and moral ethos. 'It's yours and my turn to go into mourning at present,' Mr Kenneth tells Nelly. 'Who's given us the slip now, do you think?' (I. iii. 228) The doctor's irreverent announcement of Hindley Earnshaw's death effectively conveys his sense that death and mourning are the ordinary eventualities from which no one is excluded. All the novel's main characters except its narrators, Nelly and Lockwood, and the sole surviving descendants of the Earnshaw and Linton families, Cathy Linton and Hareton, give us the slip before the novel is done, although most do so without Nelly's being present to observe and describe their going. The deaths Nelly witnesses are Mr Earnshaw's, Frances Earnshaw's, Catherine Earnshaw Linton's, Edgar Linton's, and Heathcliff's, although she is unaware of the moment of Mr Earnshaw's dying and not actually present for Heathcliff's. Everybody mourns in *Wuthering Heights*. Every romantic relationship, except that of Catherine and Heathcliff, begins when one or both of the parties to it are in mourning. Catherine is in mourning for her father when she enters Thrushcross Grange for the first time and meets Edgar Linton; Edgar is in mourning for his parents when he proposes to Catherine. Both Cathy Linton and Linton Heathcliff are in mourning for Linton's mother, Isabella, when they meet for the first time; Cathy returns to Wuthering Heights as Linton Heathcliff's wife on the evening of her father's funeral. She is in mourning for both her father and her husband, dead within the past two months, when Lockwood enters Wuthering Heights for the first time, although we can add this item to the long list of items he neglects to notice or make sense of.

In one crucial sense, Catherine's and Heathcliff's romantic relationship does begin like the others with a death. Recalling her 'great grief' following her father's burial after her own three-day brain fever in Thrushcross Grange, Catherine locates its source in Hindley's separation of her from Heathcliff. 'I was laid alone for the first time,' she tells Nelly (I. xii. 153). Catherine's love of Heathcliff begins with the lack of him. So does a fundamental change in the self, which Catherine experiences as a loss of self. Her identification of herself with Heathcliff, and of her loss of self with loss of him, is grounded in the novel's boldest coincidence: the father's death coincides with the daughter's separation from her companion and bedmate, the older brother's coming into authority, and the onset of the daughter's puberty. How much of a leap is required to cross the distance from this first experience of separation and aloneness to the last one? Not more of a leap than Catherine can manage in her delirium. 'I'll not lie there by myself,' she says, this time referring not to the oak-panelled bed but to her grave. And, addressing an absent Heathcliff: 'they may bury me twelve feet deep, and throw the church down over me, but I won't rest till you are with me ... I never will!' (I. xii. 154)

In *Wuthering Heights*, Brontë explores the unsatisfactoriness of both a spiritual survival after death, in keeping with Christian doctrine, and a biological survival that depends on generation. Spiritual survival is the specific concern of Joseph, the novel's prophet of the doctrine of the everlasting punishment of the wicked, and of Nelly Dean and Lockwood, narrators who share a view of these matters close to the doctrine of universal salvation. Nelly earns her surname by being a ready source of accepted Christian wisdom about most things. Take, for example, her response to Catherine's dream of waking up in heaven and finding herself miserable there. 'All sinners would be miserable in heaven,' Nelly informs her, anticipating the point Cardinal Newman would later make repeatedly in his sermons: 'for an "irreligious man" heaven would be nothing less than hell.'[7] Both Catherine and Heathcliff explicitly deny the relevance as well as the truth of a spiritual survival after death whether it involves the consignment of the dead to a place of punishment, purification, or reward, or allows their reunion, in another place, with those who have gone before. But they also deny the relevance of biological survival. She requires, and he agrees, that nothing of her should be deemed to survive in her daughter. In my experience teaching the novel, readers usually try to explain Heathcliff's profound dislike for Cathy Linton rationally: Heathcliff hates Edgar Linton, and Cathy resembles her father; or, she has, albeit unwillingly, caused her mother's death in childbirth. But the ground of Heathcliff's antipathy to Cathy is not rational at all: Cathy is like everyone else in being not-Catherine, and perhaps more so because others (Nelly, Edgar) insist on seeing her as what survives of her mother. For Heathcliff, Cathy's distance from her mother is as great as that of the flagstone on which he walks or the cloud above him, which also flash Catherine's image to him. Proliferating simulacra bear perpetual, mocking witness to the simple fact of Catherine's unrepeatability. Heathcliff keeps on returning to the pain of her absence and his loss of her.

Catherine Earnshaw Linton's death divides the novel's first and second volumes. This division is the foundation of most readings of *Wuthering Heights*, which, as Empson has suggested, provides a good example of the use of the double plot both for 'covert deification' and for telling the same story twice with two different endings.[8] The usual way of conceiving the double plot of *Wuthering Heights* is to contrast the relationship of Heathcliff and Catherine with that of Cathy and Hareton. Having done this, readers then agree to differ over whether the love affair of the younger pair represents a diminished alternative to the more authentic love affair of Heathcliff and Catherine, or a more fruitful version of it, modulated and humanized so as to give some promise of social happiness.[9] But such an understanding of the novel's double plot, and its juxtaposed pairs of lovers, confines the relationship of Heathcliff and Catherine to the novel's first volume. This version of things is given its fullest expression in William Wyler's classic 1939 film of the novel, which ends with Catherine's death and omits everything that follows it in the novel, including the relationship of Cathy and Hareton.

The most important thing to notice about *Wuthering Heights* is that the novel doesn't end with Catherine's death. Nor does the relationship between Catherine and Heathcliff end there. Brontë is comparing and contrasting two pairs of lovers and two versions of romantic love in *Wuthering Heights*, and she is also comparing and contrasting a love affair that takes place while both parties to it are alive with one that retains all of its charge after one of them has died. *Wuthering Heights* isn't just about Heathcliff's reaction to Catherine's death; it is about how he lives his life in relation to her death. The probability that a marriage will unite Cathy and Hareton, as a marriage has divided Catherine and Heathcliff, is less important to the structure and meaning of the novel than that death divides Catherine and Heathcliff, and fails to divide them, although it keeps them from having the physical access to each other that each most desires. Perhaps Terry Eagleton has these complications in view when he describes the love of Catherine and Heathcliff as 'an unhistorical essence which fails to enter into concrete existence and can do so, ironically, only in death,'[10] but the phrases 'unhistorical essence' and 'concrete existence' are slippery, and it is impossible to know whether the concrete existence Eagleton has in mind belongs to the period after Catherine's death, or to that after Heathcliff's.

What kind of concrete existence would a relationship between two people—one of whom is dead—have? Nothing ironic about the conclusion of Tennyson's 'Vastness':

> Peace, let it be! for I loved him, and love him for ever:
> the dead are not dead but alive.

What is unique about *Wuthering Heights* and what binds the novel to Brontë's poems and the mid-nineteenth century world out of which both emerged is her interest in representing an affair of the heart and nerves that continues after death. How exactly does one love someone who is dead? This question is still alive in Hardy's *Poems of 1912–13*. And do the dead love back? Or are they annihilated, transfigured (in the language of the Christian burial service, a natural body become a spiritual body), or existent but without consciousness, 'changed and careless' as in 'Song' ('The linnet in the rocky dell')? Can a heart that is 'earth in an earthy bed' 'beat', 'start', 'tremble' and 'blossom in purple and red', or is it only deranged lovers who think so?

I want to suggest two readings of Heathcliff's experience in the second volume of *Wuthering Heights*. First, Heathcliff is a good example of someone whose mourning can only conclude with his own death. Having ignored the Stoic-Christian warning not to love unreservedly anything that may be lost, Heathcliff is doomed to enact the depressive pattern Freud describes in 'Mourning and Melancholia': unable to retract his unlimited libidinal investment in Catherine, he is depleted by her dying. In Freud's memorable language, the melancholy ego is eclipsed by 'the shadow of the object' that falls on it. Or in Poe's close anticipation of Freud's language in his great poem about melancholy, 'The Raven': 'And my soul from out that shadow that lies floating on the floor | Shall be lifted—nevermore!'[11] In *Wuthering Heights*, this pattern of melancholy mourning is complicated by the novel's insistence on the indivisibility of Heathcliff and Catherine, and on the self's need for union with something outside it. Such complications lead to a second reading of the novel, related to the first but different from it. Wittgenstein asserts that 'death is not an event in life; we do not live to experience death,'[12] but insofar as Catherine *is* Heathcliff (as she asserts) and Heathcliff's 'life' and 'soul' are Catherine (as he avers), *Wuthering Heights* may be as close as we can get to a representation of death as an event in life. According to this reading, Heathcliff is not only the novel's central mourner but someone who lives to experience his own death, and Emily Brontë undertakes to represent not just an unresolved and inconclusive melancholy mourning in *Wuthering Heights* but an auto-mourning. Freud suggests that because our own death is unimaginable, 'whenever we make the attempt to imagine it we can perceive that we really survive as spectators.'[13] Heathcliff is such a spectator in the second half of *Wuthering Heights*, seeking and achieving the visions of Catherine that separate him from the living beings to whose senses she is forever unavailable. But Heathcliff is also the agent of so much brutal violence against the inhabitants of the Heights that Nelly wonders whether he is a 'ghoul, or a vampire' (II. xx. 403). The idea that Heathcliff is a revenant who aggressively torments the living has some basis in Yorkshire lore. According to Jean-Claude Schmitt, vampires or ghosts with 'an extraordinary "corporeity"' who terrorize and injure their former neighbours are peculiar to the Yorkshire ghost stories recorded in the Middle Ages. Although the usual remedies—prayers or promises of absolution—sometimes satisfied, there were occasions when these ghosts disappeared only when the villagers dug up their corpses and dismembered and burned them.[14]

Catherine's and Heathcliff's identification with each other finds expression in Catherine's famous 'I-am-Heathcliff' confession to Nelly and in the ambiguities that bedevil their conversational exchanges. When Heathcliff returns to Wuthering Heights after his mysterious three-year absence, for example, he tells Catherine that she must forgive him, 'for I struggled only for you' (I. x. 120). 'For *you*,' meaning that Catherine has all along been Heathcliff's object and that he has striven to win her; and '*for* you,' meaning that he has struggled on Catherine's behalf, as her agent. A few pages later, when they are discussing Isabella's passion for Heathcliff, Catherine tells him that she is 'not jealous of you' but 'jealous for you' (I. xi. 137). She means that she is jealous on Heathcliff's behalf, as if her wishes should be identified with his, including even the wish to marry Isabella Linton; she is not jealous *of* him, as if he were the object of her affections and Isabella Linton were her rival. Heathcliff's response to this distinction—'If I imagined you really wished me to marry Isabella, I'd cut my throat!'—and Catherine's retort—'Oh, the evil is that I'm *not* jealous, is it?'—reveal that she understands her relation to him differently from the way he understands it. That most readers of the novel find his point of view easier to occupy than hers is clearest in the readiness with which they dismiss as merely self-deluding her belief, earlier on, that she can marry Edgar Linton while remaining faithful to Heathcliff. Again, the 1939 film differs from the novel in representing Catherine's behaviour toward Heathcliff after her marriage to Edgar as guilty, as if adultery were really what was on her mind (as opposed, say, on Edgar's or Heathcliff's mind).

Readers of *Wuthering Heights* have not sufficiently questioned J. Hillis Miller's assertion that Heathcliff and Catherine share an understanding of their relationship. 'He speaks in exactly the same way about her as she speaks about him, and exactly the same relation is being dramatized.'[15] Or, they have misrepresented Heathcliff's relation to language entirely by failing to note that if he is barely articulate as Catherine's would-be suitor in the first volume of the novel, he is voluble when he returns from his three-year absence, carrying his own full weight in his conversations with Catherine and doing his part to keep Nelly informed about his feelings after Catherine's death. That is, Heathcliff arrives at Wuthering Heights speaking 'some gibberish that nobody could understand' (I. iv. 45), retreats into bitter silence after Catherine's stay at Thrushcross Grange, and then, in the second volume of the novel, masters a mode of expression that is precise, determined, and eloquent.[16] Heathcliff's acquisition of a language adequate to his plight is one of the stories the second volume of the novel tells. Brontë clearly distinguishes Heathcliff's accession to language from his consistent rejection of other people's language, particularly the language of books, which are the delight of the characters who are suspected of preferring mediated life to the thing itself. At the same time, absence from Catherine, not caused by her death but by his own flight from Wuthering Heights when he believes that she has abandoned him for Edgar, may be instrumental to his acquisition of language, since he requires language to mediate what was before an unmediated relation to the world outside him, an unmediated related to Catherine.

I suspect that Brontë, like D. W. Winnicott, wanted to be alive for her own death, and that she brought Heathcliff as close as she could to this experience by protracting his life after Catherine's death. This is consistent with Charlotte's account of her sister's death in a letter to Ellen Nussey:

I cannot forget Emily's death-day; it becomes a more fixed—a darker, a more frequently recurring idea in my mind than ever: it was very terrible; she was torn conscious, panting, reluctant though resolute out of a happy life.[17]

The economy of Heathcliff's gravestone—one date as well as one name serving for the usual two—recalls the Victorian convention according to which an earthly death-day is a heavenly birth-day, but does so with an irony appropriate to the mystery of Heathcliff's origins and to his anti-Christian faith: 'No minister need come; nor need anything be said over me—I tell you, I have nearly attained *my* heaven; and that of others is altogether unvalued and uncoveted by me!' (II. xx. 409)

Heathcliff's heaven recalls those heavens of others that the novel has already described: Catherine's, Cathy's, Linton Heathcliff's, and, more pointedly, Edgar Linton's. He testifies to his faith in Emily Brontë's version of the conventional Victorian deathbed scene: 'I am going to her,' he tells his daughter, 'and you, darling child, shall come to us' (II. xiv. 344). In 'I see around me tombstones grey', Brontë develops the logical contradictions of the conventional Victorian heaven Edgar anticipates:

> Let me remember half the woe
> I've seen and heard and felt below
> And heaven itself—so pure and blest
> Could never give my spirit rest—
> Sweet land of light! thy children fair
> Know nought akin to our despair—
> Nor have they felt, nor can they tell
> What tenants haunt each mortal cell
> What gloomy guests we hold within—
> Torments and madness, tears and sin!
> Well—may they live in ecstacy
> Their long eternity of joy;

Like Heathcliff—or like Catherine, whose most memorable dream has her waking in heaven and willing herself back to earth where she belongs—this poem's speaker rejects a conventional heaven for herself, while acknowledging its existence for other people, because consciousness, specifically memory, is incompatible with the peace heaven promises. But the poem goes farther. Heaven's inhabitants are like 'children' because children have no knowledge of their own inevitable deaths. Because heaven's inhabitants don't remember their own mortal pasts, they can have no comprehension of mortal life:

> Nor have they felt, nor can they tell
> What tenants haunt each mortal cell
> What gloomy guests we hold within—

Brontë's 'mortal cell' combines allusions to the 'narrow cell' of Gray's *Elegy* where each former village inhabitant is forever asleep and the cavity of the brain where Cowper locates sleeping Memory.[18] It may also recall Locke's image of ideas lodged in Memory that 'start up in our Minds of their own accord ... and very often are rouzed and tumbled out of their dark Cells, into open Day-light, by some turbulent and tempestuous Passion; our Affections bringing *Ideas* to our Memory, which had otherwise lain quiet and unregarded.'[19]

Brontë's 'long eternity' should give us pause: what would a 'short' eternity be? *Long* is qualitative, not quantitative, here. Eternity is tedious, not least because it excludes the 'turbulent and tempestuous Passion' that can tumble sleeping memories into the light of consciousness. Brontë's heavenly beings 'live in ecstacy', literally *out of themselves* because they lack any consciousness of past actions. This view declares itself in opposition to Locke, who insists that the dead man's self 'is the same *self* now it was [alive] then'.[20] Locke goes on to consider the case of someone who has forgotten some of his past actions and distinguishes between two senses of the word 'I', which may refer to either Man or Person:

if it be possible for the same Man to have distinct incommunicable consciousness at different times, it is past doubt the same Man would at different times make different Persons; which, we see, is the Sense of Mankind in the solemnest Declaration of their Opinions, Humane Laws not punishing the *Mad Man* for the *Sober Man*'s Actions, nor the *Sober Man* for what the *Mad Man* did, thereby making them two Persons; which is somewhat explained by our way of speaking in *English*, when we say such an one *is not himself*, or is *besides himself*; in which Phrases it is insinuated, as if those who now, or, at least, first used them, thought, that *self* was changed, the *self* same Person was no longer in that Man.[21]

To justify the Last Judgement, Locke requires continuous consciousness, or a self that can be held accountable for actions it can recognize as its own. Brontë is more concerned to reject what we might call the false consciousness a conventional Victorian heaven would require. From the perspective of her poem, the conventional heaven—Heathcliff's heaven 'of others'—is a vale of soul un-making. As for the reunion of the dead in heaven, what would such a reunion be like if the parties to it were no longer, by memory's warrant, the self-same persons who had been lovers in an earthly life? The dead of 'I see around me tombstones grey' are forever 'lone' and forever part of a company whose undiscriminated tombstones cast a single, vast shadow.

Earth isn't in Brontë's poem, as in Wordsworth's 'Intimations Ode', a foster mother whose aim is to compensate her charges for their lapse into mortality and help them to endure their progressive distance from the bright sun of a prenatal everlasting life. She is instead the beloved birth mother whom we betray when we prefer some 'dazzling land above' to her sphere below:

> We all in life's departing shine
> Our last dear longings blend with thine;
> And struggle still, and strive to trace
> With clouded gaze thy darling face
> We would not leave our native home
> For *any* world beyond the Tomb

No—rather on thy kindly breast
Let us be laid in lasting rest
Or waken but to share with thee
A mutual immortality—

This is a description of dying—a struggle to keep the beloved face of Nature in view, despite weakening eyesight—and an expression of longing for a particular kind of human survival. In preferring either a 'mutual immortality', a continuing earthly existence, or a lasting rest without consciousness or memory, a death that is really final, to the conventional 'Sweet land of light', 'I see around me tombstones grey' provides a helpful gloss on Heathcliff's heaven, Catherine's dream of being cast out of a heaven where she doesn't belong, and the competing visions of Catherine and Heathcliff with which *Wuthering Heights* closes. In the end, Brontë refuses to choose for us. There is the small boy's story of meeting with 'Heathcliff and a woman, yonder, under t'Nab' (II. xx. 412) to suggest that Catherine and Heathcliff achieve a mutual immortality, a mortal world without end, and there is also Lockwood's visit to the graves of Heathcliff, Catherine, and Edgar, whom he imagines in quiet sleep. *Wuthering Heights* lets us think what we will.

'Death', another poem Brontë selected for publication in 1846, is the only poem she wrote that expresses her anguish in the face of individual extinction with an urgency comparable to that of *Wuthering Heights*. Unlike the novel, it does so without the scaffolding of a great romance and without the displacement of one's own death by the death of the other, but like the novel, it draws on the resources of narrative. The poem's sources have puzzled Brontë's editors, and their efforts to find them reveal their fundamental assumptions about her creative process. Juliet Barker suggests that 'Death' belongs to Brontë's Gondal narrative, even though Brontë transcribed the poem into her Honresfeld manuscript, the fair-copy notebook she used for non-Gondal poems.[22] Derek Roper also supports an unspecified Gondal context for the poem and says why: 'It is not easy to find events in Emily Brontë's own life to match these.'[23] But 'Death' isn't a Gondal poem, its date of composition doesn't correspond to a specific external event in Brontë's life, and its narrative doesn't hold the key to one. We can guess at the *kind* of personal experience that entered into the writing of 'Death', but what we don't need to guess at is the impersonal source of the poem's anguish. It describes what Goethe identifies as the moment when death, which has been 'an impossibility', 'changes into a reality'.[24]

'Death' (see Figure 2) enacts the extinction of 'the *whole* feeling of futurity' and asserts the self's sovereignty in the face of that feeling. The poem's imagery and vocabulary—its familiar references to the tree and water of life, to seasonal and diurnal cycles, and to Guilt, Hope, Sin, and Love (all these terms appear at the beginning of lines, justifying the capital letters)—together with its exhilarated celebration of eternity—would have masked its substantial departures from Christian orthodoxy for Charlotte Brontë and for other readers at the time of the poem's publication. 'Death' posits an eternal substratum of organic forms out of which new life emerges and into which old life is absorbed, but because the boughs that flourish are 'other' than the corpse that moulders, the theory contradicts Paul's assertion (in 1 Corinthians 15) that some principle of identity unites the seed that falls and the grain that sprouts. Brontë would likely have had John's image of Christ as a vine in her mind as well—'If a man abide not in me, he is cast forth as a branch, and is withered' (John 15: 5)—but her focus, unlike John's, is on biological mortality, not spiritual death. According to her poem, every branch must wither, every sapling perish. Moreover, the individual is redeemed from Sorrow and Guilt not by God's love but by the life surging within her. Her own recuperative powers are likened to Nature's, and the 'parent's kindly bosom' is more plausibly Nature's than Christ's. The mixing of metaphors—the branch becomes a bosom and the sap flowing through it ('Life's restoring tide') becomes both milky and watery—suggests that this poem's myth of eternal life exalts the same Earth Mother as 'I see around me tombstones grey.'

Death

Death! that struck when I was most confiding
In my certain faith of joy to be—
Strike again, Time's withered branch dividing
From the fresh root of Eternity!

Leaves, upon Time's branch, were growing brightly,
Full of sap, and full of silver dew;
Birds beneath its shelter gathered nightly;
Daily round its flowers the wild bees flew.

Sorrow passed, and plucked the golden blossom;
Guilt stripped off the foliage in its pride;
But, within its parent's kindly bosom,
Flowed for ever Life's restoring tide.

Little mourned I for the parted gladness,
For the vacant nest and silent song—

Hope was there, and laughed me out of sadness;
Whispering, 'Winter will not linger long!'

And behold! with tenfold increase blessing,
Spring adorned the beauty-burdened spray;
Wind and rain and fervent heat, caressing,
Lavished glory on that second May!

High it rose—no winged grief could sweep it;
Sin was scared to distance, with its shine;
Love, and its own life, had power to keep it
From all wrong—from every blight but thine!

Cruel Death! The young leaves droop and languish;
Evening's gentle air may still restore—
No! the morning sunshine mocks my anguish—
Time, for me, must never blossom more!

Strike it down, that other boughs may flourish
Where that perished sapling used to be;
Thus, at least, its mouldering corpse will nourish
That from which it sprung—Eternity.

The poem begins sharply. Death, which has struck once, is commanded to strike again. It ends with a repetition—'Strike it down'—followed by a grudging ('Thus, at least') double rationalization. The narrative the poem's first and last stanzas encircle is brief, abstract, and scarred. Time is imagined as a tree rooted in Eternity and branching into mortal being; one blossoming and withering branch seems to represent the poem's speaker. Firmly located in a natural world defined by change and succession, and not yet recognizing her difference from that natural world, she begins her life happily. She then experiences the ravages of sorrow and guilt—terms that together cover the emotional and psychological distress caused by events over which she has no control as well as her consciousness of responsibility for actions ill-done or done to others' harm. So long as 'Life's restoring tide' flows—it seems 'for ever'—she is able to survive so harsh a winter and blossom into what she describes as a glorious 'second May'. In her revival, she feels immune to the ravages of grief. Sin is 'scared to distance.' In the end, however, human life is held hostage to death—to the human knowledge of death—which blights it, betraying the promise of renewal nature celebrates in its seasonal and diurnal cycles. Morning 'mocks my anguish'.

To 'die humanly', Bataille writes in *The Accursed Share*, 'in anguish, is to have the representation of death that enables the dividing of oneself into a present and a future: to die humanly is to have of the future being, of the one who matters most in our eyes, the senseless idea that he is not.'[25] The first stanza's memory of a time when the speaker was 'most confiding | In my certain faith of joy to be' stipulates the dramatic occasion for 'Death'. How should we understand this speaker's 'certain faith'? Much depends on the meaning of the word 'joy' and on the ambiguity of the phrase 'joy to be', which can be read either as a loose reference to the joy that is to be (the joy that the speaker anticipates feeling at some future time) or as a more pointed reference to the joy of being. If the former, then her faith comes into relation with the 'trust in Pleasure's careless guiding' that turns out to be illusory in 'E.W. to A.G.A', the only other poem in which the word 'confiding' appears. If the latter, then her faith is in the joy of being, or in the continuity of her own being, what Coleridge calls the '*whole* feeling of futurity'. It is this faith that death shatters when it strikes in 'Death'. 'To be full of being is to live as a body-soul,' Elizabeth Costello says, in one of her lectures in J. M. Coetzee's *Elizabeth Costello*. 'One name for the experience of full being is *joy*.'[26] This is how Brontë uses *joy*, though she uses it sardonically, when she describes the inhabitants of heaven as living a 'long eternity of joy' in 'I see around me tombstones grey'. The knowledge of death, not the event itself, is what separates humans from animals as well as from inanimate natural life, the things that continue to be things because they lack full being. The death 'that struck when I was most confiding' is no specific death, no death for which we could find a biographical source, but the death that brings with it the knowledge that death is in life, in my life.

The underlying metaphor in Brontë's poem is not a journey, as in so many of Emily Dickinson's poems about death, but a progress that is cyclical like the progress of the seasons or the day. Moreover, Brontë's death has nothing in common with Dickinson's 'supple Suitor' (P 1445). Death doesn't seduce us; it strikes with sudden and savage violence (tears us from life, 'conscious, panting, reluctant'). Given the inevitability of death in time, the only way Brontë's human speaker can assert her own sovereign agency and refuse the role of hapless victim is to take control: she orders Death to strike her down. No imagination of future rewards and punishments enters into this transaction. The speaker has only the consolation of self-sacrifice and the relief of firm despair. Her death makes way for other lives; her dissolution nourishes an Eternity that not only gives birth to Time but feeds on it. The tone of the poem's last stanza is problematic, for triumphant audacity doesn't displace horror and anger. The relation between Brontë's Time and her Eternity is as circular and as gruesome as that incestuous one between Milton's Sin and Death, whose progeny devour one parent on the other's behalf. If Brontë's Eternity is a devourer who requires an interminable succession of 'mouldering corpses' for its survival, it hardly differs from Death. With the transmutation of the 'perished sapling' into a 'mouldering corpse', the terms of the poem's allegory change places; human bodies, not withered branches, are food for worms.

As in 'Remembrance', the regular alternation of masculine and feminine endings in 'Death' reinforces the theme of repetition, but the metre of 'Death' is so inexorable as to suggest that this poem's speaker is bound upon a wheel. The wheel is Time, which the poem represents in its own circular progress, just as it represents Time as a tree in its allegorical narrative. Although a future event is grimly anticipated, first and last, when the speaker orders Death to strike, the future state that is realized with the poem's only future tense finite verb, 'will nourish', marks a return to organic process. The poem's only repeated rhyme of 'be' and 'Eternity' in its first and last stanzas invites us to cycle back from the end of the poem to the beginning, and, by positioning 'Eternity' next to 'Death', confirms Emily Dickinson's insight that death is at once final and first.

'Death' is connected to the last two school essays Brontë wrote in 1842, 'The Palace of Death' and 'The Butterfly'. J. Hillis Miller read 'The Butterfly' as a key to *Wuthering Heights* in *The Disappearance of God*, a reading he later recanted. Both essays were written in response to an assignment given to Charlotte as well, and the differences between what the sisters produced are instructive. The plot of 'The Palace of Death' essays was a given: both sisters describe a competition for the position of Death's prime minister, which Intemperance wins. Although both picture Intemperance as a 'gay', 'jaunty', and apparently healthy young woman, Charlotte uses her opportunity to moralize: a close examination of Intemperance reveals 'delirium' rather than joy in her eyes, a fevered complexion, and 'disorder' in her attire. 'Her disheveled head was crowned with a garland of flowers; those flowers seemed fresh and fair, but among the petals, twisted in the stems, one saw a serpent glitter.'[27] The validity of the claim Charlotte's Intemperance makes relies on her nature as 'enchantress' (a nature revealed in her deceptively attractive appearance); a vague assertion that she has more victims than the other contenders, War and Ambition; and an undeveloped notion that War and Ambition are the children of Intemperance and would not exist without her. Emily makes a stronger case by attaching Intemperance to Civilization, which will triumph over Death's other minions, including Ambition, Wrath, Fanaticism, and Famine, and by emphasizing the capacity of Intemperance to change men's 'entire nature' so as to make them 'an easier prey' for Death.

The fiercer logic of Emily's argument and its determined pessimism—she links social progress to self-destruction—is registered again in 'The Butterfly'. This time, the two sisters chose different titles. Charlotte's title, 'The Caterpillar', marks her focus on a metamorphosis she understands in conventional Christian terms. As Lonoff points out, Charlotte 'shows a penchant for triadic patterning: yesterday, today, and tomorrow; caterpillar, chrysalis, and butterfly.'[28] As in 'The Palace of Death', Charlotte takes her opportunity to point the moral. The caterpillar living its material life is a symbol for mortal man, and the butterfly, the spiritualized caterpillar, is a symbol for the man of whom Faith speaks, specifically in the language of 1 Corinthians that also appears in the Book of Common Prayer and forms a part of the Anglican burial service. Emily's title, 'The Butterfly', signals her emphasis on a reality, or an appearance, that contradicts the different reality of ordinary experience. In her essay, the butterfly appears coincidentally, just after her narrator has crushed the caterpillar in a gesture that demonstrates her own human nature and at the same time mimics divine acts of destruction. The butterfly is said to be 'like a censoring angel sent from heaven', shining momentarily and then vanishing. The lesson that the narrator's 'inner voice' produces recommends humility and patience:

As the ugly caterpillar is the origin of the splendid butterfly, so this globe is the embryo of a new heaven and a new earth whose poorest beauty will infinitely exceed your moral imagination. And when you see the magnificent result of that which seems so base to you now, how you will scorn your blind presumption, in accusing Omniscience for not having made nature perish in her infancy.[29]

The point here is violent disjunction without organic continuity. Emily Brontë's caterpillar doesn't metamorphose into a butterfly but dies violently so that the butterfly can appear. The tone of 'The Butterfly' is uncertain. Its angry, defiant narrator receives a lesson in humility. The angry speaker of 'Death' remains defiant.

'Death' turns on three connected insights that are fundamental to Brontë's vision. One, the knowledge of death is fully human and different from the fear of death that all animals feel; it is best expressed as an evacuation of faith in the unbreakable continuity of one's own being, what the poem calls the loss of our 'certain faith of joy to be'. Two, the anguish that accompanies the knowledge of death is as boundless as the

joy associated with the Christian promise of eternal life. Three, annihil-
ation sustains regeneration, and renewal in nature can be assured only
by a putrefaction that is full of life. The best-known fictional represent-
ations of Victorian deathbed scenes—Helen Burns's death in *Jane Eyre*,
or Catherine's as reported by Nelly in *Wuthering Heights*—soothe us by
showing the dying displaying their composure and 'lively hope' of sal-
vation and eternal life.[30] *Wuthering Heights* and 'Death' remind us that
the most fully human response to the incorporation of death into life
is '*irreducible anguish*'.[31] The emotional and psychological territory we
are in as readers of 'Death' belongs to a non-theological mystic whose
spiritual intelligence reaches towards the blight of her own death and
past it to the mystery of an unfathomable world, inexpressibly beautiful
and tender and also unforgiving in its demand for expenditures beyond
our bearing. 'Everything within us demands that death lay waste to us,'
Bataille writes in *The Accursed Share*:

we anticipate these multiple trials, these new beginnings, unproductive from the
standpoint of reason, this wholesale destruction of effective force accomplished
in the transfer of one individual's life to other, younger, individuals. Deep down,
we even assent to the condition that results, that is almost intolerable, in this
condition of individuals destined for suffering and inevitable annihilation ... [32]

Almost intolerable:

> Deep deep down in the silent grave
> With none to mourn above

7

Posthumous Brontë

... and She—
(How shall I sing her?)—whose soul
Knew no fellow for might,
Passion, vehemence, grief,
Daring, since Byron died,
That world-fam'd Son of Fire; She, who sank
Baffled, unknown, self-consum'd;
Whose too-bold dying song
Shook, like a clarion-blast, my soul.

Matthew Arnold's lines about Emily Brontë appear in his poem com-
memorating Charlotte Brontë, whose death in 1855 was its occasion. He
compares Emily Brontë to Byron because of the qualities they shared—
'might, | Passion, vehemence, grief, | Daring'—and contrasts their recep-
tion. He is 'That world-fam'd Son of Fire,' while she 'sank | Baffled,
unknown, self-consum'd'. Yet her 'dying song' was a revelation that
shook his soul.[1] Arnold's reverence for Emily Brontë wasn't widely
shared, or so both he and Charlotte believed. Securing more of it for
both her sisters after their deaths was Charlotte's primary objective in
1850, when she undertook a new edition of *Wuthering Heights*, together
with *Agnes Grey* and poems by both Emily and Anne. She makes her
objective evident not just in the 'Biographical Notice of Ellis and Acton
Bell' and 'Editor's Preface to the New Edition of Wuthering Heights' but
in her decision to reprint *Agnes Grey* (Anne's first novel) rather than *The
Tenant of Wildfell Hall* (her second, more challenging novel), her edit-
orial changes to *Wuthering Heights*, and her revisions to Emily's poems,
my subject in this chapter. Charlotte was less interested in making high
claims for her sisters' novels than she was in defending Anne and, espe-
cially, Emily against charges that reviewers of *Wuthering Heights* and
The Tenant of Wildfell Hall had levelled against their manners and their

morals. In a letter written to W. S. Williams less than a month before Emily's death, Charlotte pictures herself and her two sisters reacting to one of these reviews:

The North American Review is worth reading—there is no mincing the matter there—what a bad set the Bells must be! What appalling books they write! To-day as Emily appeared a little easier, I thought the Review would amuse her so I read it aloud to her and Anne. As I sat between them at our quiet but now somewhat melancholy fireside, I studied the two ferocious authors. Ellis the 'man of uncommon talents but dogged, brutal and morose,' sat leaning back in his easy chair drawing his impeded breath as best he could and looking, alas! piteously pale and wasted—it is not his wont to laugh—but he smiled half-amused and half in scorn as he listened—Acton was sewing, no emotion ever stirs him to loquacity, so he only smiled too, dropping at the same time a single word of calm amazement to hear his character so darkly portrayed.[2]

The contrast between the world's image of the ferocious Bells and Charlotte's own picture of Anne and Emily, two women in a domestic setting, calm and busy with their ordinary occupations, even though stricken, sounds the keynote of this period of her life. In her obituary for Charlotte, Harriet Martineau, another writing woman, also adduced her subject's domesticity as a sure sign of her goodness: 'She was as able at the needle as the pen.'[3] Charlotte's intimate family portrait looks ahead to the 'Biographical Notice of Ellis and Acton Bell', which is her own closest approach to writing an obituary for Emily and Anne.

With the 1850 edition of *Agnes Grey* and *Wuthering Heights*, Charlotte hoped to persuade the world that Emily and Anne were 'genuinely good and truly great'.[4] Each sister required and received a different kind of defence. Anne, Charlotte writes in the 'Biographical Notice', chose a subject for her second novel, *The Tenant of Wildfell Hall*, that was 'an entire mistake'. Although she 'hated her work', she continued it out of a commitment to her readers' moral improvement and her own didactic mission. Emily, on the other hand, didn't understand or have control over her work. She revealed 'immature but very real powers' in *Wuthering Heights*; her mind was 'original' but 'unripe'.[5] In the 'Biographical Notice', when Charlotte refers to the widespread suspicion that *Wuthering Heights* was 'an earlier and ruder attempt of the same pen which had produced *Jane Eyre*,' hurried into print to take advantage of that novel's popularity, she denies the imputed motive for publishing *Wuthering Heights*, the charge against Emily, but not the charge against Emily's novel.[6] Why couldn't Charlotte see that *Wuthering Heights* was 'singularly mature', as Peter Bayne, a critic writing as early as 1881, recognized? Bayne marks the novel's style as the achievement of a 'consummate' writer and praises its 'sentiment' for being 'free of young-mannish bravura, and, still more, of a young-womanish syllabub. The author never seems for one moment to lose her self-possession and self-command.'[7] One reason Charlotte did not, or would not, acknowledge the maturity of *Wuthering Heights* was that she had a deep investment in Emily's immaturity. Maturity, denied to Emily by an early death, would have brought her greater equanimity and happiness. So Charlotte trusted: 'Had she but lived,' she writes in her 'Editor's Preface,' the 'matured fruits of her mind would have attained a mellower ripeness and sunnier bloom; but on that mind time and experience alone could work: to the influence of other intellects, it was not amenable.'[8] *Shirley*, whose title character is based on Emily, confirms Charlotte's enthusiasm for a view of her sister in happier circumstances. These would have included time, wealth, and a husband who would tame and instruct as well as love her.

Charlotte's revisions to the poems she edited for publication in 1850 shaped Emily's reputation for the remainder of the century and longer. The seventeen poems published in 1850, together with the twenty-one poems published in 1846 and one more poem published in the *Cornhill Magazine* in 1860 ('A Farewell to Alexandria'), made up the entire canon of Emily Brontë's known poetic achievement until 1902. The 1850 poems were known to nineteenth-century readers only in Charlotte's versions of them. When Emily Dickinson asked to have 'No coward soul is mine' read at her funeral, she was asking to have the poem as altered by Charlotte read: she knew it in no other form. Although there are at least four poems Charlotte revised more substantially than 'No coward soul is mine', adding or removing lines and verses from them, her revisions to 'No coward soul is mine' are not incidental.[9] They produce a declaration of faith of the sort that Charlotte believed was required to sustain any claim for Emily's goodness and greatness. For this reason, it was also useful to identify 'No coward soul is mine', composed in January of 1846, as the last poem Emily wrote, although Charlotte knew it was not. As in 1846, all the poems published in 1850 (except 'Often rebuked, yet always back returning', for which no manuscript has ever been found) were taken from Emily's two transcript notebooks. In one of them, the *Gondal Poems* notebook, Charlotte would have seen 'Why ask to know the date—the clime', which was composed in September of 1846 (eight months after 'No coward soul is mine') and partly revised in May of 1848. Swinburne's reading of 'No coward soul is mine' in 1883 shows how much Charlotte accomplished with its publication:

Belief in the personal or positive immortality of the individual and indivisible spirit was not apparently, in [Emily Brontë's] case, swallowed up or nullifed or made nebulous by any doctrine or dream of simple reabsorption into some indefinite infinity of eternal life. So at least it seems to me that her last ardent confession of dauntless and triumphant faith should properly be read, however capable certain phrases in it may seem of the vaguer and more impersonal interpretation … [10]

Charlotte's revisions strengthen the reading on which Swinburne settles, despite 'certain phrases' in the poem that tell a different story. The competing doctrine or dream he has in view—'simple reabsorption into some indefinite infinity of eternal life'—could well be the one put forward in 'Death', published in 1846 (and so available to Swinburne) but composed before 'No coward soul is mine'. 'The Philosopher', also published in 1846, might have given him pause as well. In it, the philosopher pleads for death because he has never found the spirit whose eye lights the clouds. The last poem Emily Brontë completed—'Why ask to know the date—the clime'—doesn't explicitly challenge the faith put forward in 'No coward soul is mine' but does support a view of her imagination as 'more sombre than sunny'. [11]

The *Athenaeum's* anonymous reviewer astutely characterized the 1850 volume 'as a more than usually interesting contribution to the history of female authorship in England'. [12] I would characterize it as a more than usually interesting contribution to the history of Brontë biography. In examining Charlotte's versions of 'No coward soul is mine' and two of the four poems to which she added several lines, 'Aye there it is! It wakes tonight' and 'The Visionary', I look at what she tried to make of these poems and at what she hoped to unmake about them. In reading 'Often rebuked, yet always back returning' as a poem composed by Charlotte and attributed by her to Emily, I am interested not only in Charlotte's motives but in the composite picture of Emily-and-Charlotte (or Emily *as* Charlotte) that this poem gives us. Together with 'The Visionary', 'Often rebuked, yet always back returning' is the most important source for the familiar compound ghost who appears in place of the more elusive ghost of Emily Brontë herself in most discussions of her life and her poems.

Read in the context of Emily Brontë's poetry as a whole, and especially in relation to other poems she wrote around the same time on related topics, 'No coward soul is mine' is a consummate achievement. Why didn't Brontë publish the poem—dated 2 January 1846—in 1846? Perhaps because she had already made her selection of poems for publication when she wrote it. Perhaps because she was unwilling to have anyone, even her sisters, read it.[13] 'No coward soul is mine' may not announce her arrival in a safe port, but it finds a rock on which hope anchors. In it, she goes farther than she has before in describing the attributes and actions of the spirit that 'animates eternal years', and she locates this spirit in herself. She manages to hold eternity firmly in view and to persuade herself that her own creative spirit is indomitable. The opposite of a coward soul would be a brave one, and the poem articulates a brave belief beyond the capability of Brontë's philosopher, who chastises himself for his 'coward cry':

> 'And even for that spirit, seer,
>   I've watched and sought my life-time long;
> Sought him in heaven, hell, earth, and air—
>   An endless search, and always wrong!
> Had I but seen his glorious eye
>   *Once* light the clouds that wilder me,
> I ne'er had raised this coward cry
>   To cease to think, and cease to be;'

Here is the poem, as Emily Brontë wrote it:

> No coward soul is mine
> No trembler in the world's storm-troubled sphere
> I see Heaven's glories shine
> And Faith shines equal arming me from Fear
>
> O God within my breast
> Almighty ever-present Deity
> Life, that in me hast rest
> As I Undying Life, have power in thee
>
> Vain are the thousand creeds
> That move men's hearts, unutterably vain,
> Worthless as withered weeds
> Or idlest froth amid the boundless main
>
> To waken doubt in one
> Holding so fast by thy infinity
> So surely anchored on
> The steadfast rock of Immortality
>
> With wide-embracing love
> Thy spirit animates eternal years

Pervades and broods above,
Changes, sustains, dissolves, creates and rears

Though Earth and moon were gone
And suns and universes ceased to be
And thou wert left alone
Every Existence would exist in thee

There is not room for Death
Nor atom that his might could render void
Since thou art Being and Breath
And what thou art may never be destroyed

Faith is the element of this poem, not its subject: faith in a vital principle as opposed to faith in any of the 'thousand creeds' available to Brontë and her contemporaries. Brontë calls her vital principle 'God within my breast', 'Almighty ever-present Deity' and 'Life' (or, in a reading that I think is to be preferred, 'Almighty ever-present Deity | Life'), 'Undying Life', and 'Being and Breath'. The poem's imagery is precise. Although both heart and lungs are located within the breast, the poem questions the heart's reliability, even when it is moved (as by a creed), but not the warrant of the lungs, the organ of breath. Although only human creatures have hearts, not only humans but trees, violets, and bluebells have breath in Brontë's poems. In the fragmentary poem beginning 'And first an hour of mournful musing', a 'breathing from above' announces the brightening of 'the glorious star of love'. In 'No coward soul is mine', this love is 'wide-embracing'. Breath *pervades* all living beings and *broods* over them. Brontë may have borrowed this sense of *brood* from Wordsworth's 'Intimations Ode', where the context is related, but it is the combination of the two words, *pervade* and *brood*, that best characterizes her own vision.

When she describes her vital principle, Brontë uses the vocabulary Coleridge had used to describe the secondary imagination, which (according to Coleridge) is identical to the primary imagination in kind but differs from it in degree and in the mode of its operation:

It dissolves, diffuses, dissipates, in order to recreate; or where this process is rendered impossible, yet still, at all events, it struggles to idealize and to unify. It is essentially *vital*, even as all objects (*as* objects) are essentially fixed and dead.[14]

Coleridge's secondary imagination is the poet's imagination, but Brontë's vital principle is more like his primary imagination in not requiring an exercise of the conscious will and in not striving 'to idealize and to unify'. Like breathing, its operations are involuntary. Coleridge's secondary imagination 'dissolves, diffuses, dissipates, in order to recreate'. Brontë's vital principle 'Changes, sustains, dissolves, creates and rears'. In Brontë's poetic universe, living forms may be newly created, not just recreated as in Coleridge's.

Other readers have remarked on the similarity of Brontë's language in the poem to Catherine's language in *Wuthering Heights*, when she describes her relation to Heathcliff:[15]

I cannot express it; but surely you and everybody have a notion that there is, or should be, an existence of yours beyond you. What were the use of my creation if I were entirely contained here? My great miseries in this world have been Heathcliff's miseries, and I watched and felt each from the beginning; my great thought in living is himself. If all else perished and *he* remained, I should still continue to be; and if all else remained, and he were annihilated, the Universe would turn into a mighty stranger. I should not seem a part of it. (ɪ ix. 101)

Catherine's identification of Heathcliff as an extension of her own being differs from Jane Eyre's much more conventional reference to Rochester as her 'whole world; and, more than the world.'[16] What Catherine says is that she would continue to exist in a world in which Heathcliff was, despite the annihilation of all else, and that she would be alienated from a world from which he was absent, even if all else persisted. She would not cease to exist in a world lacking Heathcliff, but she would be self-enclosed or self-contained in such a world, an existence without an existence beyond her own. In this passage, she anticipates her own condition during Heathcliff's two absences (which she feels as abandonments) and provides the novel's clearest account of the metaphysical predicament that alienates him from everyone and everything after her death, except the ghost of Catherine, which teases him mercilessly. From Catherine's point of view, her marriage to Edgar Linton—the topic of her conversation with Nelly—is entirely compatible with her own understanding of her relation to Heathcliff. Intuitively, she recognizes that marriage is not an expression of one person's view of another as an extension of her own being but instead a means of social advancement and economic consolidation—in Jane's language, an acknowledgement that someone is your 'world'. Edgar is well qualified for this more usual kind of human relation, as Heathcliff is not. In addition to being rich, he is young, handsome, cheerful, and pleasant to be with. The territory the novel charts in its account of Catherine's relation to Heathcliff is closely connected to the territory of 'No coward soul is mine'. In the novel, the pervasive vital principle that keeps the individual soul not just from dying but from being isolated and self-contained, adrift in an alien universe, is given a human form.

We know that Brontë took the phrase 'coward soul' from an irregular ode written by Hester Chapone and dedicated to Elizabeth Carter, '*who had recommended to me the* Stoic Philosophy, *as productive of* Fortitude, *and who is going to publish a Translation of* Epictetus'.[17] Knowing this, we can not only substantiate Brontë's reading of Chapone and Epictetus in Carter's translation but look at another example of how, and why, she borrows or alludes. Chapone's ode isn't simply a source for the phrase in Brontë's poem but a necessary part of its intent, sense, and spirit. The occasion for both Chapone's and Brontë's poems is 'the world's storm-troubled sphere', an account of which takes up Chapone's first two stanzas. In her third stanza, Chapone eschews 'social, or domestic Ties' in favour of 'inward Beauty', 'God-like Reason', and 'Virtue's heavenly Form':

> But teach me in *myself* to find
> Whate'er can please or fill my Mind.

But in the fourth stanza, she rejects this doctrine as 'impious Pride', and the rest of the poem offers the Christian dispensation as a wiser and more effective response to human suffering, including death. In her last stanza, Chapone addresses Elizabeth Carter directly, pleading with her not to try to sustain Chapone's 'feeble Soul' with 'Stoic Pride, and fancied Scorn | Of human Feelings, human Pain'. It is her penultimate stanza that contains the phrase 'coward Soul':

> No more repine, my coward Soul!
> The Sorrows of Mankind to share,
> Which He who could the World controul,
> Did not disdain to bear!
> Check not the Flow of sweet fraternal Love,
> By Heav'n's high King in Bounty given,
> Thy stubborn Heart to soften and improve,
> Thy Earth-clad Spirit to refine,
> And gradual raise to Love divine
> And wing its soaring Flight to Heaven!

Brontë's poem doesn't answer Chapone by defending Epictetus, although she was deeply sympathetic to his view of the universe, but by rejecting, at the start, Chapone's characterization of her own spirit as 'feeble' or 'coward'. Brontë's poem is imbued with pride in the power of her own vision ('I see heaven's glories shine') and daunting confidence in the profoundly creative life force she embodies. Her 'God within my breast' is very like the 'God-like all-sufficient' human mind that Chapone mocks: 'Is it not foul, weak, ignorant, and blind?' 'Within *myself* does Virtue dwell?' Chapone's ode asks. *That's right*, Brontë's poem replies. In 'No coward soul is mine', she expresses her faith in an infinite, enduring life pervading the universe and in the soul brave enough to claim its participation in that life. This enduring life vested in the self cannot diminish human suffering but gives us something to praise in the face of it.

I take the poem to be the 'confession of dauntless and triumphant faith' in the 'personal or positive immortality of the individual and indivisible spirit' Swinburne took it to be. But it never risks locating its authority outside the self, although Charlotte Brontë's revised version suggests otherwise. In the revision, Charlotte's enthusiasm for a creed she wants to proclaim, or wants Emily to proclaim (in a louder than usual voice) displaces the achieved calm of Emily's poem. Emily's pronouns for the vital spirit pervading the universe are 'thy', 'thou', or 'thee'. Although Charlotte makes changes to capitalization and punctuation throughout and changes the format of the poem's stanzas, she make her most dramatic changes to the last two stanzas:

> Though earth and man were gone,
> And suns and universes ceased to be,
> And Thou wert left alone,
> Every existence would exist in Thee.

> There is not room for Death,
> Nor atom that his might could render void:
> Thou—THOU art Being and Breath,
> And what THOU art may never be destroyed.

Charlotte capitalizes the first letter of the pronouns *thou* and *thee*, and the whole of the pronoun *thou* in the poem's last two lines. Repeating 'Thou' as 'THOU' in the poem's penultimate line both distances and external-izes Emily's vital principle. We don't comfortably now, and Emily and Charlotte wouldn't comfortably then, refer to a human as 'Thou' or 'THOU'.[18] Charlotte's omission of the word 'Since' from the start of the line doesn't just make room for the emphatic repetition of 'THOU'. It also cuts this line and the following one off from the rest of the poem, and replaces the thoughtfulness of a subordinate clause with the con-viction of a creed. Standing independently, the lines constitute the sort of moral lesson with which Charlotte frequently closes her own poems.

This is striking in a poem in which a 'thousand creeds' are said to be 'worthless', not simply ineffectual but ministering to doubt rather than faith. What difference does the substitution of one vowel for two vowels—Charlotte's substitution of *man* for *moon* ('Though earth and man were gone')—make? It makes nonsense of Emily's thought. Life pervades human beings, who carry the whole of the known and unknown world—every existence—within them. What is once alive can't die, although objects *as* objects—earth, moon, suns, and universes—may disappear.

Charlotte also published three of Emily's poems that deal explicitly with creative experience and so anticipate 'No coward soul is mine'. Composed between the autumn of 1840 and the summer of 1841, they are 'The Night-Wind', which was probably considered for publication in 1846, 'Shall Earth no more inspire thee', and 'Ay—there it is! It wakes to-night'. Each of these poems represents an encounter between a poet-speaker and nature. The poet resists the seductive sighs and arguments of the wind, who seeks to 'win' her against her will in 'The Night-Wind' and the claims of Nature in 'Shall Earth no more inspire thee'. Only in 'Aye there it is! It wakes tonight' does she succumb to the wind's influence. This is the poem as it appears in Emily Brontë's manuscript:

> Aye there it is! It wakes tonight
> Sweet thoughts that will not die
> And feeling's fires flash all as bright
> As in the years gone by!—
>
> And I can tell by thine altered cheek
> And by thy kindled gaze
> And by the words thou scarce dost speak,
> How wildly fancy plays—
>
> Yes I could swear that glorious wind
> Has swept the world aside
> Has dashed its memory from thy mind
> Like foam-bells from the tide—
>
> And thou art now a spirit pouring
> Thy presence into all—
> The essence of the Tempest's roaring
> And of the Tempest's fall—
>
> A universal influence
> From Thine own influence free—
> A principle of life intense
> Lost to mortality—

> Thus truly when the breast is cold
> Thy prisoned soul shall rise
> The dungeon mingle with the mould—
> The captive with the skies—

Emily's poem does not appear incomplete (dashes frequently end poems in her manuscripts), yet Charlotte implicitly declared it so by adding five lines she composed:

> Nature's deep being, thine shall hold,
> Her spirit all thy spirit fold,
> Her breath absorb thy sighs.
> Mortal! though soon life's tale is told;
> Who once lives, never dies!

It's hard not to be struck by the hope, or wish, contained in these lines. It is that Emily will be folded in Nature's embrace, and that her sighs will disappear in a long maternal inhalation. But there is no sighing in the poem Emily wrote. The wind that sweeps the poet's mind clear of the memory of the world becomes her own spirit; her breath becomes the essence of the tempest, its roaring and its fall. Her poem ends with ideas familiar to us from her other poems: mortal beings have lost their connection to a vital principle, and this connection, which is intermittently re-established on occasions when awareness is heightened, for example in dreams, will be re-established at death, when the immortal spirit will be separated from the mortal body. One difference between this poem and 'No coward soul is mine' is that the 'principle of life intense' is not lost to mortality (or awaiting the death of the body) in the later poem. Like 'No coward soul is mine', 'Ay there it is! It wakes tonight' is heavily burdened by the extra freight of meaning Charlotte loads it with. The 'Thus' that opens Emily's last stanza requires a change of voice, but a smaller one than that required by the stanza Charlotte added. The sense of these two last stanzas is also different, since Emily's lines speak of a spiritual mingling or fusion, something like the 'simple reabsorption into some indefinite infinity of eternal life' that Swinburne had discovered in her poems, while Charlotte's image a holding and enfolding of spirit by Spirit.

Another change Charlotte made when she published the poem supports the idea that the older sister is lecturing the younger sister as well as comforting her: in revising the first stanza, she altered not just her sister's words but her sister's dramatic occasion. Emily's poem has a single speaker, probably the poet self-communing, but Charlotte's poem attributes the first stanza to one speaker and the remaining stanzas to another, thereby reinforcing the tone of instruction. The speaker of the first stanza is the poet, now beset by 'Deep feelings I thought dead' rather than 'Sweet thoughts that will not die':

> Ay—there it is! it wakes to-night
> Deep feelings I thought dead;
> Strong in the blast—quick gathering light—
> The heart's flame kindles red.

The speaker of the remaining stanzas is not the 'glorious wind' that was given a speaking voice in 'The Night-Wind' but some human observer who describes the poet's experience and, at its close, extracts a lesson from it. This is a poem about influence and resistance to it, and Charlotte's explanatory note to it in the 1850 edition recalls both her characterization of Emily's mind in her 'Editor's Preface' ('to the influence of other intellects, it was not amenable') and the plot of *Shirley*. This 'votary' has a 'wayward' spirit, but she will submit, eventually, to a beloved power greater than her own:

the Genius of a solitary region seems to address his wandering and wayward votary, and to recall within his influence the proud mind which rebelled at times against what it most loved.[19]

Charlotte's editorial control is grounded in her love for Emily and her faith in Emily's love for her, but it also expresses her confidence that her understanding—of last things as well as of poems—is more mature than her younger sister's.

In her 'Biographical Notice', Charlotte announces her conviction that an 'interpreter ought always to have stood between [Emily] and the world'.[20] While she lived, Emily had encouraged Charlotte to interpret the world for her. When Ellen Nussey remarked on her not going to London with Charlotte and Anne, Emily wondered what use her going would serve. 'Charlotte will bring it all home to me,' she told Ellen.[21] Though she refused to meet Charlotte's publisher, George Smith, and his reader, W. S. Williams, she was happy to read their letters to Charlotte and to share the books they sent to the Parsonage. The difference between the role Charlotte played in Emily's life while Emily was still alive, and the role she played after Emily's death is partly the difference between shielding Emily from contact with an outside world she chose to avoid and putting words into her mouth. But this difference is more subtle than it may sound. If Charlotte created a role for herself after Emily's death that

Emily would never have approved, she did so by improving upon a role she had played while Emily was still alive. 'Her will was not very flexible, and it generally opposed her interest,' Charlotte writes in the 'Biographical Notice'.[22] Emily's death freed Charlotte to promote Emily's interest.

With 'The Visionary', a poem consisting of twelve lines written by Emily as the opening of 'Julian M. and A. G. Rochelle'[23] and eight lines written by Charlotte herself, Charlotte seeks to serve Emily's interest even more fully than she had with her revisions to Emily's other poems. Reading 'The Visionary' and knowing which lines are Emily's and which Charlotte's, we can see that Charlotte's tone, diction, and rhythm aren't much like Emily's. These are Emily's lines:

> Silent is the House—all are laid asleep;
> One, alone, looks out o'er the snow-wreaths deep;
> Watching every cloud, dreading every breeze
> That whirls the wildering drifts and bends the groaning trees—
>
> Cheerful is the hearth, soft the matted floor
> Not one shivering gust creeps through pane or door
> The little lamp burns straight; its rays shoot strong and far
> I trim it well to be the Wanderer's guiding-star—
>
> Frown, my haughty sire, chide my angry Dame;
> Set your slaves to spy, threaten me with shame;
> But neither sire nor dame, nor prying serf shall know
> What angel nightly tracks that waste of winter snow—

Here are the eight lines Charlotte wrote, the rest of 'The Visionary':

> What I love shall come like visitant of air,
> Safe in secret power from lurking human snare;
> What loves me, no word of mine shall e'er betray,
> Though for faith unstained my life must forfeit pay.
>
> Burn, then, little lamp; glimmer straight and clear—
> Hush! a rustling wing stirs, methinks, the air:
> He for whom I wait, thus ever comes to me;
> Strange Power! I trust thy might; trust thou my constancy.

Charlotte's lines give Emily's speaker a role like that of her own Angrian heroines, who—unlike the heroines of Gondal—passively await the preference of their heroes. Charlotte's 'Visionary' awaits the sources of her power, the mighty masculine lover, to whom she is faithful even though her own death may be the consequence. She loves her visitant, and he, in turn, loves her back. She is willing to die for him. I have already commented on the way this imagination of visionary experience serves Margaret Homans's and Irene Tayler's idea that Emily Brontë's muse is not just an inspiring voice located outside her but one invested with 'Strange Power' over her.[24] This persuasive construction of Brontë relies not just on a potent feminist critical paradigm according to which women writers have habitually been disabled by their being women, but on Charlotte's strong misreading of Emily's relation to poetic inspiration in 'The Visionary' and in the 1850 volume as a whole.

The rhetoric and diction of the lines Charlotte wrote mark them as hers. We ought to register the difference between Emily's realistic details in the first eight lines—'The little lamp burns straight; its rays shoot strong and far'—and Charlotte's fussy personification—'Burn, then, little lamp; glimmer straight and clear.' Emily's syntax is characteristically simple and direct throughout; Charlotte's can be contorted: 'Though for faith unstained my life must forfeit pay.' The words *visitant, snare, unstained*, and *glimmer* appear nowhere in Emily's poems or her novel, but *snare* turns up in all of Charlotte's novels, except, surprisingly, in *Villette*, which is full of snares. The word also appears once in a poem by Patrick Brontë, once in a poem by Branwell, once in *The Tenant of Wildfell Hall*, and twice in Branwell and Charlotte's early writings. Like *snare*, the other words belong to a Brontë word kitty that Charlotte and Branwell—but not Emily—draw heavily on. Both *unstained* and *glimmer* turn up three times in Branwell's and in Charlotte's poems. *Visitant* appears only in Charlotte's and Branwell's early writings and in Charlotte's novels, twice in *Jane Eyre*.[25]

Rhythmically, there are also differences. Emily's lines have a dipodic lilt.[26] If the lines are scanned as dipodic verse, the caesura represents 'a systematically dictated systematically missing beat' (there is 'no migration across the boundary it establishes'),[27] and the second stress in each half-line can be seen to be consistently weaker than the first and third stresses in that half-line:

> / × \ × / ‖ / × \ × /
> Silent is the House—all are laid asleep;
>
> / × \ × / ‖ / × \ × /
> One alone, looks out o'er the snow-wreaths deep;

The rhythm of the last line of the first stanza and the third and fourth lines of the second and third stanzas shifts, so that these lines can be scanned as regular iambic hexameters, but they sound rhythmically consistent with the rest, both because the strong caesura continues to be positioned precisely in the middle of each line and because each half-line retains its three beats. Charlotte only twice manages (in lines 17 and 18) to imitate the dominant rhythm of Emily's lines. Awkward metrical variations in the rest of her lines destabilize their rhythm. She weakens the caesura in line 16 and lets it drift backwards from the centre in lines 15, 18, and 20. She recovers somewhat in her last line, which imitates Emily's iambic hexameter lines, although the spondee in the first foot has no precedent in Emily's lines.

To turn from 'The Visitant' to 'Often rebuked, yet always back returning' is to turn to a poem that has even more powerfully shaped our understanding of Emily Brontë. For generations of readers, as for T. J. Wise and J. A. Symington, the early purveyors of the Brontës to the world, 'Often rebuked, yet always back returning' sounded the 'keynote to her character'.[28] Significantly, 'Often rebuked, yet always back returning' is the only poem attributed to Emily Brontë for which no holograph manuscript survives or has ever been seen. If the poem is Emily's, it is anomalous in not belonging to either of the transcript books from which Charlotte took the other poems she made public in 1850. Although there could be no final proof of its authorship apart from the discovery of a holograph manuscript in Emily's hand (even a manuscript in Charlotte's hand would not prove that she wrote the poem, but only that she copied it), I believe that the author of this poem has to be Charlotte. The only good reason for believing that Emily wrote the poem turns out to be no reason at all: it is the belief that Charlotte would not have attributed a poem to Emily that Emily didn't write. Would an editor who did not scruple to publish 'The Visionary' as Emily's poem, although she herself created it by adding eight lines of her own to twelve of her sister's, hesitate to publish as Emily's a poem entirely of her own devising?[29]

The jury (not composed of peers but of Brontë critics and editors) is still out. Edward Chitham argues for Emily's authorship on the grounds that the 'general content of the poem is quite characteristic of Emily in certain ways' and that 'some of its language resembles that of other poems written by her'.[30] Victor Neufeldt, the most recent editor of Charlotte's poems, thinks that the language as well as the content of the poem are 'characteristically Emily's, especially the last two stanzas' and believes that Charlotte ' "edited" the poem, as she did others, in preparation for the 1850 edition'.[31] Hatfield anticipated my view long ago. He printed the poem in an appendix to his edition of Emily Brontë's poems in 1941, believing that it sounded more like Charlotte than Emily and seemed to express Charlotte's feelings about her sister rather than Emily's own thoughts.[32] In my edition of Emily Brontë's poems, I print the poem, together with one other, in a section titled 'Poems of Doubtful Authority', suggesting in my note that 'resemblances between this poem and others by Emily Brontë are not striking'.[33]

How we view the authorship of 'Often rebuked, yet always back returning' bears on our understanding of the form and content of Emily Brontë's poems and on our understanding of what to make of her creative life. The poem is crucial for coming to terms with Emily's importance for Charlotte, and with Charlotte's understanding of what Emily's interest was. I suggest that Charlotte wrote 'Often rebuked, yet always back returning' sometime between 1 November 1849, after reading the first review of *Shirley*, and September 1850, when she wrote to her publisher about the 1850 edition of *Wuthering Heights* and *Agnes Grey*. The chronology for that month in 1850 is as follows: on 13 September, Charlotte mentions adding a 'few poetical remains' to the new edition of her sisters' novels; by 20 September, she has sent off a rough draft of the 'Biographical Notice'; on 27 September, she mentions her 'intention to write a few lines of remark on "Wuthering Heights"'.[34] She may have begun 'Often rebuked, yet always back returning' in the autumn of 1849, without planning to attribute it to her sister. Perhaps she subsequently revised the poem with the attribution to Emily in mind. Or she may have written the poem in the autumn of 1850, when the occasion for publishing poems by Emily and Anne presented itself.

Establishing that Charlotte is the author of 'Often rebuked, yet always back returning' is more complicated than confirming that she wrote the lines she added to Emily's other poems published in 1850. There is no evidence that Charlotte was attempting to sound like Emily when she revised or contributed to these other poems. She was attempting to improve them, according to a better model of her own. The composition of 'Often rebuked, yet always back returning' resulted from a different kind of application by a writer who was well acquainted with her sister's work and talented enough to be able to imitate another poet credibly and creditably. Charlotte makes use of her new knowledge of Emily's poems, the fruit of rereading them in connection with her plan to publish poems in 1850, and succeeds admirably in writing a poem that might almost have been written by Emily Brontë:

> Often rebuked, yet always back returning
> To those first feelings that were born with me,

And leaving busy chase of wealth and learning
    For idle dreams of things which cannot be:

To-day, I will seek not the shadowy region;
    Its unsustaining vastness waxes drear;
And visions rising, legion after legion,
    Bring the unreal world too strangely near.

I'll walk, but not in old heroic traces,
    And not in paths of high morality,
And not among the half-distinguished faces,
    The clouded forms of long-past history.

I'll walk where my own nature would be leading:
    It vexes me to choose another guide:
Where the grey flocks in ferny glens are feeding;
    Where the wild wind blows on the mountain side.

What have those lonely mountains worth revealing?
    More glory and more grief than I can tell:
The earth that wakes *one* human heart to feeling
    Can centre both the worlds of Heaven and Hell.

Read as autobiography, the poem strengthens the case that Emily Brontë is 'genuinely good and truly great'. It shows her resolute but uncomplaining, however much maligned. These are the characteristics Charlotte emphasizes in the 'Biographical Notice' and, as we have seen, in the family portrait she provides in her letter to W. S. Williams. Emily, she says, would have viewed reproaches or complaints as 'an unworthy, and offensive weakness'.[35] Unlike Anne, who was upheld by endurance, Emily was nerved by energy despite the reviewers' rebukes.[36] They were 'both prepared to try again'. Emily was 'always back returning' to her native feelings; she was determined to set her own course. In the poem, her unbending spirit and inflexible will are enabled by association with the 'wild winds' and softened by association with 'grey flocks in ferny glens', pairings equally at home in Charlotte's imaginary world and in Emily's. In her 'Editor's Preface', Charlotte has difficulty locating the moral wisdom of *Wuthering Heights*, but 'Often rebuked, yet always back returning' attributes a moral purpose to all of Emily Brontë's work: she wrote to reveal a lasting truth, however often it escaped full articulation.

    The language and content of this poem, even the language and content of its last two stanzas, are not characteristic of Emily. They are more characteristic of Charlotte and of Charlotte's idea of Emily, which is sometimes on the mark, sometimes off it. On the one hand, the 'lonely mountains' and the 'wild wind' are regular features of a Gondal land-scape, which is more sublime than that of Charlotte's Angria. On the other, the poem's praise of the earth because it 'wakes *one* human heart to feeling' sounds a note more familiar in Charlotte's writing than in Emily's. Her Roe Head journals record her flights from the schoolroom to those twin places of imagination, Haworth and Angria:

> that wind I know is heard at this moment far away on the moors of Haworth. Branwell & Emily hear it and as it sweeps over our house down the church-yard & round the old church, they think perhaps of me & Anne— <Nort> Glorious! that blast was mighty it reminded me of Northangerland ... O it has wakened a feeling that I cannot satisfy—a thousand wishes rose at its call which must die with me for they will never be fulfilled. now I should be agonized if I had not the dream to repose on, its existences, its forms its scenes do fill a little of the craving vacancy.[37]

'Often rebuked, yet always back returning' speaks of 'idle dreams of things which cannot be', a formulation long familiar to Charlotte, who struggled—as Emily never did—with the morality of preferring a glamorous and enthralling visionary world to a 'real' world of homely duties. When Charlotte is self-approving, she writes about solacing herself 'with the dream of creations whose reality I shall never behold'. When she isn't, she feels 'only shame and regret'.[38] Most readers will associate the idea expressed in the poem's last line—that earth centres heaven and hell—with Emily rather than Charlotte. And rightly so, for several of Emily's poems pair heaven and hell, and Charlotte only manages this thought with Emily's help. One of Emily's poems that may have influenced Charlotte's composition of 'Often rebuked, yet always back returning' is 'My Comforter', published in 1846. In it, Emily writes in her own way about vexation and moody resentment:

> So stood I, in Heaven's glorious sun,
>   And in the glare of Hell;
> My spirit drank a mingled tone,
> Of seraph's song, and demon's moan;
> What my soul bore, my soul alone
>   Within itself may tell!

The characteristic note of these lines is their location of the human spirit at the confluence of Heaven and Hell, making it a channel for the warring energies of each realm. The human spirit somehow contains these forces; like a battleground, it is alternately laid waste and redeemed.

But this isn't the same idea as the one expressed in 'Often rebuked, yet always back returning', where Charlotte draws on poets other than Emily. The mountain scenery there assumes a more Wordsworthian function familiar to us from lines like these from 'The Tables Turned':

> One impulse from a vernal wood
> May teach you more of man,
> Of moral evil and of good,
> Than all the sages can.

Readers of Romantic poetry familiar with its praise of a natural world that whispers lessons to us may have an additional reason for admiring the last stanza of 'Often rebuked, yet always back returning', but it is not a reason for attributing the poem to Emily Brontë.

In the note to 'Often rebuked, yet always back returning' in my edition of Emily Brontë's poems, I point out that Charlotte wrote many poems in iambic pentameter, Emily very few. One of these is 'Remembrance'. I have described the extraordinary skill of this poem's rhythmic effects in Chapter 3: its repeated substitution of a trochee for an iamb in the first foot of each line, the strong caesura after the second foot, the regular alternation of feminine and masculine endings 'Often rebuked, yet always back returning' lacks the recurring metrical variations that account for the stalled, haunting music of 'Remembrance'. Its cadences are settled and even. Although both 'Remembrance' and 'Often rebuked, yet always back returning' alternate masculine and feminine endings, 'Often rebuked, yet always back returning' relies on the easiest of these in English, the *ing*-ending that 'Remembrance' avoids. The logical and syntactical structure of the last quatrain of 'Often rebuked, yet always back returning' also points to Charlotte. When Emily asks and answers a question, the question is simpler, and the answer less portentous. Riddles are in the background of some of these questions and their answers:

> Tell me tell me smiling child
> What the past is like to thee?
> An Autumn evening soft and mild
> With a wind that sighs mournfully

Questions that come at the end of Emily Brontë's poems are usually rhetorical and lack explicit answers, as in 'Remembrance'—'Once drinking deep of that divinest anguish, | How could I seek the empty world again?'—or 'Plead for Me', a poem in which the question comes near the end and is succeeded by a plea, not an answer:

And am I wrong to worship, where
Faith cannot doubt, nor hope despair,
Since my own soul can grant my prayer?
Speak, God of visions, plead for me,
And tell why I have chosen thee!

'Often rebuked, yet always back returning' ends like a poem by Charlotte, not like a poem by Emily. It is resolved, even dogged in its conclusiveness. No hard or troubling destiny overcomes its speaker or catches its reader unawares. No seraph's song or demon's moan disturbs its even surface. No wild, tender, or harsh music distinguishes the poem's lines from those of sensible prose.[39]

'Often rebuked, yet always back returning' tells too much, and more than Emily Brontë ever does. Its three middle stanzas, explicit and comprehensive in their assertions about her poetic intentions and practice, are especially unlikely to have been written by her. Much of the language in them is foreign to her poems. She never uses 'traces' in this sense, and never uses 'heroic' at all. She never uses 'high' as an adjective (Charlotte, we remember, titled one of her early stories 'High Life in Verdopolis'), and never mentions 'morality' either in her poems or in *Wuthering Heights*. History is frequently a subject in Charlotte's poems, but Emily's mention history only once (in 'E. W. to A. G. A.'), and there the reference is to an individual's past rather than a collective record. There is no other mention of 'first feelings' in Emily's writing, although the phrase turns up twice in Branwell's poems.

We cannot readily locate the vocabulary of 'Often rebuked, yet always back returning' in Charlotte's poems either. I can explain this. Emily continues to write poems while she is writing *Wuthering Heights* and after, but Charlotte virtually stops writing them once she begins writing prose. The vocabulary and some of the syntactical patterns of 'Often rebuked, yet always back returning' belong not to Charlotte's poems but to her novels and to the letters she writes after the publication of *Shirley*. Charlotte writes about 'morality' in both *Jane Eyre* and *Shirley*, and the odd locution in the poem's fourth stanza—'It vexes me'—doesn't figure in Emily's writing but turns up twice in *Shirley*, where Robert Moore's secrecy 'vexes' Shirley and Mrs Pryor's dress annoys Caroline: 'it vexes me even.'[40] Emily does use 'centre' as a verb once (in 'Geraldine'—'My whole heart centred there'), but Charlotte also uses 'centre' as a verb in *Jane Eyre* as does Anne in 'Self-Communion', the last poem she wrote and one that Charlotte read but didn't select for publication in 1850. The gratuitous syntactic inversion in the poem's second stanza—'To-day I will seek not the shadowy region'—is unlike Emily but very like Charlotte. The same point might be made about the preponderance of negative constructions in the second and third stanzas of the poem. Margot Peters points out that in her novels Charlotte 'is as disposed to describe things in terms of what they *are not*, as in terms of what they are'.[41]

We can establish a deeper context for elements of 'Often rebuked, yet always back returning' in Charlotte's novels and letters, where these elements are related to a complex of feelings associated with Charlotte's life after Emily's death or to an 'unflinching' stance taken by her or by one of her heroines.[42] In the letters, they minister to Charlotte's idea of Emily and to her increasingly close identification with Emily after her death. The word *unsustaining*, for example, doesn't appear elsewhere in poems by either Emily or Charlotte, but *unsustained* appears in *Jane Eyre*, when Jane justifies her refusal to marry Rochester:

Still indomitable was the reply—'*I* care for myself. The more solitary, the more friendless, the more unsustained I am, the more I will respect myself.' (III. i. 404)

In a letter to W. S. Williams, after finishing *Shirley*, Charlotte writes that the novel 'took me out of a dark and desolate reality to an unreal but happier region'.[43] When she writes to him about her fears that her anonymity will not survive the publication of *Shirley*, she sounds like the voice of 'Often rebuked, yet back returning', even slipping once into an internal rhyme:

No matter—whether known or unknown—misjudged or the contrary—I am resolved not to write otherwise. I shall bend as my powers tend. The two human beings who understood me and whom I understood are gone: I have some that love me yet and whom I love without expecting or having a right to expect that they shall perfectly understand me: I am satisfied; but I must have my own way in the matter of writing.[44]

Should we rebuke Charlotte for writing as her sister and then attributing what she had written to her? 'The crisis of bereavement is an acute pang which goads to exertion—the desolate after feeling sometimes paralyses.'[45] So Charlotte describes her state of mind after Emily's death. We would do better to imagine Charlotte as she was in 1849 and 1850, goaded to the exertion that produced the wonderful letters of those years; *Shirley*; the 1850 edition of *Wuthering Heights*, *Agnes Grey*, and her sisters' poems; and her own most successful poem, 'Often rebuked, yet always back returning.' Emily's death, Anne's death, and *Shirley*'s publication, three events that occurred in rapid succession between December 1848 and October 1849, confirmed Charlotte's identification with both her sisters, but especially her 'primitive adhesiveness' with Emily.[46] Rebuke (the reviews of *Shirley* stunned, then stirred Charlotte), exposure (Charlotte's mask of anonymity slipped after the publication of *Shirley*), and isolation (Emily had demanded it during her lifetime, and Charlotte felt it newly after Emily's death) combined to set the tone of the 1850 volume as a whole and of 'Often rebuked, yet always back returning' specifically. When Charlotte read the first review of *Shirley* in the *Daily News*, she wrote to W. S. Williams: 'It is not a good review—it is unutterably false,' plucking a word from 'No coward soul is mine'. 'Were my Sisters now alive they and I would laugh over this notice,' she writes, recalling their responding together to the review in the *North American Review*, 'but they sleep—they will wake no more for me ... '[47] 'I fear that I am not so firm as I used to be,' she writes (probably thinking of Emily, her model for firmness), 'nor so patient,' she continues (probably thinking of Anne, her model for patience).[48]

Charlotte writes as Emily in 'Often rebuked, yet always back returning' because she feels like Emily, especially after Emily's death and the rebuke that followed the publication of *Shirley*. Before Emily's death, she had written about her closeness to this sister, telling Ellen Nussey that she 'seems the nearest thing to my heart in this world'[49] and W. S. Williams that her own happiness depended on Emily's well-being:

When she is ill there seems to be no sunshine in the world for me; the tie of sister is near and dear indeed, and I think a certain harshness in her powerful, 'and' peculiar character only makes one cling to her more. But this is all family egotism (so to speak) excuse it—and above all, never allude to it, or to the name, Emily, when you write to me; I do not always show your letters, but I never withhold them when they are inquired after.[50]

In his letter to Charlotte after Emily's death, W. S. Williams perceptively and soothingly refers to Emily as 'one who was your other self'.[51] After the death, Charlotte discovered Emily's likeness in places likely and unlikely. In Elizabeth Gaskell's nature, she discovered 'a remote affinity to my sister Emily', in G. H. Lewes's face, a resemblance.[52] When she saw George Richmond's portrait of herself, she wept, perhaps because of the resemblance to Anne (as George Smith remembered) but more likely because of the resemblance to Emily (as John Richmond, the artist's son, told the story).

We do not know much about the illness that preceded Emily Brontë's death. Charlotte's letter to Dr Epps about Emily's symptoms and her self-medication of them survives but is incomplete. The first sheet has been torn, just at the place where details of her symptoms are about to be given. If Charlotte censored this part of the letter, Cassandra Austen anticipates her by expurgating such physical facts from her famous sister's letters.[53] We know that Emily refused to see a doctor until a few hours before her death. When she agreed to see a doctor, she did so as one might ask for a priest, to preside over her death, not to forestall it. In Carter's translation of Epictetus, the philosopher notes that to be very ill is to be near the separation of soul and body. 'What harm is there in this, then?' Why flatter your physician, or 'furnish an Occasion to his Pride?' Why not treat him, 'with regard to an insignificant Body, which is not yours, but by Nature mortal, like a Shoemaker, about your foot or a Carpenter about a house?'[54] During her illness, Emily took no medicine apart from 'a mild aperient—and Locock's cough wafers' and regulated her own diet.[55] For purposes of contrast, take Anne. She followed the medical recommendation to dose herself with cod liver oil and carbonate of iron, which nauseated her, and endured blisters applied to her chest. When the medicines did her no good, kept her 'always sick', and made eating impossible, she gave them up and tried hydropathy, which had also been recommended.[56] Yet Charlotte believed that Anne, 'from her childhood, seemed preparing for an early death', while Emily 'was torn conscious, panting, reluctant though resolute out of a happy life'.[57] The different ways in which Anne and Emily faced death have a history in the different ways they faced life when they were still in good health. Emily's tone in the diary papers is tranquil and optimistic about the future; sometimes it is buoyant. While Anne writes in 1845, 'I for my part cannot well be *flatter* or older in mind than I am now,' Emily expresses considerable satisfaction with her circumstances and prospects:

I am quite contented for myself—not as idle as formerly, altogether as hearty and having learnt to make the most of the present and hope for the future with less fidgetiness that I cannot do all I wish—seldom or [n]ever troubled with nothing to do <illegible> and merely desiring that every body could be as comfortable as myself and as undesponding and then we should have a very tolerable world of it—[58]

Though Emily Brontë's genius was yoked with death, even her anguish in response to a life with death was more exhilarated than gloomy.[59]

On Emily's last night, Charlotte read to her from the second series of Emerson's essays, one of several books her publisher had recently sent her: 'the very evening before her last morning dawned I read to her one of Emerson's essays—I read on till I found she was not listening—I thought to recommence next day—Next day, the first glance at her face told me what would happen before night-fall.'[60] It is tempting to imagine that she read from 'The Poet', an essay Emily would have found congenial. In it, Emerson speaks of the substances that poets use and abuse—alcohol, mead, opium: 'they help him to escape the custody of that body in which he is pent up, and of that jail-yard of individual relations in which he is enclosed'.[61] She was not one of those poets Emerson criticizes for being 'contented with a civil and conformed manner of living', and with writing 'poems for the fancy, at a safe distance from their own experience'.[62] As Brontë might have, Emerson bemoans the feebleness with which the 'impressions of nature' fall on us: 'Every touch should thrill. Every man should be so much an artist, that he could report in conversation what had befallen him.'[63] In his final paragraph, he rises to exhort the Poet and hands down his own commandments. These bear reading as a defence of Emily Brontë's reclusive habits and her willingness to leave so many matters in Charlotte's capable hands:

Thou shalt leave the world, and know the muse only. Thou shalt not know any longer the times, customs, graces, politics, or opinions of men, but shalt take all from the muse. For the time of towns is tolled from the world by funereal chimes, but in nature the universal hours are counted by succeeding tribes of animals and plants, and by the growth of joy on joy. God wills also that thou abdicate a manifold and duplex life, and that thou be content that others speak for thee. Others shall be thy gentlemen, and shall represent all courtesy and worldly life for thee; others shall do the great and resounding actions also.[64]

In the 1850 volume, Charlotte acted not just as Emily's 'near and dear' sister but as her gentleman.

Emily would have understood Emerson's distinction between the 'time of towns', which is 'tolled from the world by funereal chimes', and 'the universal hours', which 'are counted by succeeding tribes of animals and plants, and by the growth of joy on joy'.[65] Writing about *Shirley*, but probably thinking about Emily, Charlotte registers her heroine's access to an earth like an Eden, a life like a poem, and a joy that gives her the highest kind of experience that Charlotte can imagine, 'experience of a genii-life'.[66] The reference to 'a genii-life' transports us back to the storytelling that for a time engaged the imaginations of all four Brontë children, who called themselves Genius Brannii, Tallii, Emmii, and Annii. They collaborated in telling these stories, but Charlotte could claim to be their leader. She was the one who introduced the idea of the Genii, those superhuman beings who had the power not just to take life, but to restore it. In an unfinished poem composed in 1839, 'How long will you remain? The midnight hour', two characters argue about whether one of them had better go to sleep rather than remaining barely awake or entertaining her 'blissful dream that never comes with day'. The other reminds her that the world will be transformed by breaking day, birdsong, and the 'merry voices' of her children:

> Aye speak of these—but can you tell me why
> Day breathes such beauty over earth and sky
> And waking sounds revive restore again
> Dull hearts that all night long have throbbed in pain
>
> Is it not that the sunshine and the wind
> Lure from its self the mourner's woe worn mind
> And all the joyous music breathing by
> And all the splendour of that cloudless sky
>
> Regive him shadowy gleams of infancy
> And draw his tired gaze from futurity [67]

The final couplet holds two opposing states of being in balance and resists the pressure of two more near rhymes that would have been clearly in view: *infinity* and *eternity*. Brontë's sketches surround the poem and give us some information about the dreamwork that produced it. There is a winged serpent, a frond or feather, a cross like a Celtic cross but lacking any circle, and then, below the poem, a circle within a circle. Below the poem, she has also written the word *regive* and the phrase *regive him* several times, as if she cannot or will not let it go.

Notes

INTRODUCTION: AND FIRST

1. Woolf praised Brontë's poems in 'Jane Eyre and Wuthering Heights', *Collected Essays*, 4 vols. (New York: Harcourt, Brace & World, 1966), i. 189.

2. Mary Taylor's exchange with Emily Brontë is recorded in T. J. Wise and J. A. Symington (eds.), *The Brontës: Their Lives, Friendships & Correspondence in Four Volumes* (Oxford: Shakespeare Head Press, 1932), ii. 276. Keats's remark comes from a letter to J. H. Reynolds (3 Feb. 1818) in *The Letters of John Keats*, ed. Hyder Edward Rollins, 2 vols. (Cambridge, Mass: Harvard Univ. Press, 1958), i. 224.

3. The first remark is from 'A General Introduction for my Work', the second from his *Autobiographies*. Robert Pack quotes both in 'Lyric Narration: The Chameleon Poet', *Hudson Review* 37/1 (Spring 1984), 54–70.

4. Woolf, *Collected Essays*, i. 189.

5. 'The Poetry of Thomas Hardy', *Athenaeum* (1919), quoted in Dennis Taylor, *Hardy's Metres and Victorian Prosody* (Oxford: Clarendon Press, 1988), 202.

6. Housework did not keep her from reading a great deal or from studying German and Latin.

7. *Glass, Irony and God* (New York: New Directions, 1995), 4.

8. Quoted by Christopher Ricks, in *Allusion to the Poets* (Oxford: Oxford Univ. Press, 2002), 268.

9. *The Life of Charlotte Brontë*, ed. Alan Shelston (London: Penguin, 1985), 230. Cf. Gaskell's account in *Cranford:* 'the last gigot, the last tight and scanty petticoat in wear in England, was seen in Cranford—and seen without a smile.' *Cranford/Cousin Phillis*, ed. Peter Keating (London: Penguin, 1976), 40.

10. Algernon Charles Swinburne, *A Note on Charlotte Brontë* (London: Chatto & Windus, 1877), 74.

11. *Literature and Evil*, trans. Alistair Hamilton (London: Marion Boyars, 2001), 28.

12. In *The Brontës and Religion*, Marianne Thormählen disagrees with Stevie Davies's characterization of Brontë as a heretic and with Barbara Prentis's

view that Brontë's 'essential fidelities were to Christian orthodoxy'. Nevertheless, she reads *Wuthering Heights* as a confirmation of 'fundamental Christian tenets' and 'No coward soul is mine' as evidence of Brontë's rejection of 'the very possibility of doubt' (Cambridge: Cambridge Univ. Press, 1999), 6–14; 72–85.

13. The phrase is Swinburne's, *A Note on Charlotte Brontë*, 74.
14. Michael Richardson, *Georges Bataille* (London: Routledge, 1994), 12.
15. Charlotte Brontë and Emily Brontë, *The Belgian Essays*, ed. and trans. Sue Lonoff (New Haven: Yale University Press, 1996), 65.
16. I am contrasting the King James version with Brontë's. See ibid. 15, and comments, 160–62.
17. 'Our Attitude towards Death', *The Standard Edition of the Complete Psychological Works of Sigmund Freud*, trans. and ed. James Strachey, 14 (1914–16) (London: Hogarth Press, 1957, repr. 1981), 296.
18. Quoted in Juliet Barker, *The Brontës* (London: Phoenix, 1994), 454. It seems likely, though not certain, that Anne and Emily would have shared Gondal poems earlier on.
19. The phrase is Stevie Davies's in *Emily Brontë: Heretic* (London: The Women's Press, 1994), 8.
20. Edward Chitham, *The Birth of Wuthering Heights* (London: Macmillian, 1998), 174.
21. The usual number of poems by Emily Brontë published in 1850 is given as eighteen, not seventeen, but in my edition of her poems, I print the paired poems beginning 'Heavy hangs the rain-drop' and 'Child of delight, with sun-bright hair' under Charlotte's single title, 'The Two Children'.
22. Wise and Symington (eds.), *The Brontës*, ii. 275.
23. This distinction, and its use to discourage a biographical interpretation of the famous lines in 'A Prisoner (A Fragment)' in which the prisoner describes her mystical experience, still survives in Lucasta Miller's account of the Brontës, *The Brontë Myth* (New York: Alfred A. Knopf, 2003), 252.
24. See Christopher Bollas, *Being a Character: Psychoanalysis and Self Experience* (London: Routledge, 1997), especially 'Aspects of Self Experiencing', 11–32.

1. LAST THINGS

1. Susan Howe quotes Dickinson's Prose Fragment 30 in *My Emily Dickinson* (Berkeley: North Atlantic Books, 1985), 23–4.
2. Allen Grossman, *Summa Lyrica: A Primer of the Commonplaces in Speculative Poetics*, in Allen Grossman with Mark Halliday, *The Sighted Singer: Two Works on Poetry for Readers and Writers* (Baltimore: Johns Hopkins Univ. Press, 1992), 281.

3. *Complete Writings of Oscar Wilde: Reviews* (New York: The Nottingham Society, 1909), 200.

4. Virginia Blain, *Victorian Women Poets: A New Annotated Anthology* (Harlow: Pearson Education Limited, 2001), 1.

5. *Contingencies of Value: Alternative Perspectives for Critical Theory* (Cambridge, Mass: Harvard Univ. Press, 1988), 46.

6. Blain, *Victorian Women Poets*, 2.

7. 'Biographical Notice of Ellis and Acton Bell', in Emily Brontë, *Wuthering Heights*, ed. Hilda Marsden and Ian Jack (Oxford: Clarendon Press, 1976), 435.

8. Isobel Armstrong, *Victorian Poetry: Poetry, Poetics and Politics* (London: Routledge, 1993), 323. Armstrong devotes a chapter to women poets and two pages in it to Brontë's poems. Angela Leighton's *Victorian Women Poets: Writing against the Heart* (Charlottesville: University Press of Virginia, 1992) devotes chapters to Felicia Hemans, L. E. L., Elizabeth Barrett Browning, Christina Rossetti, Augusta Webster, Michael Field, Alice Meynell, and Charlotte Mew, but not Emily Brontë. Kathleen Hickok's *Representations of Women: Nineteenth-Century British Women's Poetry* (Westport, Conn.: Greenwood Press, 1984) is organized thematically and acknowledges Emily Brontë, along with Barrett Browning and Rossetti as 'the best known' nineteenth-century women poets; it devotes a chapter each to Barrett Browning and Rossetti, but gives no chapter to Brontë.

9. Isobel Armstrong and Virginia Blain (eds.), *Women's Poetry, Late Romantic to Victorian* (Basingstoke: Macmillan, 1999). Citations of Brontë occur in Virginia Blain, 'Sexual Politics of the (Victorian) Closet; or No Sex Please—We're Poets', 143, and in Robert P. Fletcher, ' "I leave a page half-writ": Narrative Discourse in Michael Field's Underneath the Bough', 165.

10. See, especially, Margaret Homans's discussion of 'The Night-Wind' and 'Shall earth no more inspire thee' in *Women Writers and Poetic Identity: Dorothy Wordsworth, Emily Brontë, and Emily Dickinson* (Princeton: Princeton Univ. Press, 1980), 124–7, and Irene Tayler's *Holy Ghosts: The Male Muses of Emily and Charlotte Brontë* (New York: Columbia Univ. Press, 1990), 2f.

11. Picasso's words are written at the end of one of his notebooks, probably in 1963 (Picasso Museum, Paris 75004). Freud is defending the use of the impersonal pronoun it (or id) on the basis of 'certain forms of expression used by normal people. "It shot through me," people say; "there was something in me at that moment that was stronger than me." "C'était plus fort que moi." ' *The Question of Lay Analysis*, trans. James Strachey (New York: W. W. Norton & Co., 1950, repr. 1964), 18.

12. Miller, *The Brontë Myth*, 205.

13. *Feminism and Psychoanalytic Theory* (New Haven: Yale Univ. Press, 1989), 196.

14. I use Lonoff's translation of Brontë's French, *The Belgian Essays*, 68.

15. *Emily Brontë: The Artist as a Free Woman* (Manchester: Carcanet, 1983), 89. Sexual longing has also been taken to be the subject of poems, not just a metaphor for their subject. Derek Roper assumes that four poems that 'tell the story of a love once joyful but now lost' refer to a human lover, even though no likely candidate has presented himself. *The Poems of Emily Brontë*, ed. Derek Roper with Edward Chitham (Oxford: Clarendon Press, 1995), 4. I read these poems as addressed to inspiration or imagination. They are 'If grief for grief can touch thee', 'O Dream, where art thou now', 'It is too late to call thee now', and 'The wind I hear it sighing'.

16. *Heretic*, 227–8.

17. *Selected Poems 1957–1994* (New York: Farrar, Straus & Giroux, 1995, repr. 2002). The poem first appeared in *Remains of Elmet* (1979). Of the several poems Hughes wrote in which Emily Brontë figures, this is the only one included in *Selected Poems*.

18. 'The Gender of Sound', in *Glass, Irony and God*, 130.

19. 'Wuthering Heights', in *Birthday Letters* (New York: Farrar, Straus & Giroux, 1998), 59–61.

20. *Heretic*, 23 and 25.

21. *Literature and Evil*, 17.

22. Ibid 26.

23. 'Approaching the Lyric,' in Chaviva Hošek and Patricia Parker (eds.), *Lyric Poetry beyond New Criticism*, and Patricia Parker (Ithaca, N.Y.: Cornell Univ. Press, 1985), 32.

24. *Guilty*, trans. Bruce Boone (San Francisco: The Lapis Press, 1988), 93. The French reads as follows: 'l'angoisse nue, évidemment, n'a pas d'objet, sinon que l'être est dans le temps, qui le détruit.' *Le Coupable*, in *Œuvres Complètes*, vol. 5 (Paris: Éditions Gallimard, 1973), 337.

25. See 'O mother I am not regretting'.

26. *Lyric Time: Dickinson and the Limits of Genre* (Baltimore: Johns Hopkins Univ. Press, 1981), 207. *The Prelude*, Book V, ll. 3–4. Barbara Hardy's observation that lyric poems often have 'the privacy of love-speech' or the 'greater privacy of inner discourse' is related. See *The Advantage of Lyric: Essays on Feeling in Poetry* (London: University of London Press, 1977), 12 f.

27. Mikhail Bahktin, quoted by Clare Cavanagh, 'Poetry and Ideology: The Example of Wislawa Szymborska', in *Literary Imagination*, 1/2 (1999), 180; Mark Jeffreys summarizes criticism levelled against the lyric from this perspective in 'Ideologies of Lyric: A Problem of Genre in Contemporary Anglophone Poetics', *PMLA* 110/2 (Mar. 1995), 197 f.

28. *A Backward Glance* (New York: D. Appleton-Century Company, 1934), 184–5.

29. 'The Avoidance of Love: A Reading of *King Lear*', in *Must We Mean What We Say: A Book of* Essays (New York: Scribner, 1969), 269.

30. See, for example, Barbara Hardy, 'The Lyricism of Emily Brontë,' in Anne Smith (ed.), *The Art of Emily Brontë* (London: Vision Press, 1976), 94–118.

31. The text for Dickinson's poems is *The Complete Poems of Emily Dickinson*, ed. Thomas H. Johnson (Boston: Little, Brown & Co., 1960). P stands for 'Poem'.

32. *The Discovery of the Mind*, trans. T. G. Rosenmeyer (Cambridge, Mass: Harvard Univ. Press, 1953), 57.

33. Dickinson, P 650.

34. In my edition of the poems, I followed Hatfield's transcription of the difficult-to-decipher fourth line of the poem: 'Through rain and [through the] wailing wind.' In my note, I present an alternative, but not very plausible, reading that better approximates what I saw in the MS: 'Through rain and weir and wailing wind.' Roper reads 'Through rain and hail and wailing wind' (*The Poems of Emily Brontë*, ed. Roper, 213–14). The new reading—'Through rain and air and wailing wind'—is the result of another look at the manuscript in the Berg Collection of the New York Public Library and seems to me the best. The difficult-to-decipher four-letter word that I originally read as 'weir' clearly (to my eye) ends in an 'r', not an 'l'. In 'The Death of A.G.A', composed in 1841 and 1844, the words 'air', 'winds', and 'rain' appear together to describe A.G.A., who is 'Left to the wild birds of the air | And mountain winds and rain!' (ll. 319–20) The letter that begins the word, a 'w' or an 'h', has not been cancelled. Perhaps the 'h' is a clue to the way Brontë voiced 'air' in this line, as it may be to her breathy pronunciation of 'watch', which she spells as 'whach'. Perhaps she had both 'air' and 'hail' in mind when she wrote the line. 'Hail' as weather doesn't appear anywhere else in her poems.

35. The text of this poem is based on Keats's manuscript and has been taken from *John Keats: The Complete Poems*, ed. John Barnard (London: Penguin Books, 1981). As Barnard points out in his note to the poem, the first published version of the poem alters line 1 to 'In a drear-nighted December', and line 21 to 'To know the change and feel it' (P. 587).

36. Bollas, *Being a Character*, 3.

37. Robin Grove, ' "It Would Not Do": Emily Brontë as Poet', in Smith, *The Art of Emily Brontë*, 63.

38. Emerson, 'The Poet', in *Essays First and Second Series: English Traits, Representative Men, Addresses* (New York: Hearst's International Library Company, 1914), 264.

39. Grossman, *Summa Lyrica*, 261–2.

40. Bollas, *Begin a Character*, 14–15.

41. Ibid. 14.

42. *Preface to Lyrical Ballads*, in *William Wordsworth*, ed. Stephen Gill (Oxford: Oxford Univ. Press, 1984, repr. 1989), 598.
43. I'm paraphrasing Charlotte Brontë's 'Editor's Preface to the New Edition of *Wuthering Heights*': 'on that mind time and experience alone could work: to the influence of other intellects, it was not amenable' (443).
44. Gaskell, *The Life of Charlotte Brontë*, 231.
45. *The Figure of Echo: A Mode of Allusion in Milton and After* (Berkeley: Univ. of California Press, 1981), ix.
46. *The Standard Edition of the Complete Psychological Works of Sigmund Freud*, xiv. 305–7.
47. See J. Stephen Russell, *The English Dream Vision: Anatomy of a Form* (Columbus: Ohio State Univ. Press, 1988), for an account of this form in the late medieval period.

2. FATHOMING REMEMBRANCE

1. The other occurrence of the phrase—'Where wilt thou go my harassed heart'—is in 'A little while, a little while.'
2. 'If, as Freud's description of the ego as a defensive structure suggests, we only pretend to forget, then what kind of remembering is psychoanalysis aiming to promote? And one answer would be: psychoanalysis is a cure by means of the kind of remembering that makes forgetting possible.' See Adam Phillips, 'Freud and the Uses of Forgetting', in *On Flirtation: Psychoanalytic Essays on the Uncommitted Life* (Cambridge, Mass.: Harvard Univ. Press, 1994), 23–5. Phillips's essay, which covers a lot of ground very quickly, has stimulated my thinking about remembering as a double-bind.
3. Quoted ibid., with the italics omitted, 26.
4. (London: John Murray, 1851), 47–8.
5. Pat Jalland, *Death in the Victorian Family* (Oxford: Oxford Univ. Press, 1996), 284, 336. Jalland assembles a rich body of evidence on bereavement and mourning from Victorian archives. The chapters titled 'Christian Consolations and Heavenly Reunions' and 'Chronic and Abnormal Grief: Queen Victoria, Lady Frederick Cavendish, and Emma Haden' support the distinction I am making here.
6. *On the Genealogy of Morals*, trans. Walter Kaufmann and R. J. Hollingdale (New York: Random House, 1989), 61.
7. Gaskell, *The Life of Charlotte Brontë*, 91.
8. Juliette Mitchell, unpublished talk, 'Memory and Psychoanalysis', delivered at Cornell University in the autumn of 1996.
9. For an account of the vogue of the annuals, see Anne Renier, *Friendship's Offering: An Essay on the Annuals and Gift Books of the Nineteenth Century* (London: Private Libraries Association, 1964).

10. Renier quotes Southey, ibid. 12–13. Frederic Shoberl, *Forget Me Not Verses* (London: [no publisher provided; printed for private circulation only], 1850), 4.

11. Jalland quotes Emma Darwin's insight that most men 'do not like remembering' (*Death in the Victorian Family*, 286–7).

12. *Revaluation: Tradition and Development in English Poetry* (London: Chatto & Windus, 1936), 6; 'Reality and Sincerity' (1952), repr. in *The Living Principle: 'English' as a Discipline of Thought* (London: Chatto & Windus, 1975), 125.

13. *The Lyric Impulse* (Cambridge, Mass.: Harvard Univ. Press, 1965), 21.

14. Wharton, *A Backward Glance*, 184–5.

15. *Fragmentation and Redemption: Essays on Gender and the Human Body in Medieval Religion* (New York: Zone Books, 1991), 187.

16. *The Hour of Our Death*, trans. Helen Weaver (Harmondsworth: Penguin Books, 1983), 445.

17. *The English Elegy: Studies in the Genre from Spenser to Yeats* (Baltimore: Johns Hopkins Univ. Press, 1985), 22–3.

18. Neele's poem was published under the title 'Stanzas' as the opening poem in the *Forget Me Not* annual for 1826. Frederic Shoberl criticizes it for 'inculcating downright materialism' in *Forget Me Not Verses*, 3–5. Neele was a barrister and poet who published articles, stories, poems, and essays in the annuals and committed suicide at the age of 31.

19. Sacks, *English Elegy*, 15.

20. *The Bonds of Love: Psychoanalysis, Feminism, and the Problem of Domination* (New York: Pantheon Books, 1988), 166.

21. Arthur Hallam, quoted by Christopher Ricks in a talk about Bob Dylan's endings given in Berkeley, California, on 22 May 1989, and subsequently published as 'Bob Dylan' in *The Threepenny Review*, 10/4 (winter 1990), 33.

22. 'Swinburne', in *A. E. Housman: Collected Poems and Selected Prose*, ed. Christopher Ricks (London: Penguin Books, 1988), 286–7.

23. Arthur Hallam, quoted by Ricks, *Allusion to the Poets*, 33.

24. 'The Poetry of Emily Brontë', in *Brontë Society Transactions* 13/2 (1965), 91.

25. Ricks, *Allusion to the Poets*, 34.

26. Quoted in Taylor, *Hardy's Metres*, 33.

27. *Poetry of Mourning: The Modern Elegy from Hardy to Heaney* (Chicago: Univ. of Chicago Press, 1994), 4. 'Sometimes punishing themselves, thereby avenging the dead and deflecting hostility inward, at other times modern elegists turn their rage outward, attacking and debasing the dead' (5).

28. *Byron and the Victorians* (Cambridge: Cambridge Univ. Press, 1995), 142–3. Support for this reading comes from an analysis of the character of

the poem's speaker (identified in the manuscript as R. Alcona) that relies less on her self-presentation in 'Remembrance' than on her appearances in two other poems, 'Rosina' and 'From a Dungeon Wall in the Southern College', in which a speaker identified as JB (Julius Brenzaida) addresses Rosina. On the basis of these two poems, Elfenbein concludes that 'Rosina is Gondal's Becky Sharp, a woman scheming for power.' A reading like Elfenbein's that represents a woman driven by ambition rather than disabled by her lover's death has some appeal for feminist readers seeking examples of powerful, self-sufficient, and even self-serving women. 'This poem rejects Emily's earlier revision of Byron by projecting a woman who gains her future because she can do what A.G.A. could not: imagine agency for herself apart from men.'

29. Phillips, *On Flirtation*, 27–8.
30. *The Letters of Charlotte Brontë*, 3 vols., ed. Margaret Smith (Oxford: Clarendon Press, 1995–2004), ii (1848–51), 186.
31. 'The Philosophy of Composition', in *Essays and Reviews* (New York: Literary Classics of the United States, Inc., 1984), 25.

3. OUTCOMES AND ENDINGS

1. Mary Visick, 'The Last of Gondal', in *Classics of Brontë Scholarship: The Best from One Hundred Years of Transactions of the Brontë Society*, ed. Charles Lemon (Haworth: The Brontë Society, 1999), 155–6.
2. 'Cold clear and blue the morning heaven' is conjecturally dated 12 July 1836 or earlier on the evidence of the date written above 'Will the day be bright or cloudy', which follows it in the manuscript. Many poems lack composition dates, and Derek Roper notes that we cannot be sure how much poetry Brontë had written before the first stipulated date. *Poems*, ed. Roper, 1.
3. *Collections from the Greek Anthology*, ed. Robert Bland et al., A New Edition by J. H. Merivale (London: Longman, Reese, Orme, Brown, Green, & Longman; and John Murray, 1833), 18, includes the following stanza in Sappho's Poem X:

> The silver moon is set;
> The Pleiades are gone;
> Half the long night is spent,—and yet,—
> I lie alone.

Lawrence I. Lipking also attributes this phrase to Sappho in *Abandoned Women and Poetic Tradition* (Chicago: Univ. of Chicago Press, 1988), 98. For an account of the reception and influence of Sappho in the nineteenth century, see Yopie Prins, *Victorian Sappho* (Princeton: Princeton Univ. Press, 1999).

4. Lipking, *Abandoned Women*, 98. Prins refers to the Sapphic model of a leap into 'an abyss of visual and verbal representation' (*Victorian Sappho*, 188).

5. The first theory is Tayler's in *Holy Ghosts*; the second is Barker's in *The Brontës*.

6. All quotations from Anne's poems have been taken from *The Poems of Anne Brontë: A New Text and Commentary*, ed. Edward Chitham (London: Macmillan Press Ltd., 1979).

7. Visick suggests that 'Why ask to know what date what clime' is a complete poem, but this is unlikely. Visick, 'Last of Gondal', 162.

8. Famine was being predicted as early as the previous year, and reports of distress were appearing in newspapers and magazines entering the Parsonage. An article in *Blackwood's* for May of 1846 argues that the regular reports of misery and distress in Ireland have been much exaggerated. 'Ireland—Its Condition—The Life and Property Bill—The Debate, and the Famine', *Blackwood's Edinburgh Magazine*, 367/59 (May 1846), 572–603. For Brontë's dependence on Scott, see *Poems*, ed. Roper, 271.

9. 'Wordsworth and the Poetry of Emily Brontë', *Brontë Society Transactions*, 16 /82 (1972), 85–6.

10. *The Complete Poems of Emily Jane Brontë*, ed. C. W. Hatfield (New York: Columbia Univ. Press, 1941); C. Day Lewis, 'The Poetry of Emily Brontë', *Brontë Society Transactions*, 13/2 (1965), 86.

11. Bland (ed.), *Greek Anthology*, 17.

12. *All the Works of Epictetus*, trans. Elizabeth Carter (London: S. Richardson, 1758), pp. xiii–xiv. It is likely that Brontë was familiar with Epictetus and with Carter's popular translation; Carter prefaces her translation with an ode by Hester Chapone, her friend and an opponent of Stoicism, that includes the phrase 'my coward Soul'. For Brontë's familiarity with Chapone, see the note to 'No coward soul is mine' in my edition of the poems, 279, and Chapter 7 below.

13. *Anatomy of Criticism: Four Essays* (Princeton: Princeton Univ. Press, 1957), 239.

14. 'The Notion of Expenditure', in *The Bataille Reader*, ed. Fred Botting and Scott Wilson (Oxford: Blackwell Publishers, 1997), 168.

15. *Contingencies*, 135.

16. Poem 1196: 'Capacity to Terminate | Is a Specific Grace—'.

17. I develop these arguments in Chapter 7.

18. *The Romantic Fragment Poem: A Critique of a Form* (Chapel Hill, NC: Univ. of North Carolina Press, 1986), 22–3 and 57–8. In this chapter, I make use of the substantial literature now available on fragments and Romantic fragments in particular. This literature includes, in addition to Levinson's study, Thomas McFarland's more widely ranging account of the Romantic ruin in *Romanticism and the Forms of Ruin: Wordsworth, Coleridge, and*

Modalities of Fragmentation (Princeton: Princeton Univ. Press, 1981); Balachandra Rajan's *The Form of the Unfinished: English Poetics from Spenser to Pound* (Princeton: Princeton Univ. Press, 1981); and the work of Anne Janowitz in 'The Romantic Fragment', in Duncan Wu (ed.), *A Companion to Romanticism* (Oxford: Blackwell, 1998), 442–51, and *England's Ruins: Poetic Purpose and the National Landscape* (Oxford: Basil Blackwell, 1990). In *The Unfinished Manner: Essays on the Fragment in the Later Eighteenth Century* (Charlottesville, Va.: Univ. of Virginia Press, 1994), Elizabeth Wanning Harries recovers the pre-Romantic life of the fragment.

19. Rajan, *Form of the Unfinished*, 7.
20. Lewis, 'Poetry of Emily Brontë', 92; Caroline F. E. Spurgeon, *Mysticism in English Literature* (Cambridge: Cambridge Univ. Press, 1913), 83.
21. 'The Lyricism of Emily Brontë', in Smith, *The Art of Emily Brontë*, 98–100.
22. Homans, *Women Writers*, 116–17. In 'The Night-Wind', one of the poems transcribed into Brontë's collection of non-Gondal poems, the inspiring breeze is called the Wanderer. While Homans suggests that the poet speaks these lines, Tayler attributes them to A. G. Rochelle. I find no evidence in the poem to support this reading.
23. Homans, who charges Julian with being self-serving and self-righteous, makes a strong case for seeing him as A. G. Rochelle's oppressor (*Women Writers*, 117–19).

4. FRAGMENTS

1. See Janowitz, 'The Romantic Fragment', 442, where the Romantic fragment poem is said to be 'either a remnant of something once complete and now broken or decayed, or the beginning of something that remains unaccomplished'.
2. Zachary Leader, *Revision and Romantic Authorship* (Oxford: Clarendon Press, 1996), 78; Leader associates the idea of poetry as process and expression with Clare as well as Byron, 218.
3. Helen Vendler, quoting Stevens in *Wallace Stevens: Words Chosen out of Desire* (Knoxville, Univ. of Tennessee Press, 1984), 38.
4. I have taken these terms from Harries, Levinson, and Rajan respectively.
5. *The Literary Absolute: The Theory of Literature in German Romanticism*, trans. Philip Barnard and Cheryl Lester (New York: State Univ. of New York, 1988), 41.
6. Novalis, quoted ibid. 49.
7. Levinson, *Romantic Fragment Poem*, 14.
8. Brontë's critics and anthologizers have represented her primarily by poems published in 1846 and 1850, although Christopher Ricks anthologizes

fragmentary poems in both *Victorian Verse* and *English Verse*. Barbara Hardy, who comments grudgingly on the number of 'lyrical fragments filched from bad verse', is not concerned with discrete fragments. Smith, in *The Art of Emily Brontë*, 96–7.

9. Ludwig Wittgenstein, *Culture and Value*, trans. Peter Winch and ed. G. H. Von Wright with Heikki Nyman (Oxford: Basil Blackwell, 1980, repr. 1984), 65ᵉ–66ᵉ. Wittgenstein quotes from Schiller's letter to Goethe, 17 Dec. 1795.

10. The formulation is Wordsworth's in *The Prelude* (1805), Book II, ll. 403–5.

11. See the section of the introduction to my edition of the poems headed 'Poems and Poetical Fragments' (pp. xxi–xxiii) for a fuller discussion of the editorial disagreements about where poems begin and end.

12. See *A Defense of Poetry, or, Remarks Suggested by an Essay Entitled 'The Four Ages of Poetry'*, in *Shelley's Poetry and Prose*, ed. Donald H. Reiman and Neil Fraistat (New York: W. W. Norton & Co., 2002), 509–35.

13. See *Poems*, 66–77, and notes to those pages.

14. See Derek Attridge, *Poetic Rhythm: An Introduction* (Cambridge: Cambridge Univ. Press, 1995), 148.

15. *Eros the Bittersweet* (Normal, Ill.: Dalkey Archive Press, 1998), 48–9.

16. 'The Name and Nature of Poetry', in Housman, *Collected Poems and Selected Prose*, 352–3.

17. *The Lyric Impulse*, 25, 94.

18. Wordsworth, in the headnote to the 'Intimations Ode', Fenwick notes.

19. Emerson, *Essays*, 354.

20. Andrew Welsh identifies riddles as one of the roots of lyric poetry in *Roots of Lyric: Primitive Poetry and Modern Poetics* (Princeton: Princeton Univ. Press, 1978), 27.

21. See Miles, in Smith, *The Art of Emily Brontë*, 69–70.

22. The opposite point of view has so far been more common among Brontë scholars. Rosalind Miles is one of those who believes that some of Brontë's poems would be improved by the recovery of a Gondal context for them. 'It is highly possible that some of the poems now rather loftily dismissed as weak and pretentious would gain in strength if we knew, as Emily Brontë did, the supportive context in which they were conceived and written.' In Smith, *The Art of Emily Brontë*, 72.

23. Barbara Herrnstein Smith, *Poetic Closure: A Study of How Poems End* (Chicago: Univ. of Chicago Press, 1968), 178.

24. Janowitz refers to 'incompletion' and 'inexpressibility' in 'The Romantic Fragment', 444 and 448; Leslie Brisman, who is writing about 'Kubla Khan', refers to 'interruption' and is quoted in Harries, *Unfinished Manner*, 160.

25. Miles, in Smith, *The Art of Emily Brontë*, 87.

26. Chitham, *Birth of Wuthering Heights*, 110.
27. Brontë's language here echoes that of Carlyle, who is the chief interpreter of German Romantic writers for English readers. In an essay on Schiller in *Fraser's Magazine* (1831), Carlyle describes Schiller as 'a genuine interpreter of the Invisible'. 'Every Poet, be his outward lot what it may, finds himself born in the midst of Prose; he has to struggle from the littleness and obstruction of an Actual world, into the freedom and infinitude of an Ideal . . . .' (271). In one of Carlyle's quotations from the *Life of Schiller* (London, 1824), poetry is said to be the 'radiant guiding-star of [Schiller's] turbid and obscure existence' (282). Compare Brontë's reference in the opening lines of 'Julian M. and A. G. Rochelle' to Julian's little lamp: 'I trim it well to be the Wanderer's guiding-star' (l. 8). In an essay on Novalis published in the *Foreign Review* (1829), Carlyle describes Novalis as 'in good part a Mystic' (104) and 'the most ideal of all Idealists' (111): 'His poems are the devout breathings of a high devout soul, feeling always that here he has no home, but looking, as in clear vision, to a "city that hath foundations." He loves external Nature with a singular depth; nay, we might say, he reverences her: for Nature is no longer dead, hostile Matter, but the veil and mysterious Garment of the Unseen; as it were, the Voice with which the Deity proclaims himself to man' (112). Brontë might easily have read Carlyle's essays, which were collected in *Critical and Miscellaneous Essays*, 4 vols. (Boston: James Munroe & Co., 1938). The essays on Novalis and Schiller are published in vol. ii.
28. 'Novalis', in *Foreign Review* (1829), collected in *Critical and Miscellaneous Essays*, ii. 82–142. See n. 27.
29. *Letters*, i (1829–47), 182.
30. Hardy, in Smith, *The Art of Emily Brontë*, 101.
31. Juliet Barker, *The Brontës: Selected Poems* (London: Dent, 1985), 121–2.
32. Levinson, *Romantic Fragment Poem*, 57.
33. C. W. Hatfield and Derek Roper agree on this.
34. Cf. Robert Graves's 'The Foreboding'.
35. Letter to Bailey, 27 Feb. 1818, in *Letters*, ed. Rollins, i. 238.
36. *Poetic Closure*, 36.

5. THE FIRST LAST THING

1. (London: Longman, Rees, Orme, Brown, Green, & Longman, 1835, repr. 1840), 318; 1050. Patrick Brontë owned a copy of *Human Physiology* (Charlotte Brontë, *Letters*, ii. 151 n. 1).
2. Quoted in Geoffrey Rowell, *Hell and the Victorians* (Oxford: Clarendon Press, 1974), 127 and 62. 'Maurice has been mentioned as an influence on Emily: more than a hundred years ago, the poet A. Mary F. Robinson's biography of Emily Brontë claimed that she had "[called] herself a disciple

of the tolerant and thoughtful Frederick Maurice". No available documentation supports this statement, though' (Thormählen, *The Brontës and Religion*, 48–9).

3. In 'Emily Brontë and the Enthusiastic Tradition', Emma Mason assumes too much when she writes that 'No coward soul is mine' rejects the ' "thousand creeds" of orthodox Anglican religion as "withered weeds." ' Mason's useful account of Methodist and eighteenth-century poetic discourses on enthusiasm as sources for Brontë's poetry substantiates my view that Brontë was well informed about the religious controversies of her time. My representation of Brontë as a nontheological mystic and an unusually intelligent one, however, differs sharply from her effort to make Brontë's 'religious values' and 'theological principles' accord with those of Methodism. See 'Emily Brontë and the Enthusiastic Tradition', *Romanticism on the Net*, 25 (February 2002): 19 pars. http://users.ox.ac.uk/-scat0385/25mason.html.

4. See Thormählen, *The Brontës and Religion*, 100–15, for a discussion of heaven and hell in *Wuthering Heights*. Although Thormählen acknowledges that Catherine and Heathcliff seem 'destined for a heaven of their own making, with each other and without God—the latter circumstance making it a state that any Christian would regard as hellish' (107–8), she finds other reasons for declaring that the plot line of *Wuthering Heights*, like that of the other Brontë novels, 'confirm[s] fundamental Christian tenets' (6). Unlike Thormählen, I find no evidence that the poems and *Wuthering Heights* are imbued with the 'idea of a loving and merciful God' or that Emily Brontë is much interested in 'the interplay between human struggle and Divine grace' (115).

5. Barker, *The Brontës*, 102.

6. BL Additional MS 70949, published in *Letters*, ii. 150–1.

7. Quoted in Rowell, *Hell and the Victorians*, 94.

8. See *Some Versions of Pastoral* (New York: New Directions, 1974), 86.

9. Patricia Parker disrupts while confirming this binarism when she describes the two couples as 'two possibilities within the model of the line,' the second of which 'only approximately repeats the first' and is always shadowed by it. 'The (Self-) Identity of the Literary Text: Property, Propriety, Proper Place, and Proper Name in *Wuthering Heights*', in Mario J. Valdès and Owen Miller (eds.), *Identity of the Literary Text* (Toronto: Univ. of Toronto Press, 1985), 111–12.

10. *Myths of Power: A Marxist Study of the Brontës* (London: Macmillan, 1975), 109.

11. 'Mourning and Melancholia', in *A General Selection from the Works of Sigmund Freud*, ed. John Rickman (New York: Doubleday & Co., 1957), 131. The Poe lines are taken from 'The Raven'.

12. *Tractatus logico-philosophicus*, trans. D. F. Pears and B. McGuinness (New York: Humanities Press, 1961), 147: 6.4311.

13. 'Thoughts for the Times on War and Death' (1915) in *Collected Papers* (1925), iv. 304–5.

14. *Ghosts in the Middle Ages: The Living and the Dead in Medieval Society*, trans. Teresa Lavender Fagan (Chicago: Univ. of Chicago Press, 1998), 82–3; 142–7.

15. *The Disappearance of God: Five Nineteenth-Century Writers* (Cambridge, Mass.: Harvard Univ. Press, 1982), 173–4.

16. See Regina Barreca's 'The Power of Excommunication: Sex and the Feminine Text in *Wuthering Heights*', in Barreca, *Sex and Death in Victorian Literature* (Bloomington: Indiana Univ. Press, 1990), 227–40, for a different point of view: 'the male characters in contrast can barely articulate their simplest thoughts' and 'Heathcliff appears entirely separated from language, having, as Stevie Davies notes, "no mother country and no mother tongue"' (231). Margaret Homans's concern with language in *Bearing the Word: Language and Female Experience in Nineteenth-Century Women's Writing* (Chicago: Univ. of Chicago Press, 1986) focuses elsewhere, specifically on the double plot as embodying two different relations of women to language.

17. *Letters*, ii. 200.

18. *The Task*, vi. 11.

19. *An Essay Concerning Human Understanding*, ed. Peter H. Nidditch (Oxford: Clarendon Press, 1975, repr. 1979), II. x.152–3.

20. Ibid., II. xxvii. 335.

21. Ibid. 342–3.

22. Barker, *Selected Poems*, 251.

23. *Poems*, ed. Roper, 267.

24. Quoted in Bataille, *The Accursed Share*, vol. iii, *Sovereignty* (New York: Zone Books, 1991), 209.

25. Ibid. 219.

26. The portion of *Elizabeth Costello* from which I have taken this passage appeared previously in *The Lives of Animals* and is subtitled 'The Philosophers and the Animals' (New York: Viking Press, 2003), 77–8.

27. Lonoff, *Belgian Essays*, 221–2.

28. Ibid. 187.

29. Ibid. 178.

30. The phrase is Rowell's, *Hell and the Victorians*, 10.

31. This is Bataille's phrase, from *Guilty*, 93: 'I can't justify this principle: *irreducible anguish*. In such cases, we refuse to recognize *the unjustified*, however inevitable it may be.'

32. Georges Bataille, *The Accursed Share*, vol. ii, *The History of Eroticism*, 85–6. I have silently corrected an obvious typographical error in the translation ('almot' for 'almost').

6. POSTHUMOUS BRONTË

1. 'Haworth Churchyard', quoted in Miriam Allott (ed.), *The Brontës: The Critical Heritage* (London: Routledge & Kegan Paul, 1974), 306–10. Arnold's poem was first published in *Fraser's Magazine* in 1855. We can trace the line of descent from Arnold's 'too-bold dying song' to Hughes's 'Her death is a baby-cry on the moor'.
2. Letter to W. S. Williams, 22 Nov. 1848, in *Letters*, ii. 142.
3. Quoted in Allott, *Critical Heritage*, 304.
4. 'Biographical Notice of Ellis and Acton Bell',reprinted in the Clarendon edition of *Wuthering Heights*, 440.
5. Ibid. 437 and 438.
6. Ibid. 438. 'That writer who could attempt to palm off an inferior and immature production under cover of one successful effort, must indeed be unduly eager after the secondary and sordid result of authorship, and pitiably indifferent to its true and honourable meed.' Charlotte Brontë's actual 'earlier and ruder attempt' was *The Professor*, which no publisher could be induced to bring out until after her death, despite her continuing efforts.
7. Peter Bayne, in *Two Great Englishwomen: Mrs Browning and Charlotte Brontë* (1881), quoted in Allott, *Critical Heritage*, 427–8.
8. 'Editor's Preface', reprinted in the Clarendon edition of *Wuthering Heights*, 443. When I presented a shortened version of this chapter as a talk for the American Brontë Society meeting in New York, Sue Lonoff suggested that 'sibling rivalry' also affected Charlotte's response to *Wuthering Heights*. I agree (see below).
9. In addition to adding lines of her own to the poem she titled 'The Visionary' and to 'Aye there it is! It wakes tonight', which are discussed in this chapter, Charlotte Brontë composed stanzas for 'The Two Children' and 'The Elder's Rebuke'. She also omitted several stanzas from the poems that were the basis for 'The Elder's Rebuke' and 'The Bluebell'.
10. Quoted in Allott, *Critical Heritage*, 442. Swinburne was reviewing Mary Robinson's *Emily Brontë* in the *Athenaeum* (16 June 1883). In her headnote to this entry, Allott quotes from Swinburne's defence of Emily Brontë in a letter to T. W. Reid (24 Sept. 1877): 'Seeing that Emily Brontë was a tragic poet ... I cannot think that anything in her book is at all excessive or unjustifiable ...' (Allott, *Critical Heritage*, 438).

11. 'Editor's Preface', 442.
12. Quoted in Allott, *Critical Heritage*, 295.
13. In my edition of the poems, I have assigned the composition of this poem to 2 Jan. 1846, after Charlotte's discovery of the *Gondal Poems* notebook in the autumn of 1845. According to Roper, 'Barker reads "Jan 25" or possibly "Jan 23", following the 1934 facsimile (p. 928 n. 18). But "2d" is clear in the Brontë Parsonage Museum Library photographs and in Davidson Cook's 1926 transcript.' *Poems*, ed. Roper, 271. Charlotte Brontë sent the poems for publication to Aylott & Jones on 6 Feb. 1846. *Letters*, i. 451.
14. *Biographia Literaria*, ed. J. Shawcross, 2 vols. (Oxford: Oxford University Press, 1907), i, ch. 13, 202. Brontë would have known this passage.
15. Chitham suggests that the poem's composition precedes the novel's by some weeks. *Birth of Wuthering Heights*, 124.
16. Charlotte Brontë, *Jane Eyre*, ed. Jane Jack and Margaret Smith (Oxford: Clarendon Press, 1969), II. ix. 346.
17. Carter prints Chapone's ode, together with the dedication to her, at the beginning of *All the Works of Epictetus*. Margaret Maison was the first to point this out in 'Emily Brontë and Epictetus', *Notes and Queries*, NS 25 (June 1978), 230–1. Maison also notes that Ellen Nussey received a copy of Chapone's *Letters on the Improvement of the Mind* (1773) as a prize while she was a pupil at Roe Head.
18. 'Aye there it is! It wakes tonight' once capitalizes the *t* in a pronoun referring to a human spirit. It is difficult to decide whether this capitalization indicates intentional emphasis. Roper notes that Brontë sometimes uses capital letters because they are easier to form without making a blot (*Poems*, ed. Roper, 22).
19. See my edition of the poems, 265.
20. 'Biographical Notice', 440.
21. *Letters*, i. 290.
22. 'Biographical Notice', 440.
23. See Ch. 3 for a discussion of this poem.
24. See Ch. 1.
25. I made some of these points first in 'Brave New Digital World', in *Essays in Criticism*, 59/4 (Oct. 1999), 292.
26. I owe the idea that Brontë is writing dipodic verse to Charles Hartman, whose scansion of them revealed the diagnostic signs. I have borrowed the phrase 'dipodic lilt' from Dennis Taylor, whose discussion of Hardy's verse in relation to the Victorian theory of dipody has been helpful to me.
27. Charles Hartman's account of this.
28. Wise and Symington, *The Brontës*, ii. 275.
29. Christopher Ricks corrects this editorial error by citing Emily Jane Brontë and Charlotte Brontë as the authors of 'The Visionary' in *The New Oxford Book of Victorian Verse* (Oxford: Oxford University Press, 1987).

30. ' "Often Rebuked…" ': Emily's after All?', *Brontë Society Transactions*, 18/93 (1983), 222, 224.
31. *The Poems of Charlotte Brontë: A New Text and Commentary* (New York: Garland Press, 1985), 374.
32. *Complete Poems*, ed. Hatfield, 255.
33. Roper comments as follows: 'In view of CB's revisions and expansions of EB's poems in 1850, there is nothing improbable about her producing a complete poem in her sister's behalf to set her in a desired light… Stylistically, as Gezari points out, the iambic pentameter is uncharacteristic of EB; so is the wealth of feminine rhymes … and the jingle of "more glory and more grief". But there is no firm evidence either way, and some reasons for accepting the poem as authentic are set out by Chitham …' (*Poems*, ed. Roper, 277).
34. See *Letters*, ii. 466, 473, and 479.
35. 'Biographical Notice', 438.
36. Ibid. 439.
37. Quoted in Barker, *The Brontës*, 255–6.
38. Both statements are quoted ibid. 237 and 263. The first is from the Roe Head Journal; the second is from Brontë's reply to Southey's letter containing the famous rebuke: 'Literature cannot be the business of a woman's life, and it ought not to be.' See ibid. 262–3.
39. Cf. Peter Bayne's description of Emily Brontë's poetry in 1857 as 'characterized by strength and freshness, and by that original cadence, that power of melody, which, be it wild, or tender, or even harsh, was never heard before, and comes at first hand from nature, as her sign of the born poet'. Quoted in Allott, *Critical Heritage*, 325.
40. *Shirley*, ed. Herbert Rosengarten and Margaret Smith (Oxford: Clarendon Press, 1979), ii vi. 353 and iii ii. 505.
41. *Charlotte Brontë: Style in the Novel* (Madison: Univ. of Wisconsin, 1973), 66. See also Peters's chapter on syntactic inversion.
42. She uses the word to describe Emily, *Letters*, ii. 168.
43. Ibid. 241.
44. Ibid. 260.
45. Ibid. 193.
46. The phrase is Terry Castle's in *Boss Ladies, Watch Out!* (New York: Routledge, 2002). Her idea of the 'primitive adhesiveness—and the underlying eros—of the sister-sister bond' revises James Edward Austen-Leigh's description of Cassandra's and Jane's relation: 'Their sisterly affection for each other could scarcely be exceeded' (126–8).
47. *Letters*, ii. 272.
48. Ibid. 272.
49. Ibid., 23 November 1848, ii. 145.
50. Ibid., 2 November 1848, ii. 132–3.

51. *Letters*, 21 December 1848, ii. 156.
52. Ibid., ?17 November 1849, ii. 286; 12 June 1850, ii. 414.
53. According to Deirdre Le Faye, the editor of the Oxford edition of Jane Austen's letters, Cassandra Austen's censorship of them often had to do with omitting references to her physical ailments. See Castle, *Boss Ladies*, 126.
54. Carter, *All the Works of Epictetus*, 257.
55. British Library Additional MS 70949. 9 Dec. 1848, published in *Letters*, ii. 150–1.
56. *Letters*, ii. 168 and 201.
57. Ibid. 216 and 200.
58. Quoted in Barker, *The Brontës*, 455–6.
59. I have taken the phrase 'yoked with death' from the review by Sydney Dobell, quoted in Allott, *Critical Heritage*, 279.
60. *Letters*, ii. 225.
61. Emerson, *Essays*, 256.
62. Ibid. 240.
63. Ibid. 241.
64. Ibid. 265.
65. *Letters*, ii. 168.
66. *Shirley*, iii. xi. 437.
67. In his edition of the poems, Derek Roper does not represent stanza breaks, but the MS (and Brontë's usual practice) provide support for them. I follow Roper in not enclosing the word 'Dull' in brackets, although I include the brackets in my edition of the poems to indicate that my reading of the holograph is uncertain.

Bibliography

ABERCROMBIE, JOHN, *Inquiries Concerning the Intellectual Powers and the Investigation of Truth* (Edinburgh: Waugh & Innes, 1830).

ALLOTT, MIRIAM, *The Brontës: The Critical Heritage* (London: Routledge & Kegan Paul, 1974).

ARIÈS, PHILIPPE, *The Hour of our Death*, trans. Helen Weaver (Harmondsworth: Penguin Books, 1983).

ARMSTRONG, ISOBEL, *Victorian Poetry: Poetry, Poetics, and Politics* (London: Routledge, 1993).

_____ and BLAIN, VIRGINIA (eds.), *Women's Poetry, Late Romantic to Victorian* (Basingstoke: Macmillan, 1999).

ATTRIDGE, DEREK, *Poetic Rhythm: An Introduction* (Cambridge: Cambridge Univ. Press, 1995).

BAILIN, MIRIAM, *The Sickroom in Victorian Fiction: The Art of Being Ill* (Cambridge: Cambridge Univ. Press, 1994).

BARKER, JULIET, *The Brontës: Selected Poems* (London: Dent, 1985).

_____ *The Brontës* (London: Phoenix, 1994).

BARRECA, REGINA, *Sex and Death in Victorian Literature* (Bloomington: Indiana Univ. Press, 1990).

BATAILLE, GEORGES, *Guilty*, trans. Bruce Boone (San Francisco: The Lapis Press, 1988).

_____ *Inner Experience*, trans. Leslie Anne Boldt (Albany: State Univ. of New York Press, 1988).

_____ *The Accursed Share: An Essay on General Economy*, trans. Robert Hurley, 3 vols. (New York: Zone Books, 1991).

_____ *The Bataille Reader*, ed. Fred Botting and Scott Wilson (Oxford: Basil Blackwell, 1997).

_____ *Literature and Evil*, trans. Alistair Hamilton (London: Marion Boyars, 2001).

BELL, RUDOLPH M., *Holy Anorexia* (Chicago: Univ. of Chicago Press, 1985).

BENJAMIN, JESSICA, *The Bonds of Love: Psychoanalysis, Feminism, and the Problem of Domination* (New York: Pantheon Books, 1988).

BERMAN, JEFFREY, *Narcissism and the Novel* (New York: New York Univ. Press, 1990).

BLAIN, VIRGINIA, *Victorian Women Poets: A New Annotated Anthology* (Harlow: Pearson Education Limited, 2001).

BLAND, ROBERT et al. (eds.), *Collections from the Greek Anthology*, A New Edition by J. H. Merivale (London: Longman, Reese, Orme, Brown, Green, and Longman; and John Murray, 1833).

BLOCH, MAURICE, and PARRY, JONATHAN (eds.), *Death and the Regeneration of Life* (Cambridge: Cambridge Univ. Press, 1982).

BOLLAS, CHRISTOPHER, *Being a Character: Psychoanalysis and Self-Experience* (London: Routledge, 1997).

BOWLBY, JOHN, *Attachment and Loss*, 3 vols. (New York: Basic Books, 1980).

BOYM, SVETLANA, *Death in Quotation Marks: Cultural Myths of the Modern Poet* (Cambridge, Mass.: Harvard Univ. Press, 1993).

BRONFEN, ELISABETH, *Over Her Dead Body* (Manchester: Manchester Univ. Press, 1992).

_____ and GOODWIN, SARAH WEBSTER, *Death and Representation* (Baltimore: Johns Hopkins Univ. Press, 1993).

BRONTË, ANNE, *The Poems of Anne Brontë*, ed. Edward Chitham (London: Macmillan Press, 1979).

BRONTË, CHARLOTTE, *Jane Eyre*, ed. Jane Jack and Margaret Smith (Oxford: Clarendon Press, 1969).

_____ *Shirley*, ed. Herbert Rosengarten and Margaret Smith (Oxford: Clarendon Press, 1979).

_____ *The Poems of Charlotte Brontë: A New Text and Commentary*, ed. Victor A. Neufeldt (New York: Garland Press, 1985).

_____ *An Edition of the Early Writings of Charlotte Brontë*, 3 vols., ed. Christine Alexander (London: Basil Blackwell, 1991).

_____ *The Letters of Charlotte Brontë*, 3 vols., ed. Margaret Smith (Oxford: Clarendon Press, 1995–2004).

_____ British Library, Additional MS 70949.

BRONTË, EMILY JANE, *The Complete Poems of Emily Jane Brontë*, ed. C. W. Hatfield (New York: Columbia Univ. Press, 1941).

_____ *Wuthering Heights*, ed. Hilda Marsden and Ian Jack (Oxford: Clarendon Press, 1976).

_____ *Emily Jane Brontë: The Complete Poems*, ed. Janet Gezari (London: Penguin Books, 1992).

_____ *The Poems of Emily Brontë*, ed. Derek Roper with Edward Chitham (Oxford: Clarendon Press, 1995).

BRUMBERG, JOAN JACOBS, *Fasting Girls: The Emergence of Anorexia Nervosa as a Modern Disease* (Cambridge, Mass.: Harvard Univ. Press, 1988).

BYNUM, CAROLINE WALKER, *Holy Feast and Holy Fast: The Religious Significance of Food to Medieval Women* (Berkeley: Univ. of California Press, 1987).

_____ *Fragmentation and Redemption: Essays on Gender and the Human Body in Medieval Religion* (New York: Zone Books, 1991).

CAMERON, SHARON, *Lyric Time: Dickinson and the Limits of Genre* (Baltimore: Johns Hopkins Univ. Press, 1981).

CARLYLE, THOMAS WELSH, *Critical and Miscellaneous Essays*, 4 vols. (Boston: James Munroe & Co., 1938).

CARSON, ANNE, *Eros the Bittersweet* (Normal Ill: Dalkey Archive Press, 1988).

_____ *Glass, Irony and God* (New York: New Directions, 1995).

CARTER, ELIZABETH (trans.), *All the Works of Epictetus* (London: S. Richardson, 1758).

CASTLE, TERRY, *Boss Ladies, Watch Out!* (New York: Routledge, 2002).

CAVANAGH, CLARE, 'Poetry and Ideology: The Example of Wislawa Szymborska', *Literary Imagination*, 1/2 (fall 1999), 174–90.

CAVELL, STANLEY, *Must We Mean What We Say: A Book of Essays* (New York: Scribner, 1969).

CHITHAM, EDWARD, ' "Often Rebuked ... ": Emily's after All?' *Brontë Society Transactions*, 18/93 (1983), 222–6.

_____ *The Birth of Wuthering Heights* (London: Macmillan, 1998).

_____ and WINNIFRITH, TOM, *Brontë Facts and Brontë Problems* (London: Macmillan, 1983).

_____ _____ (eds.), *Selected Brontë Poems* (Oxford: Basil Blackwell, 1985).

CHODOROW, NANCY J., *Feminism and Psychoanalytic Theory* (New Haven: Yale Univ. Press, 1989).

COETZEE, J. M., *Elizabeth Costello* (New York: Viking Press, 2003).

DAVIE, DONALD, *Thomas Hardy and British Poetry* (New York: Oxford Univ. Press, 1972).

DAVIES, STEVIE, *Emily Brontë: The Artist as a Free Woman* (Manchester: Carcanet, 1983).

_____ *Emily Brontë: Heretic* (London: The Women's Press, 1994).

DICKINSON, EMILY, *The Poems of Emily Dickinson: Variorium Edition*, ed. R. W. Franklin, 3 vols. (Cambridge, Mass.: Harvard Univ. Press, 1998).

EAGLETON, TERRY, *Myths of Power: A Marxist Study of the Brontës* (London: Macmillan, 1975).

ELFENBEIN, ANDREW, *Byron and the Victorians* (Cambridge: Cambridge Univ. Press, 1965).

ELLIOTSON, JOHN, *Human Physiology* (London: Longman, Rees, Orme, Brown, Green, and Longman, 1835, repr. 1840).

EMERSON, RALPH WALDO, *Essays First and Second Series: English Traits, Representative Men, Addresses* (New York: Hearst's International Library Co., 1914).

EMPSON, WILLIAM, *Some Versions of Pastoral* (New York: New Directions, 1974).

Forget Me Not, A Christmas and New Year's Present for 1823 (no place of publication, publisher, or date).

Forget Me Not, A Christmas and New Year's Present for 1825 (London: R. Ackerman, 1825). Subsequent editions for the years 1826–9.

Forget Me Not: A Christmas, New Year's, and Birth-Day Present for 1830 (London: R. Ackerman, 1830). Subsequent editions for the years 1831–46.

FRADENBURG, LOUISE O., ' "Voice Memorial": Loss and Reparation in Chaucer's Poetry', *Exemplaria* 2/1 (1990), 169–202.

FREUD, SIGMUND, *The Question of Lay Analysis*, trans. James Strachey (New York: W. W. Norton & Co., 1950, repr. 1964).

——— 'Mourning and Melancholia', in *A General Selection from the Works of Sigmund Freud*, ed. John Rickman (New York: Doubleday & Co., 1957).

——— *The Standard Edition of the Complete Psychological Works of Sigmund Freud*, trans. and ed. James Strachey, xiv (1914–916) (London: The Hogarth Press, 1957, repr. 1981).

——— 'Thoughts for the Times on War and Death' (1915), in *Collected Papers*, trans. Joan Riviere, vol. iv (New York: Basic Books, 1959).

——— *Letters of Sigmund Freud*, ed. E. L. Freud. (New York: Basic Books, 1960).

——— 'On Narcissism: An Introduction', in *General Psychological Theory: Papers on Metapsychology*, ed. Philip Rieff (Baltimore: Johns Hopkins Univ. Press, 1983), 1–24.

FRIEDMAN, ALAN WARREN, *Fictional Death and the Modernist Enterprise* (Cambridge: Cambridge Univ. Press, 1995).

Friendship's Offering: A Literary Album, ed. Thomas K. Hervey (London: Lupton Relfe, 1826).

Friendship's Offering: A Literary Album and Christmas and New Year's Present for 1825 (London: R. Ackerman, 1825). Subsequent editions for the years 1829–31.

FRYE, NORTHROP, *Anatomy of Criticism: Four Essays* (Princeton: Princeton Univ. Press, 1957).

GALLANT, CHRISTINE, 'The Archetypal Feminine in Emily Bronte's Poetry', *Women's Studies*, 7 (1980), 79–94.

GASKELL, E. C., *The Life of Charlotte Brontë*, ed. Alan Shelston (London: Penguin, 1985).

GEZARI, JANET, 'Brave New Digital World', *Essays in Criticism*, 59/4 (Oct. 1999), 285–99.

GILLIGAN, CAROL, 'Remapping the Moral Domain: New Images of Self in Relationship', in *Restructuring Individualism: Autonomy, Individuality, and the Self in Western Thought*, ed. Thomas C. Heller, Morton Sosna, and David E. Wellbury (Stanford: Stanford Univ. Press, 1986), 237–52.

GREENBERG, JAY R., and MITCHELL, STEPHEN A., *Object Relations in Psychoanalytic Theory* (Cambridge, Mass.: Harvard Univ. Press, 1983).

GROSSMAN, ALAN, *Summa Lyrica: A Primer of the Commonplaces in Speculative Poetics*, in Alan Grossman with Mark Halliday, *The Sighted Singer: Two Works on Poetry for Readers and Writers* (Baltimore: Johns Hopkins Univ. Press, 1992).

HARDY, BARBARA, *The Advantage of Lyric: Essays on Feeling in Poetry* (London: Univ. of London Press, 1977).

HARRIES, ELIZABETH WANNING, *The Unfinished Manner: Essays on the Fragment in the Later Eighteenth Century* (Charlottesville, Va.: Univ. of Virginia Press, 1994).

HEWISH, JOHN, *Emily Brontë: A Critical and Biographical Study* (London: Macmillan, 1969).

HICKOK, KATHLEEN, *Representations of Women: Nineteenth-Century British Women's Poetry* (Westport, Conn.: Greenwood Press, 1984).

HOLLANDER, JOHN, *The Figure of Echo: A Mode of Allusion in Milton and After* (Berkeley: Univ. of California Press, 1981).

HOMANS, MARGARET, *Women Writers and Poetic Identity: Dorothy Wordsworth, Emily Brontë, and Emily Dickinson* (Princeton: Princeton Univ. Press, 1980).

_____ ' "Syllables of Velvet": Dickinson, Rossetti, and the Rhetorics of Sexuality', *Feminist Studies*, 11/3 (1985), 569–93.

_____ *Bearing the Word: Language and Female Experience in Nineteenth-Century Women's Writing* (Chicago: Univ. of Chicago Press, 1986).

HOŠEK, CHAVIVA, and PARKER, PATRICIA (eds.), *Lyric Poetry beyond New Criticism* (Ithaca, NY: Cornell Univ. Press, 1985).

HOUSMAN, A. E., *Collected Poems and Selected Prose*, ed. Christopher Ricks (London: Penguin, 1988).

HOWE, SUSAN, *My Emily Dickinson* (Berkeley: North Atlantic Books, 1985).

HUGHES, TED, *Birthday Letters* (New York: Farrar, Straus & Giroux, 1998).

_____ *Selected Poems 1957–1994* (New York: Farrar, Straus & Giroux, 1995, repr. 2002).

HUMPHREY, S. C., and KING, HELEN (eds.), *Mortality and Immortality: The Anthropology and Archaeology of Death* (London: Academic Press, 1981).

'Ireland—Its Condition—The Life and Property Bill—The Debate, and the Famine', *Blackwood's Edinburgh Magazine*, 367/59 (May 1846), 572–603.

JALLAND, PAT, *Death in the Victorian Family* (Oxford: Oxford Univ. Press, 1996).

JANOWITZ, ANNE, *England's Ruins: Poetic Purpose and the National Landscape* (Oxford: Basil Blackwell, 1990).

_____ 'The Romantic Fragment', in Duncan Wu (ed.), *A Companion to Romanticism* (Oxford: Basil Blackwell, 1998).

JEFFREYS, MARK, 'Ideologies of Lyric: A Problem of Genre in Contemporary Anglophone Poetics', *PMLA* 110/2 (1995), 196–205.

KAVALER-ADLER, SUSAN, *The Compulsion to Create: A Psychoanalytic Study of Women Artists* (New York: Routledge, 1993).

KAY, DENNIS, *Melodious Tears: The English Funeral Elegy from Spenser to Milton* (Oxford: Oxford Univ. Press, 1990).

KEATS, JOHN, *The Letters of John Keats*, ed. Hyder Rollins, 2 vols. (Cambridge: Mass.: Harvard Univ. Press, 1958).

_____ *The Complete Poems*, ed. John Barnard (London: Penguin Books, 1981).

LACOUE-LABARTHE, PHILIPPE, and NANCY, JEAN-LUC, *The Literary Absolute: The Theory of Literature in German Romanticism*, trans. Philip Barnard and Cheryl Lister (New York: State Univ. of New York, 1988).

LEADER, ZACHARY, *Revision and Romantic Authorship* (Oxford: Clarendon Press, 1996).

LEAR, JONATHAN, *Love and its Place in Nature: A Philosophical Interpretation of Freudian Psychoanalysis* (New York: Farrar, Straus & Giroux, 1990).

LEAVIS, F. R., *Revaluation: Tradition and Development in English Poetry* (London: Chatto & Windus, 1936, repr. 1953).

—— *The Living Principle: 'English' as a Discipline of Thought* (London: Chatto & Windus, 1975).

LEIGHTON, ANGELA, *Victorian Women Poets: Writing against the Heart* (Charlottesville: Univ. Press of Virginia, 1992).

LEVINSON, MARJORIE, *The Romantic Fragment Poem: A Critique of a Form* (Chapel Hill, NC: Univ. of North Carolina Press, 1986).

LEWIS, C. Day, *The Lyric Impulse* (Cambridge, Mass.: Harvard Univ. Press, 1965).

—— 'The Poetry of Emily Brontë', *Brontë Society Transactions*, 13/2, (1965), 83–95.

LIPKING, LAWRENCE I., *Abandoned Women and Poetic Tradition* (Chicago: Univ. of Chicago Press, 1988).

LOCKE, JOHN, *An Essay Concerning Human Understanding*, ed. Peter H. Nidditch (Oxford: Clarendon Press, 1975, repr. 1979).

LONOFF, SUE (ed. and trans.), *The Belgian Essays of Charlotte and Emily Brontë: A Bilingual, Annotated, Critical Edition* (New Haven: Yale Univ. Press, 1996).

LYNCH, THOMAS, *The Undertaking: Life Studies from the Dismal Trade* (New York: W. W. Norton & Co., 1997).

McCANNELL, COLLEEN, and LANG, BERNHARD, *Heaven: A History* (New Haven: Yale Univ. Press, 1988).

McFARLAND, THOMAS, *Romanticism and the Forms of Ruin: Wordsworth, Coleridge, and Modalities of Fragmentation* (Princeton: Princeton Univ. Press, 1981).

MAISON, MARGARET, 'Emily Brontë and Epictetus', *Notes and Queries*, NS 25 (June 1978), 230–1.

MASON, EMMA, 'Emily Brontë and the Enthusiastic Tradition', *Romanticism on the Net*, 25 (Feb. 2002): 19 pars. http://users.ox.ac.uk/-scat0385/25mason.html.

MELLOR, ANNE K., *Romanticism and Feminism* (Bloomington: Indiana Univ. Press, 1988).

—— *Romanticism and Gender* (New York: Routledge, 1993).

MILES, JOSEPHINE, *Wordsworth and the Vocabulary of Emotion* (Berkeley: Univ. of Calif. Publications in English, vol. 12, no. 1 [1942]).

MILLER, J. HILLIS, *The Disappearance of God: Five Nineteenth-Century Writers* (Cambridge, Mass.: Harvard Univ. Press, 1982).

___ *Fiction and Repetition: Seven English Novels* (Cambridge, Mass.: Harvard Univ. Press, 1982).

MILLER, LUCASTA, *The Brontë Myth* (New York: Alfred A. Knopf, 2003).

MITCHELL, JULIET, 'Memory and Pyschoanalysis', unpublished talk at Cornell University (autumn 1996).

MORLEY, JOHN, *Death, Heaven and the Victorians* (London: Studio Vista, 1971).

NEITZSCHE, FRIEDRICH WILHELM, *On the Genealogy of Morals*, trans. Walter Kaufmann and R. J. Hollingdale (New York: Random House, 1989).

The New Forget Me Not, or Ladies Fashionable Remembrancer for 1843 (London: Peacock & Mansfield, 1842).

NOCHLIN, LINDA, *Realism* (Harmondsworth: Penguin, 1971).

NUSSBAUM, FELICITY A., *The Autobiographical Subject: Gender and Ideology in Eighteenth-Century England* (Baltimore: The Johns Hopkins Univ. Press, 1989).

PACK, ROBERT, 'Lyric Narration: The Chameleon Poet', *Hudson Review* 37/1 (Spring 1984), 54–70.

PARKER, PATRICIA, 'The (Self-) Identity of the Literary Text: Property, Propriety, Proper Place, and Proper Name in *Wuthering Heights*', in Mario J. Valdès and Owen Miller (eds.), *Identity of the Literary Text* (Toronto: Univ. of Toronto Press, 1985), 92–116.

PENNINGTON, MONTAGU, *Memoirs of the Life of Mrs. Elizabeth Carter, with a new edition of her poems, to which are added Miscellaneous Essays in Prose, together with her Notes on the Bible and answers to objections concerning the Christian Religion* (London: F. C. and J. Rivington, 1807).

PETERS, MARGOT, *Charlotte Brontë: Style in the Novel* (Madison: Univ. of Wisconsin, 1973).

PETERSON, LINDA (ed.), *Wuthering Heights: Case Studies in Contemporary Criticism* (Boston: St. Martin's Press, 1992).

PETIT, JEAN-PIERRE, *L'Œuvre d'Emily Brontë: la vision et les thèmes* (Lyon: Éditions L'Hermès, 1977).

PHILLIPS, ADAM, *Winnicott* (Cambridge, Mass.: Harvard Univ. Press, 1988).

___ *On Flirtation: Psychoanalytic Essays on the Uncommitted Life* (Cambridge, Mass.: Harvard Univ. Press, 1994).

PLATH, SYLVIA, *The Collected Poems*, ed. Ted Hughes (New York: Harper & Row, 1981).

POE, EDGAR ALLEN, *Essays and Reviews* (New York: Literary Classics of the United States, Inc., 1984).

PRINS, YOPIE, *Victorian Sappho* (Princeton: Princeton Univ. Press, 1999).

RAJAN, BALACHANDRA, *The Form of the Unfinished: English Poetics from Spenser to Pound* (Princeton: Princeton Univ. Press, 1981).

RAMAZANI, JAHAN, *Poetry of Mourning: The Modern Elegy from Hardy to Heaney* (Chicago: Univ. of Chicago Press, 1994).

RENIER, ANNE, *Friendship's Offering: An Essay on the Annuals and Gift Books of the Nineteenth Century* (London: Private Libraries Association, 1964).

RICHARDSON, MICHAEL, *Georges Bataille* (London: Routledge, 1994).

RICKS, CHRISTOPHER, 'Bob Dylan', *Threepenny Review*, 10/4 (1990).

——*Allusion to the Poets* (Oxford: Oxford Univ. Press, 2002).

ROBINSON, A. MARY, *Emily Brontë* (London: W. H. Allen & Co., 1883).

ROSCOE, THOMAS (ed.), *The Remembrance* (London: Jennings & Chaplin, 1831). Further editions: London: Thomas Holmes, 1836; London: Thomas Albin, 1843.

ROWELL, GEOFFREY, *Hell and the Victorians* (Oxford: Clarendon Press, 1974).

ROWTON, FREDERIC, *The Female Poets of Great Britain* (London: Longman, Brown, Green, & Longmans, 1848).

RUSSELL, STEPHEN J., *The English Dream Vision: Anatomy of a Form* (Columbus: Ohio State Univ. Press, 1988).

SACKS, PETER, *The English Elegy: Studies in the Genre from Spenser to Yeats* (Baltimore: Johns Hopkins Univ. Press, 1985).

SCHAPIRO, BARBARA, 'The Rebirth of Catherine Earnshaw: Splitting and Reintegration of Self in *Wuthering Heights*', *Nineteenth-Century Studies* (1989), 37–51.

SCHIESARI, JULIANA, *The Gendering of Melancholia: Feminism, Psychoanalysis, and the Symbolics of Loss in Renaissance Literature* (Ithaca, NY: Cornell Univ. Press, 1992).

SCHMITT, JEAN-CLAUDE, *Ghosts in the Middle Ages: The Living and the Dead in Medieval Society*, trans. Teresa Lavender Fagan (Chicago: Univ. of Chicago Press, 1988).

SCHOR, ESTHER, *Bearing the Dead: The British Culture of Mourning from the Enlightenment to Victoria* (Princeton: Princeton Univ. Press, 1988).

SCODEL, JOSHUA, *The English Poetic Epitaph: Commemoration and Conflict from Jonson to Wordsworth* (Ithaca, NY: Cornell Univ. Press, 1991).

SEAFIELD, FRANK, *The Literature and Curiosities of Dreams: A Commonplace Book of Speculations Concerning the Mystery of Dreams and Visions*, 2 vols. (London: Chapman & Hall, 1865).

SHELLEY, PERCY BYSSHE, *Shelley's Poetry and Prose*, ed. Donald H. Reiman and Neil Fraistat (New York: W. W. Norton & Co., 2002).

SHOBERL, FREDERIC, *Forget Me Not Verses* (London: printed for private circulation only, 1850).

SMITH, ANNE (ed.), *The Art of Emily Brontë* (London: Vision Press, 1976).

SMITH, BARBARA HERRNSTEIN, *Poetic Closure: A Study of How Poems End* (Chicago: Univ. of Chicago Press, 1968).

—— *Contingencies of Value: Alternative Perspectives for Critical Theory* (Cambridge, Mass.: Harvard Univ. Press, 1988).

SNELL, BRUNO, *The Discovery of Mind*, trans. T. G. Rosenmeyer (Cambridge, Mass.: Harvard Univ. Press, 1953).

SOUTHEY, ROBERT, *The Poetical Works of Robert Southey, Collected by Himself*, 10 vols. (London: Longman, Orne, Brown, Green, & Longman, 1838).

SPURGEON, CAROLINE F. E., *Mysticism in English Literature* (Cambridge: Cambridge Univ. Press, 1913).

STATEN, HENRY, *Eros in Mourning: Homer to Lacan* (Baltimore: Johns Hopkins Univ. Press, 1995).

STILLINGER, JACK, *Coleridge and Textual Instability: The Multiple Versions of the Major Poems* (New York: Oxford Univ. Press, 1994).

STONEMAN, PATSY, 'Feminist Criticism of *Wuthering Heights*', *Critical Survey*, 4/2 (Oxford: Oxford Univ. Press, 1992), 147–53.

SWINBURNE, ALGERNON CHARLES, *A Note on Charlotte Brontë* (London: Chatto & Windus, 1877).

SYMONDS, JOHN ADDINGTON, *Sleep and Dreams* (London: John Murray, 1851).

TAYLER, IRENE, *Holy Ghosts: The Male Muses of Emily and Charlotte Brontë* (New York: Columbia Univ. Press, 1990).

TAYLOR, DENNIS, *Hardy's Metres and Victorian Prosody* (Oxford: Clarendon Press, 1988).

TAYLOR, JENNY BOURNE, and SHUTTLEWORTH, SALLY (eds.), *Embodied Selves: An Anthology of Psychological Texts 1830–1890* (Oxford: Clarendon Press, 1998).

THORMÄHLEN, MARIANNE, *The Brontës and Religion* (Cambridge: Cambridge Univ. Press, 1999).

TRENCH, R. C. (ed.), *Sacred Poems for Mourners* (London: Francis & John Rivington, 1846).

VENDLER, HELEN, *Wallace Stevens: Words Chosen out of Desire* (Knoxville: Univ. of Tennessee Press, 1984).

VISICK, MARY, 'The Last of Gondal', in Charles Lemon (ed.), *Classics of Brontë Scholarship: The Best from One Hundred Years of Transactions of the Brontë Society* (Haworth: The Brontë Society, 1999), 154–64.

WELSH, ANDREW, *Roots of Lyric: Primitive Poetry and Modern Poetics* (Princeton: Princeton Univ. Press, 1978).

WHARTON, EDITH, *A Backward Glance* (New York: D. Appleton-Century Company, 1934).

WHEELER, MICHAEL, *Death and the Future Life in Victorian Literature and Theology* (Cambridge: Cambridge Univ. Press, 1990).

WILDE, OSCAR, *Complete Writings of Oscar Wilde: Reviews* (New York: The Nottingham Society, 1909).

WINNICOTT D. W., *The Maturational Processes and the Facilitating Environment* (London: Hogarth Press and the Institute of Psychoanalysis, 1965).

—— *Playing and Reality* (Harmondsworth: Penguin Books, 1974).

Wion, Philip K., 'The Absent Mother in Emily Bronte's *Wuthering Heights*', *American Imago*, 42/2 (Summer 1985), 143–64.

Wise, T. J., and Symington, J. A. (eds.), *The Brontës: Their Lives Friendships & Correspondence in Four Volumes* (Oxford: Shakespeare Head Press, 1932).

Wittgenstein, Ludwig, *Culture and Value*, trans. Peter Winch, ed. G. H. Von Wright with Heikki Nyman (Oxford: Basil Blackwell, 1980, repr. 1984).

—— *Tractatus logico-philosophicus*, trans. D. F. Pears and B. McGuiness (New York: Humanities Press, 1961).

Wolfson, Susan J., *Formal Changes: The Shaping of Poetry in British Romanticism* (Stanford, Calif: Stanford Univ. Press, 1997).

Woolf, Virginia, *Collected Essays*, 4 vols. (New York: Harcourt, Brace & World, 1966).

Wordsworth, Jonathan, 'Wordsworth and the Poetry of Emily Brontë', *Brontë Society Transactions*, 16/82 (1972), 85–100.

Wordsworth, William, *Preface to Lyrical Ballads*, in *William Wordsworth*, ed. Stephen Gill (Oxford: Oxford Univ. Press, 1984, repr. 1989).

Wright, George T., 'The Lyric Present: Simple Present Verbs in English Poems', *PMLA* 89/3 (May 1974), 563–79.

Index